HERITAGE KNOWLEDGE IN THE CURRICULUM

Moving beyond the content integration approach of multicultural education, this text powerfully advocates for the importance of curriculum built upon authentic knowledge construction informed by the Black intellectual tradition and an African episteme. By retrieving, examining, and reconnecting the continuity of African Diasporan heritage with school knowledge, this volume aims to repair the rupture that has silenced this cultural memory in standard historiography in general and in PK-12 curriculum content and pedagogy in particular. This ethically informed curriculum approach not only allows students of African ancestry to understand where they fit in the world but also makes the accomplishments and teachings of our collective ancestors available for the benefit of all. King and Swartz provide readers with a process for making overt and explicit the values, actions, thoughts, and behaviors reflected in an African episteme that serves as the foundation for African Diasporan sociohistorical phenomenon/ events. With such knowledge, teachers can conceptualize curriculum and shape instruction that locates people in all cultures as subjects with agency whose actions embody their ongoing cultural legacy.

Joyce E. King holds the Benjamin E. Mays Endowed Chair for Urban Teaching, Learning and Leadership at Georgia State University, USA, where she is Professor of Educational Policy Studies in the College of Education and Human Development.

Ellen E. Swartz is an independent scholar and educational consultant in curriculum development and the development of culturally informed instructional materials for K-12 teachers and students.

HERITAGE KNOWLEDGE IN THE CURRICULUM

Retrieving an African Episteme

Joyce E. King and Ellen E. Swartz

Routledge
Taylor & Francis Group

NEW YORK AND LONDON

First published 2018
by Routledge
711 Third Avenue, New York, NY 10017

and by Routledge
2 Park Square, Milton Park, Abingdon, Oxon, OX14 4RN

Routledge is an imprint of the Taylor & Francis Group, an informa business

© 2018 Taylor & Francis

The right of Joyce E. King and Ellen E. Swartz to be identified as authors
of this work has been asserted by them in accordance with sections 77 and
78 of the Copyright, Designs and Patents Act 1988.

Library of Congress Cataloging-in-Publication Data
Names: King, Joyce Elaine, 1947– author. | Swartz, Ellen, author.
Title: Heritage knowledge in the curriculum : retrieving an African
    episteme / Joyce E. King and Ellen E. Swartz.
Description: New York, NY : Routledge, 2018. | Includes bibliographical
    references and index.
Identifiers: LCCN 2017056529 | ISBN 9780815380429 (hardback :
    alk. paper) | ISBN 9780815380436 (pbk. : alk. paper) |
    ISBN 9781351213233 (ebook)
Subjects: LCSH: African Americans—Education—Curricula. |
    Afrocentrism—Study and teaching—United States.
Classification: LCC LC2771 .K555 2018 | DDC 371.829/96073—dc23
LC record available at https://lccn.loc.gov/2017056529

ISBN: 978-0-815-38042-9 (hbk)
ISBN: 978-0-815-38043-6 (pbk)
ISBN: 978-1-351-21323-3 (ebk)

Typeset in Bembo
by Apex CoVantage, LLC

This book is dedicated to emancipatory educators who "re-member" school knowledge by applying the same standards of scholarly integrity to the history and heritage of all cultures and groups. In so doing, they enact the African cultural concepts of *knowing as a communal experience in which everyone has something to contribute* and *exhibiting self-determination that considers the needs of the collective.*

CONTENTS

A NOTE ABOUT THE PAPERBACK COVER IMAGE

The symbol on the paperback cover is an Adinkra symbol called *Dwennimmen*. Adinkra is an indigenous Akan (West Africa) script whose many symbols are epistemic expressions of Akan philosophy, cosmology, values, and cultural concepts. *Dwennimmen* (djwin-knee-mann) translates as Ram's Horns and stands for strength of mind, body, and soul and for wisdom, humility, and learning. Chapter 5 provides more information about the meaning of this and other Adinkra symbols that can be used to teach the qualities needed to develop good character.

FOREWORD

Each year during my fall doctoral level course I ask students to raise their hands if they have heard of W.E.B. DuBois or Carter G. Woodson. For the most part, the only hands that go up are from African American students. I hold up two books, *The Souls of Black Folks* and *The Mis-education of the Negro*, and say, "If you are unfamiliar with these volumes, you are ignorant of the intellectual history of this nation." Most students do not receive this statement graciously. How dare I refer to them as "ignorant?" They have been admitted to the nation's number one public School of Education. They study with some of the world's best education scholars. They are a "special" group of up-and-coming scholars. Yet, I contend their education lacks serious perspectives and understandings about the intellectual traditions of African descent people in the United States.

In my undergraduate social studies methods course I do something a little different. I ask the students to take out a sheet of paper and make a list of all of the European countries they can name. I let them know they have ten minutes to complete this task. My mostly White, monolingual, female, and Wisconsin native students sit writing gleefully and frantically. Each is certain s/he has an impressive list. After the ten minutes are up I ask students to raise their hands if they can name only between one and ten countries. No hands go up. I continue in intervals of 10 (11–20, 21–30, 31–40, 41–50) and each interval contains more students. While the students are raising their hands, I document the numbers and plot a histogram on a piece of chart paper based on their responses. The histogram results in a line with a steadily upward slope with many more students in the final group (41–50) than in other groups. My students smile at each other and look to me for approval. Can't I see how smart they are? I congratulate them on their basic knowledge of Europe and quickly ask them to turn their papers over. Next I say, "Write down as many African countries as you can. Again, you have ten minutes." This time I watch the consternation and panic that come across their faces. A few minutes into the task I perceive looks of frustration and defeat. When the ten-minute time passes I again say, "Raise your hand if you were able to list only between one and ten countries." This time more than half of the class raises its hands. I continue on asking in intervals. How many listed between 11 and 20 countries? 21 and 30? 31 and 40? 41 and 50+? Once again I create a histogram but this time the slope of the line is a steadily downward one. I place the two graphs on top of each other and the students can easily see a figure that looks like an X.

"How is this possible?" I ask the students. "You are among the state's brightest students. I asked you a basic geography question. I did not ask you to name countries' presidents or kings. I did not ask you any questions of history or government about the countries. I only asked you to name countries you can easily see on a map or globe. Why don't you know this?"

Both of the aforementioned examples—one in a graduate class and the other in an undergraduate class—sit as the essential problems this volume by King and Swartz addresses. These authors speak to knowledge construction and the hegemony and privileging of one kind of knowledge in our schools and classrooms. The two main themes of the book, the need to center African Diasporic peoples and their knowledge in school curriculum and the cultural continuity of a Black intellectual tradition, based on an ancient episteme that reaches back into antiquity, are sorely missing from the PK-12 and teacher education curriculum. These omissions and distortions form the basis of Carter G. Woodson's assertion:

> The same educational process which inspires and stimulates the oppressor with the thought that he is everything and has accomplished everything worthwhile, depresses and crushes at the same time the spark of genius in the Negro by making him feel that his race does not amount to much and never will measure up to the standards of other peoples.
>
> *(1934/1969, p. 21)*

As the modern civil rights movement (c. 1954–1969) began to come to a close, some exciting activities started to happen in the classrooms at both the PK-12 and collegiate level. The nation had been in turmoil. College and university campuses erupted. Student strikes happened at campuses like San Francisco State and the University of California–Berkeley. Protests against the Vietnam War, for Black rights and women's rights occurred across the nation. This dissension provided the foundation for an entire set of "new studies" (Wynter, 1984). We began to see courses in Black studies, Women's studies, and Chicano studies. At San Francisco State University we witnessed the first university Ethnic Studies Department. On some historically Black colleges and universities' (HBCU) campuses courses that had been on the books with the modifier "Negro" were revived and now called "Black." We now had Black History, Black Culture, and Blacks in Film, as well as courses in Swahili, and the Black Aesthetic.

The activists of the civil rights movement were the catalyst for curricular change. In education, scholars began to expand the curriculum (King, 2003) to make clear the intellectual, historical, and cultural contributions of peoples beyond those of European descent. But, as King makes clear in her explication, expanding the knowledge did not interrogate or interrupt the extant regime of truth (Foucault, 1995). Thus, we began to think of groups outside of the dominant paradigm in terms of "us too" rather than a total epistemic rupture of the way knowledge and thinking are organized.

In this volume Joyce King and Ellen Swartz offer an important departure from Eurocentric paradigms and epistemology. They identify "heritage knowledge" as the missing thinking systems in school curriculum. And they point out that this knowledge is available and helps us to locate African Peoples as "historical agents whose ideas and actions remain connected to their heritage" (preface, this volume). Much of the Eurocentric historical record suggests the process of "seasoning" in the European slave trade on the continent of Africa was so complete that there were no vestiges of culture from the various Black African ethnic groups that could be made available for building knowledge systems in the "New World."

Over and over we have heard that Africans who arrived on the shores of the Americas were stripped of languages, histories, cultures, and customs. However, in 1941 Jewish anthropologist Melville J. Herskovitz published *The Myth of the African Past*, in which he argued that African Americans retained what he termed "Africanisms" that established the relationship between Africans and African Americans. What Herskovitz was saying is exactly what cognitive scientists argue regarding prior knowledge. Consider the facts. Africans who are transported across an ocean as adults have language, thought, culture, history, religion, rituals, and customs in their minds. Placing them with other Africans from different ethnic and linguistic groups does not mean they lose the ability to maintain aspects of their histories and cultures. They do not arrive in the Americas "empty-headed." They do not arrive in the Americas speaking English. They continue to use their own epistemological systems to make sense of a new and terrifying world. Indeed, their own systems are the only thing they possess as a sense-making strategy. And they do what they can to transmit these systems to their offspring. Yes, some cultural practices change but they change in the same ways every new generation's practices change. Changing practices does not mean no such practices exist.

King and Swartz offer us a marvelous opportunity to see what recapturing and reconstructing the knowledge and cultural practices can do to ensure our children experience academic success on their own terms. This volume helps us see how African diasporic knowledge was used by people like Benjamin Banneker, how knowledge and use of African languages support historical consciousness and allow African descent people to retrieve group memory and identity. This work offers us an opportunity to see a different regime of truth—one that centers the African subject in his/her own worldview. The work also reminds us all (both African descent and non-African descent) that the contributions of African heritage knowledge are not peripheral to the advances and developments that made America a world power.

Consider a reimagined Martin Luther King Jr. who used his African memory in combination with his understanding of Gandhi as a vehicle for promoting high moral principles that reflect an expansive view of democracy. Think about a Fannie Lou Hamer who does not succumb to the "cult of White woman-hood" but instead has a vision of a powerful Queen Nzinga, who understands that power is not limited by gender positionality. Entertain the idea of three Black women—Katherine Johnson, Mary Jackson, and Dorothy Vaughn—who are smart enough to help NASA put a manned rocket in orbit because they pull upon the heritage knowledge that Benjamin Banneker and their African ancestors already knew about mathematics and science.

This volume offers us an important opportunity to reconstruct the knowledge and cultural connections of African descent peoples that may ultimately move us away from the "achievement gap" discourse and toward an authentic and deeper understanding of the ways African epistemologies help us disrupt Euro-centric hegemonic paradigms that depend on oppression and hierarchy in opposition to justice and human freedom.

Gloria Ladson-Billings
Kellner Family Distinguished
Chair in Urban Education
University of Wisconsin–Madison

References

Foucault, M. (1995). *Discipline and punish: The birth of prison.* New York: Vintage Books.

King, J. E. (2003). Culture centered knowledge: Black studies, curriculum transformation and social action. In J. A. Banks & C. M. Banks (Eds.), *Handbook of research on multicultural education* (2nd ed., pp. 349–379). San Francisco: John Wiley.

Woodson, C. G. (1934/1969). *The miseducation of the Negro.* Washington, DC: Association Press.

Wynter, S. (1984). The ceremony must be found: After humanism. *Boundary 2, 12/13*(3), 19–70.

PREFACE

The unequivocal stance of this book is that standard eurocratic school practices are harmful to all students. They are harmful to the students they marginalize and to the students they privilege by failing to recognize the inherent worth of all Peoples—a supremacist practice that destroys the integrity of school knowledge and the practices that could support it. This volume proposes that an African worldview and cultural concepts constitute an indigenous epistemic foundation needed to identify the "re-membered" content and emancipatory pedagogies able to create schools as sites of democratic practice where inclusive, representational, and more accurate and engaging curriculum is the norm.

As educators—both PK-12 and higher education—we need to broaden our historical knowledge—really all kinds of knowledge—that has been either omitted or agreed upon for so long that we think it is true. To do this we use an African episteme of theoretical concepts and culturally informed principles. This episteme is conceptually broad enough to replace the limited worldview and cultural concepts that were cemented into the foundation of schooling in this society centuries ago for the purpose of creating a hierarchy of human worth that benefits the few at the expense of the many. The state proprietors of the existing educational system—and their corporate sponsors—have maintained this preferential race, class, and gender epistemology that originated with Europeans and that they established in schooling in the Americas. This system has been quite effective at inducting children into societies where inequalities and dominance are taught as inevitable, conformity and obedience are rewarded, cultural heritage is erased or distorted, and profit is favored over ethical standards. Children don't know precisely what is being done to them, but they experience (and often resist) its effects every day in and outside of school. Decades have been spent critiquing this impoverished and harmful system of education. It is past time to replace it.

Changing the epistemic foundation of school knowledge means no
presenting historically oppressed Peoples as either voiceless victims reac
one abuse after another or as "exceptions to the rule" when their intelligence,
courage, industriousness, and excellence are too obvious to ignore. And the
civilizational accomplishments and heritages of African, Indigenous, and Asian
Peoples—which preceded and seeded Europe's development—are no longer
omitted or distorted to the extent that Europe is inaccurately and absurdly taught
as the standard-bearer of civilization. The continued construction of school
knowledge within a narrow, dislocating lens is untenable within an African
episteme, which "re-members" multiple lived experiences by applying the same
standards of accurate scholarship to the history and heritage of all cultures and
groups. This process of reconnection ends the privileging of dominant accounts
whose narrators speak for and have effectively silenced all others.

As academics who have critiqued the current eurocratic system of education,
we typically view our role as theorizing and even envisioning a new system, but
ultimately it is PK-12 educators who must enact it. That we have failed to
develop stronger partnerships with the very people who do this work is one
reason why real change has remained out of reach. Whereas we *need and use*
teachers and their classrooms and youth and families for our research, we rarely
acknowledge the expertise they have and seek ways to support those who know
or are open to knowing that current school practices are not inevitable and can
be replaced. We have also been remiss in making connections to knowledge
holders in our communities—to the very people who carry the history, traditions, and lived experiences we write about. Their knowledge provides educators
with opportunities to connect students to heritage knowledge about their own
communities as contexts for learning in diverse subject areas.

In Chapter 1 the conversation between a fifth-grade teacher and academic/
author demonstrates what a mutually supportive relationship might look like. It
provides details about the foregoing ideas and the agency needed to replace the
educational system we inherited, and includes summaries of the chapters that
follow. In those chapters we provide specific examples of the praxis needed to
construct learning experiences that positively shape students' perceptions of their
location in the world; and we retrieve, examine, and reconnect the continuity
of African Diasporan heritage with school knowledge in order to repair the
rupture that has distorted this heritage by removing Diasporan connections with
Africa in standard historiography in general and in PK-12 curriculum in particular. When all students learn about their own and others' history, languages,
and culture, their humanity is affirmed and they can see themselves as belonging
to a continuous heritage. This reconnection gives students whose history and
heritage have been distorted and ruptured a way to see how they fit in the
world—in their families, communities, classrooms, and beyond. This reconnection
gives students who have been falsely taught to accept myths about white/Euro-
pean superiority a more accurate measure of their own humanity.

We selected an African episteme, in which the Black intellectual tradition of ethically informed scholarship is rooted, since this episteme enacts the principle of a collective humanity. Any episteme and scholarship grounded in this principle can guide us in the process of centering African Diasporan, Indigenous, and *all* other Peoples as historical agents whose ideas and actions remain connected to their heritage. These ideas and actions are informed by heritage knowledge, which is a group's intergenerational cultural memory. Through examples of how ethically informed scholarship and heritage knowledge shape the ideas, actions, languages, and movements of African Diasporan people, this volume supports teachers in conceptualizing curricula and developing instruction that (1) center all students culturally and individually; (2) use African worldview elements and cultural concepts to frame the teaching of content and skills as a context for gaining knowledge and developing good character; (3) foster community building through ethical ideals and right action; (4) develop relationships with students and families that build on who they are and what they know; (5) communicate that student success is a communal responsibility by bringing family presence and ideas into curriculum development and assessment practices; (6) teach students' ancestral languages as a source of making meaning about cultural concepts and practices; and (7) stimulate students' critical thinking, intrinsic motivation, and agency. In these ways educators can be part of "Returning What We Learn to the People," which is the title of our last chapter. By viewing family, community, and language as sites of memory we show how educators can return practical, healing knowledge to their students and their families and communities through the curriculum, and in so doing, create conditions for human freedom and collective well-being that are shared and sustained.

ACKNOWLEDGMENTS

We acknowledge all those women and men of agency and self-determination—activists, thinkers, and wisdom keepers—who have informed us throughout our careers. Their theories and practices have marked the trail that guides our actions in pursuit of education that expands the life chances of all children. Their light invites the development of historical and critical consciousness and the identification of an epistemic context that enacts the African cultural concept of *pursuing knowledge as inseparable from pursuing wisdom.* In particular we wish to acknowledge Nannie Helen Burroughs, who understood that knowing your past was essential to knowing yourself and being successful in the present; W.E.B. Du Bois, whose prolific and long career demonstrated how change and consistency are not mutually exclusive; Carter G. Woodson, whose integrity was as uncompromising as his critiques of both white supremacy and the miseducation of his people; Dr. Beverly M. Gordon, for her early theorizing of emancipatory pedagogy and African American epistemology; Dr. Wade W. Nobles, for his unceasing scholarly efforts in recovering the African mind; and Maulana Karenga, whose scholarship unearthed and decolonized knowledge about ancient Kemetic, Yoruba, and other African philosophical systems. This knowledge offers the principles, values, and virtues that lead to "human freedom and flourishing."

We thank Geneva Smitherman, "Dr. G.," Professor Emerita at the University of Michigan, for her assistance with sources regarding the Black oral tradition, and Sylvia Wynter, for her fierce insistence on rewriting academic knowledge and her commitment to Black studies theorizing for human freedom; and we remember that Baba Asa G. Hilliard, III made his transition ten years ago but his legacy continues to inspire us to keep pressing on. We also thank Dr. Susan Goodwin and Dr. Rosenna Bakari for reviewing portions of the manuscript and the staff of the Patron Services Interlibrary Loan Section at the University of

Rochester Libraries for their outstanding efforts in providing requested research materials. Finally, we acknowledge teachers, students, families, and community knowledge holders who are willing to participate in replacing the eurocratic model of education. Of course this volume would not be possible without the Routledge editorial and production staff, including our first editor, Naomi Silverman, whose steadfast support during the process of preparing and finalizing this manuscript has carried us to our destination a third time.

Chapter 6 is an adaption of a 2017 article entitled "A Call for a Reparatory Justice Curriculum for Human Freedom: Re-writing the Story of Our Dispossession and the Debt Owed," published in the 2017 issue of *Journal of African American History, 102*(2), 213–231.

Chapter 7 is an adaption of a 2017 article entitled "Education Research in the Black Liberation Tradition: Return What You Learn to the People," published in *The Journal of Negro Education 87*(2), 95–114.

1

INTRODUCTION

A Conversation

Joyce E. King and Ellen E. Swartz

What do Africa—its peoples, its culture—have to offer to the ongoing historical project of improving the human condition and enhancing the human future? Answering
this question requires that we constantly engage African texts—continental and
diasporan, ancient and modern, oral, written, and living-practice texts . . . This
means using our culture as a resource rather than as a reference . . . In this process,
one does not simply make a historical reference to Harriet Tubman as a major leader
of the Underground Railroad. Rather, one stands at the crossroads of history with
her, at the moment of her self-liberation, when she moves from elation over being
free to sadness at having left all those she loved in the Holocaust of enslavement. It
is when she decides that freedom is a shared good, that the profound happiness in
freedom she first felt should be shared by all, and then chooses to return and free
others that offers such a fruitful field for philosophic engagement.

(Karenga, 2006, pp. 246–247)

This book is about shifting the ground we stand on by reaching back to retrieve
an old but unacknowledged debt to an episteme—forgotten by many—but
brought from Africa to the Diaspora and passed from one generation to the
next as African heritage knowledge (a group's cultural memory) (Clarke, 1992).
To "go back and fetch what we need" is a philosophical construct conveyed by
the Adinkra symbol *Sankofa* (from an Akan language, Ghana, West Africa) (Willis,
1998, p. 189). According to W. Bruce Willis (1998), "*Sankofa* is the repossession
of something that was forgotten and the initiation of a process to return to the
place where the object was lost in order 'to fetch it' and 'then move forward'
into the future" (p. 189). The repossession of this African episteme makes it
possible to produce more historically accurate and ethically and culturally

informed curriculum about the diverse histories, languages, and cultures that influenced all of our ancestors and informed what they accomplished and taught the world. In fact, curriculum based on an African Diasporan epistemic foundation has the capacity to extricate *all* students and educators from the hegemonic straitjacket that controls school knowledge. Importantly, this foundation is a location from which to democratize the school experience so that students have possibilities to see and know the world in ways that standard school knowledge has hidden far too long.

We begin with a recorded conversation between Dr. King and Ms. Singleton, who was part of our recent text, *The Afrocentric Praxis of Teaching for Freedom: Connecting Culture to Learning* (King & Swartz, 2016). In that text, we constructed scenarios featuring her and Ms. Hart—another fifth-grade teacher in her school—that are instructional composites of culturally responsive teachers and classrooms that we have observed over the years. As a practitioner of Teaching *for* Freedom, we asked Ms. Singleton to begin the conversation by sharing how she views this model of teaching. After reviewing the recording, we decided to use this conversation as our introductory chapter, since it not only introduces many of the concepts and content needed to teach within an African epistemic framework, but also shows how collaboration with PK-12 teachers is essential to scholarship that intends to influence what goes on in PK-12 classrooms. Toward the completion of the book manuscript we did some minor editing and added clarifying information and a few citations in brackets. So, dear readers, we invite you to listen to, critically think about, and discuss the conversation that follows:

Ms. Singleton: It's my pleasure to be here with you, Dr. King. Some readers met me in your last book where I had the opportunity to demonstrate how I guided and supported Ms. Hart, another fifth-grade teacher who began her career at our school. She is now more experienced and soon will be guiding and supporting other new teachers in our school community. I want to begin by saying that being community-minded has always made sense to me. As a person of African ancestry, this communal way of looking at things is part of my heritage knowledge [a group's cultural memory]. I've been passing along my knowledge, experience, and expertise to new teachers for years, which is what elders in African cultures do. In Teaching *for* Freedom, the pedagogy called "Eldering" is modeled after this African understanding. So I see more clearly now that what I was doing came from my African heritage knowledge. For a White teacher like Ms. Hart, communal ideas and the concept of eldership have become part of the cultural knowledge she has gained about people of African ancestry so that we are both able to teach and pass on our knowledge of African people's worldview in ways that strengthen our relationships with students, families, and colleagues.

I understand that Teaching *for* Freedom is a model based on African worldview and cultural concepts, so at the same time as teaching content and skills we teach students to be community-minded and to share in the responsibility of bringing good into the world by being compassionate and caring about each other and the communities in which they live. I want to say more about this, but first, let me assure readers that the content of our curriculum and the way we teach it have dramatically increased my students' engagement, excitement for learning, and achievement. The curriculum is the context for making connections between the content we teach, the pedagogies we use, the students we teach, and their families. This model puts students in the center, and that makes it possible for us to guide them to know themselves, think critically, and work together. If we are going to have any impact on the imposed and often unjust conditions our students and families are facing, we too need knowledge and experiences that strengthen our cultural and individual selves and give us opportunities to think and work together.

Dr. King: I couldn't agree more. Needless to say, it's quite affirming to hear your thoughts about how you and Ms. Hart have been using the praxis of Teaching *for* Freedom, and how you are thinking about what it means. In the book we are writing now, we want to build on our last book by presenting and discussing examples of African Diasporan cultural continuity that can guide PK-12 teachers and teacher educators to use heritage and cultural knowledge that can inform content and pedagogy. We've sketched out ideas for several chapters, but thought that sharing our ideas and getting your feedback would help us as we continue to work on the manuscript.

Ms. Singleton: I'd be glad to share my thoughts. Let me first say how valuable the concept of "African Diasporan cultural continuity" has been in my teaching—that is, knowing about the connections between Africa and the Diaspora. Cultures or nations of people have existed on the African continent for millennia; and the Diaspora refers to all the places outside the African continent where people of African ancestry live. So, this idea of continuity between Africa and the Diaspora means that geography doesn't restrict where African ideas, concepts, and knowledge can be found. They are found wherever African people live.

All of us have an ongoing heritage or cultural legacies that have shaped who we are. So when students learn about their history and culture—and the history and culture of others—they learn about what *all* our ancestors accomplished and taught the world. They see themselves as belonging to a continuous heritage, which gives them a way to see how they fit in the world—in their classrooms, families, and communities.

Dr. King: Yes, and cultural continuity is essential to holding on to the foundation of a culture, or what scholars like Jacob Carruthers (1995) and Asa Hilliard (1997) call "deep thought." Holding on to this foundation involves understanding how worldview and cultural concepts shape not only what we know, but what we are like and what we do.

Ms. Singleton: We're seeing how building our lessons around cultural concepts is very important in our teaching. For example, when Ms. Hart and I taught a unit on the environment and the ways in which communities of color experience more environmental pollution than other communities, we organized our lessons around African Diasporan concepts like self-determination that considers what a community needs and everyone in a community being responsible for justice and for protecting children [see Chapter 6 in King & Swartz, 2016, for an excerpt from that unit]. Students understood that the environmental activists we were studying were trying to make the air quality better for everyone, and that they wanted to take care of their children by working together to bring about change. We explained how concepts that were part of African heritage—like the inherent worth of all people and self-determination that considers the needs of others—gave African American activists the strength to stand up to powerful corporations that were polluting their communities. We also explained how the worldview of these activists—which influenced their ideas and actions—had endured across time and place.

Dr. King: For new readers, let me explain that you can see the elements of a worldview among people who share a cultural heritage. These elements are the central tendencies of a culture even though individual members of a cultural group don't exhibit these tendencies to the same degree and don't all necessarily live in ways that are determined by them. For example, given the communal worldview within African Diasporan cultures, people who are not relatives are often regarded as family members. While the practice of extended family kinship varies among African Diasporan people and is also seen in other communal cultures, it is accepted as a norm in communities where people of African ancestry live. This norm is an example of heritage knowledge or what Dr. Clarke (1992) has described as group memory, which makes a feeling of belonging to one's people possible. This feeling of belonging—of being part of a common humanity—is often referred to by the term *Ubuntu* [in Zulu in South Africa and other Nguni languages spoken in southern Africa], which can be translated as "We are, therefore I am." In other words, it's the group and the interconnectedness of its members that bring a sense of belonging and well-being to individuals.

Ms. Singleton: There are two things I'm thinking. One is that I've noticed that African American children are typically group-oriented, especially at young ages. But, by fifth grade, if their previous school experiences have involved a lot of competition, I have to encourage and structure activities around collaboration. You might say that I have to let students know that working together as a group is something you can do in school, too. I've noticed that it doesn't take long for students of African ancestry to shift back to that approach. The second thing I'm thinking is that a group of people can have a worldview, even if they're not consciously aware of it, and everyone in the group doesn't share the tendencies of that worldview to the same extent. I know there is some confusion around this point and that some scholars say that the discussion of worldview essentializes culture [see King & Swartz, 2016, pp. 120–124, for an analysis of essentializing culture].

Dr. King: Yes, some do, but worldview is a useful tool; it's a cultural framework for identifying and learning about the ideas, productions, and practices of specific cultures and world regions. You can "see" a people's worldview through concepts that consistently "show up" across time and in different places. These cultural concepts express the worldview elements of a People.

As you know from our last book, we have identified five elements of worldview. We've put together a graphic [Figure 1.1] that shows how a worldview that includes these elements is at the foundation of numerous African cultural concepts that shape ideas and practices in African Diasporan cultures. So, when people care about and learn from interacting with others in their community, make decisions that foster justice, and come together to consider the collective needs of their people, they are guided by concepts in their group's cultural memory like *exhibiting self-determination that considers the needs of the collective* [specific cultural concepts are italicized throughout]. Another concept that comes from an African worldview is the one you mentioned a few minutes ago— *the inherent worth of all humans*. When people are guided by these concepts—think of Harriet Tubman and Rosa Parks—they make decisions and take actions to bring about justice that are in the best interests of everyone. And when people come together to protest environmental racism like you were just talking about, you can see how *sharing responsibility for communal well-being and belonging*

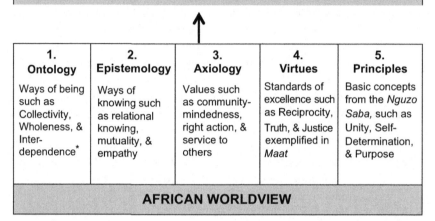

exhibiting self-determination that considers the needs of the collective	the inherent worth of all people	sharing responsibility for communal well-being and belonging	knowing that cultural sovereignty is a common right of all Peoples

AFRICAN CULTURAL CONCEPTS

1. Ontology	2. Epistemology	3. Axiology	4. Virtues	5. Principles
Ways of being such as Collectivity, Wholeness, & Inter-dependence*	Ways of knowing such as relational knowing, mutuality, & empathy	Values such as community-mindedness, right action, & service to others	Standards of excellence such as Reciprocity, Truth, & Justice exemplified in *Maat*	Basic concepts from the *Nguzo Saba,* such as Unity, Self-Determination, & Purpose

AFRICAN WORLDVIEW

* Ontological orientations, *Maatian* Virtues, and *Nguzo Saba* Principles are capitalized, but epistemologies and values are not capitalized throughout this volume. The former have been identified by scholars cited herein as "the" elements of specific sets of ontological orientations, virtues, and principles; the latter are selected by the authors among many possible examples of epistemologies and values.

FIGURE 1.1 African Cultural Concepts: Expressions of African Worldview

and *knowing that cultural sovereignty is a common right of all Peoples* are other African concepts that guide their actions. While these concepts are part of the heritage knowledge of people of African ancestry, everyone can learn about them and from them. When you think about the elements of African worldview—which have been part of African civilizations over centuries—and how the mid-twentieth-century Diasporan Kwanzaa Principles [see Karenga, 1998] reflect the elements of that worldview, you can see how worldview exists across time and space.

Ms. Singleton: Just the other day I read an article about Esther Calhoun, a woman who lives in a rural Black community in Alabama (Bogado, 2016). She is speaking out and organizing a community group against a landfill company that makes its money by receiving coal ash shipped in from across the country. People in her town are getting sick and dying from the ash dust that covers everything, and it's no longer possible to grow your own food, which people depend on . . . They have been speaking out on a Facebook page and the company is suing her group, saying their reputation is being damaged! Really! As I look at this chart, I can see her heritage knowledge in what she's doing. Her actions suggest that she knows that cultural sovereignty is a common right. In fact Ms. Calhoun exhibits all of the African worldview elements and cultural concepts in this chart. If you haven't seen the article I'll get you a copy.

Dr. King: Actually, I did see the article and I agree with you. Ms. Calhoun identified that environmental racism was at work in her town. I think I remember her saying that it was like the 1950s. And you're right about her actions being examples of the African worldview elements and cultural concepts on the chart. I remembering her saying something like the only thing she was asking for was peace and a chance to live a healthy and long life; and that if there was justice you would have clean air and water whether you were rich or poor. She was advocating not only for herself but for her community. So you can see her African heritage knowledge in her ideas and actions, whether or not she has consciously connected her actions with her African heritage.

Ms. Singleton: That makes me think of Rosa Parks, who you mentioned earlier. Maybe I can connect her actions to those of Esther Calhoun. If I were planning lessons using the four cultural concepts in this chart [pointing to Figure 1.1] to teach about the Montgomery Bus Boycott, I could ask students to think about what the efforts of Black leaders and everyday people in Montgomery were *for*—which was to be self-determined and to act collectively in ways that considered the needs and well-being of the whole community—just like Esther Calhoun.

Usually the boycott is taught with a focus on what Black people in Montgomery were *against* or trying to stop, which included the daily indignities and terror they experienced under segregation. Of course the goal was to end segregation on the buses and all the abuse that came with it—and the goal of Calhoun and her group is to end the pollution and the devastation it is causing—but as I see it, the *impetus to act* had to do, in both cases, with changing what the practices of segregation and pollution were doing to destroy the well-being and integrity of the *whole* community. In Montgomery, Black people's African heritage knowledge moved almost the entire Black community, that was joined by a few White people, to work toward recognizing the worth of all people in the community; and while we don't yet know the outcome of Esther Calhoun's efforts, she is organizing people in her community in ways that reflect the same African concept . . . the worth of all people. If I use these concepts to frame my lessons, I can show how African heritage knowledge influenced what happened in Montgomery—which seems long ago to our students—and connect that heritage knowledge to the heritage knowledge evident in the actions of Esther Calhoun, who recognizes the worth of all people today. The inherent worth of all humans is so obvious—something anyone would agree with—yet so much goes on that contradicts what is obvious.

Dr. King: Well, that speaks to why we are talking about teaching that provides access to ways of knowing, values, virtues, and principles that not only can be used to identify such contradictions, but to provide a different set of standards for what it means to be part of a common humanity. Lessons like you're describing do this, and they show cultural continuity because you're teaching how Black people in the Diaspora express their African heritage knowledge in the past and present. What's important about doing this is that Black people become the center of their own story as subjects with agency who are not just reacting to what was or is being done to them.

I want to say something more about the term "heritage knowledge." Becoming more conscious of our heritage knowledge makes it possible to identify with and know ourselves and the world as people of African ancestry. Earlier I mentioned Dr. John Henrik Clarke (1992) in connection with the idea of belonging. He explained that "heritage teaching" [p. 86] permits African people to "locate ourselves on the map of human geography" [p. 104]. All cultures have heritage knowledge, and when this cultural legacy is taught and presented with accuracy and scholarly integrity, it represents each culture's worldview, history, philosophy, language(s), and cultural concepts. We propose that curriculum and pedagogy be built around heritage knowledge because it is a way to include the cultural patterns and legacies of all children and their families, since it is families that convey heritage knowledge across the generations.

Ms. Singleton: Your point about families gives teachers a different way to think about connecting families with what's going on in school. And I don't just mean coming to parent-teacher conferences or chaperoning field trips—not that there is much money for field trips anymore. What I'm saying is that teachers can learn about families' heritage knowledge, and we can work together to explore this knowledge, which then becomes a cultural asset that can strengthen our instructional program. I always invite family members to participate in my lessons, and in teaching about the Montgomery Bus Boycott, I might ask those who participate to be part of producing a culturally authentic assessment (King & Swartz, 2014). This means that we would discuss how to use African Diasporan cultural concepts as criteria for evaluating what students are learning. In this case, we might ask students to connect a list of the cultural concepts they have learned with current topics. For example, we could involve students in demonstrating how several of these concepts influence the actions of groups like Black Lives Matter as they protest the denial of voting rights in some states and police abuses and killings of unarmed Black people in many communities. Most of my African American parents will resonate with African cultural concepts about justice, which are part of their heritage knowledge; and it will be a way for them to see what activists are trying to achieve, rather than how the media usually portrays them as being against things. In the process other parents, whose heritage is different, will be gaining cultural knowledge about people of African ancestry. I would need to refine this basic idea as I work with a group of parents, but I think you see where I'm going.

Dr. King: Yes, I do. Heritage knowledge takes the unjust system out of the center and puts the cultural foundation that generates people's agency to change that system in the center. All groups demonstrate such agency at some time or another. You're seeing families with cultural assets—with heritage knowledge—that can support instruction so that family knowledge becomes a part of school knowledge. A culturally authentic assessment project like the one you just shared makes it possible to see African Diasporan cultural continuity and its relevance for teaching and learning. While this continuity naturally exists, evidence of it has been erased from school knowledge and so it's not available for teachers' use in standard curriculum and pedagogy.

Ms. Singleton: Yes, Ms. Hart and I collaborate about how to make connections between all children and their ancestral cultures. Collaboration is essential and so is the availability of student materials with accurate content and indigenous voice. If we're going to show African Diasporan cultural continuity and make connections to what matters in the lives of students, families, and communities, we need instructional materials that help us connect what students are learning to their heritage as well as to current realities like what's going on with Black Lives Matter and people like Esther Calhoun.

This idea of African Diasporan cultural continuity is not in our district's curriculum or state standards, and it's definitely not in any textbooks. I know that textbooks are not the curriculum, but too many teachers view them as the knowledge that needs to be taught.

Publishers closely align their products with state standards and use these standards to produce district curriculum or corporate curriculum packages sanctioned by states. While some state standards are useful, they provide no support for African Diasporan cultural continuity . . . none. I also know that social studies textbooks have responded to pressure for inclusion of historically marginalized groups but this usually takes the form of sidebars, photos with captions, vignettes, and biographies of "famous" people—and they're still doing it. These "outside of the main text" approaches are still the primary form of inclusion, if you can call it that, with a growing list of possible figures deemed "worthy" of such treatment. I could count on seeing George Washington Carver, Harriet Tubman, Frederick Douglas, and Sojourner Truth in such "features" in my earlier years as a teacher. Now there are these same people as well as Benjamin Banneker, Thurgood Marshall, Zora Neale Hurston, and Mae Jemison. The problem is that these inclusions still lack indigenous voice and disconnect these "famous" people from their ancestral heritage. And the content is too limited to stimulate critical thinking—let alone thinking grounded in an African worldview. Apparently some authorities have decided that certain people are credible enough to be included, but what is African about them is always excluded.

Dr. King: We are thinking about a chapter that compares two accounts of Benjamin Banneker using Afrocentric concepts and culturally informed principles as criteria [Chapter 2, "Locating Democracy and Benjamin Banneker: Theory and Practice"]. One account is from an elementary textbook (Boyd et al., 2011a). Just as you say, it lacks indigenous voice and disconnects Banneker from his African heritage. The other is from a "re-membered" or democratized account published a year later that maintains Banneker's connection to his African ancestry (Swartz, 2013). We thought we'd ask you and Ms. Hart to teach the "re-membered" account of Banneker so readers can see how it illustrates Banneker's connection to his African heritage, is more accurate, has indigenous voice, and encourages critical thinking about social and racial justice. Learning about Banneker's heritage knowledge and how it connects to his accomplishments might also be a way for students to identify and use aspects of their own cultural background and heritage knowledge in response to a current local or national issue that affects them and their families.

Ms. Singleton: I like that idea, and I'm sure we can show how to make connections between content about Banneker and students' lives today. I've been teaching for almost three decades and what I've noticed during that time is that this idea of cultural continuity has existed, but only for White students. Cultural continuity between Europe and the Americas is assumed and constantly celebrated. It begins with the colonial period, when elementary students learn about the European countries that explorers and colonists came from and are taught something about those countries. Through the years, all students are taught—either directly or indirectly—that just about everything in the United States is connected to Europe in some way, since information about the influences of other cultures is so limited.

Dr. King: So even though there is a lot of scholarship about African influences and African cultural retentions in the Americas, very little of this information is in PK-12 curricula and pedagogy. This means that while there is assumed continuity between Europeans and their descendants, there is no assumed continuity between Africans and their descendants. Thus, there is no way for students to appreciate the debts we owe to African and Native American Peoples. Students never learn how African and Indigenous American our society actually is! The massive omissions and distortions we are talking about in school curricula—and academic scholarship— are largely responsible for this. One way to restore more accurate knowledge of cultural continuity is through scholarship that shows African worldview and influences that have shaped Diasporan people's experiences in this country and countries throughout the world [e.g., Brazil, Canada, Mexico, Haiti, Jamaica, and England; and other European, Asian, Caribbean, and South American nations]—even if people aren't consciously aware of those influences.

Ms. Singleton: Over the summer I've been reading about the pre-Columbian African presence in Mexico, the Caribbean, and South America. There is so much evidence of this early African presence and the relationship between Indigenous American and African civilizations hundreds and thousands of years ago. Wait [turning to her computer] . . . I made some notes about some of this evidence . . . let me pull it up . . . I've provided some information for students about this early African presence in the Americas, but with all this specific content, including some charts, pictures, and maps, I can do a much better job. Okay, here it is. Let me read some points from my notes:

- There are the huge Olmec heads of men with African physiognomy [carved in stone]—some with Kemetic [Egyptian] helmets, others with Ethiopian ear pendants and braids—found at several sites in Mexico and carbon-dated to as early as 800 BCE.

- There are comparative studies of pyramids in Mexico and Africa, finding them to be similar in purpose and construction, with the first Mexican pyramids at the site [La Venta] where the Olmec heads were found (Lumpkin, 2007/1992).
- There are words from West African languages in Indigenous American languages.
- Ivan Van Sertima (1976) has provided written evidence of two early fourteenth-century Mandinka [Mali Empire, West Africa] ocean voyages in search of lands to the west, with fleets of ships carrying provisions, gold, and other materials for trade, and—during the same century—carbon-dated sculptural likenesses of Mandinka sailors found in Mexico.
- There is knowledge about underwater ocean currents that carry ships from the West Coast of Africa into the Caribbean Sea (Lawrence, 2007/1992).
- There are numerous African portraits in clay, stone, and jadite carbon-dated from around 1,000 BCE (von Wuthenau, 1975, 2007/1992).

It just goes on and on . . .

- At the beginning of the twentieth century, John Boyd-Thacher (1903–1904) used the records of Columbus to explain how Taíno people in Quisqueya [called Española by Columbus and now called the Dominican Republic and Haiti] told Columbus about trading with Black men who came from the south or southeast and whose spears had metal tips. When Columbus had this metal tested in Europe, it was made with 18 parts of gold, 6 of silver, and 8 of copper. These same metals in these exact proportions were used in the metal alloying process in the Mali Empire [West Africa] at that time.
- Columbus also observed woven garments of cotton worn by Indigenous people in the Antilles and he wrote about them as having a similar style, design, and use as garments imported from West Africa into Morocco, Spain, and Portugal.

While textbooks omit all of this evidence of an early African presence in the Americas—as well as a pre-Columbian Asian presence, they include an early Viking presence around the year 1000 [BCE]. And guess what the evidence is for this? Viking sagas, legends, or tales, and a few objects found at one site in Newfoundland. I'm not kidding!

Dr. King: Well, it doesn't get any clearer. Evidence is omitted if it contradicts agreed-upon and false assumptions—in this case, that Europeans had advanced seafaring technology before anyone else. So, even though there's all this evidence to the contrary, students and teachers have no access to this example of African Diasporan continuity in state-sanctioned curriculum and textbooks. This absence is also evident in representations of the *Maafa* [the European enslavement of African people] that disconnect enslaved African people from their cultures of origin—a disconnection that continues in distorted depictions of each era that followed. Europeans are also disconnected from their heritage of enslavement—before they became "European" (Painter, 2011). When you think about it, U.S. history and social studies textbooks have been omitting and distorting content at the conceptual and factual level for over two centuries. These omissions and distortions contribute to a false narrative about cultural superiority and what it means to be White and what it means to be Black.

Ms. Singleton: Although it is omitted from our professional preparation as teachers, a number of scholars have done research and published information to correct many of these omissions and distortions. That should help us make more connections between Africa and the Diaspora.

Dr. King: Yes, it does help. Take the idea of democracy. Black philosophers and educators like W.E.B. Du Bois and Carter G. Woodson advocated for democracy that applied to all, not only some. Typically, however, the eurocratic filter for viewing their work is that it was a reaction to oppression, rather than a stance of agency based on their African worldview. [We use the term "eurocratic" rather than the general term "Eurocentric" because it more specifically refers to the process of imposing officially sanctioned constraints, in this case on knowledge, through systems that maintain Euro-American authority and hegemony.] As you know, eurocratic ideas, assumptions, policies, and practices position Europeans and their descendants as the official deciders of whose knowledge is worth knowing and how that knowledge is to be thought about. This official, agreed-upon knowledge or socially produced ignorance becomes a script—what we call a master script. In this script, Black advocacy for a democracy that includes all groups is presented merely as a reaction to oppression, not as actions that come from an African Diasporan worldview. This representation remains squarely within the eurocratic episteme, which philosophers describe as the "epistemology of ignorance" (Sullivan & Tuana, 2007). The assumption that I just mentioned about Europeans having advanced seafaring technology before Africans is an example of how eurocratic constraints on knowledge make false assumptions possible.

So, in the case of Du Bois, which we plan to develop in another chapter [Chapter 4, "Worldview, Scholarship, and Instructional Agency"], knowing that his scholarship—and all scholarship—exists within a cultural framework gives us a way to look for a cultural voice or presence in his work. There's a big difference between the eurocratic view of Black scholarship as a response to victimization or as a corrective to biases and omissions of White scholarship and the indigenous view of Black scholarship as reflecting African heritage knowledge that locates African Diasporan people at the center of their realities.

Ms. Singleton: So if teachers learn how heritage knowledge has shaped the thoughts and actions of some of our scholars and leaders, they too can act [e.g., plan units of instruction, write lesson plans, gather or write "re-membered" student materials] with a focus on the culturally informed agency of African Diasporan people.

Dr. King: Yes, with an African worldview and cultural concepts as an epistemic foundation, you can avoid content that presents people of African ancestry as either voiceless victims reacting to one abuse after another or "exceptions to the rule" when their intelligence, bravery, industriousness, and excellence are too obvious to ignore. Guided by your understanding of heritage knowledge you know to look for the agency of African Diasporan people and what their actions mean. For example, on the continent and in the United States, Brazil, and other countries in the Americas there was immediate and ongoing resistance to enslavement by African men and women. They were called Maroons in this country and parts of the Caribbean and *Quilombolas* in Brazil. They liberated themselves and formed hidden African communities that embodied African cultural concepts about the inherent right of freedom and cultural sovereignty and about freedom and justice as communal responsibilities. We can see the same agency, self-determination, and cultural definition today in the Black Lives Matter movement here and *Quilombismo* in Brazil that both aim to end the marginalization and injustices still experienced by people of African ancestry. At all levels educators need to broaden their historical knowledge—really all kinds of knowledge—that has either been omitted or agreed upon for so long that it seems true.

Ms. Singleton: Yes, and when we fail to see beyond eurocratic scripts, we continue to teach them to our students. Like democracy . . . at all levels children are still taught that the origins of democracy were in ancient Greece, and that democracy is about individuals having the right to make choices through voting. This script ignores the existence of indigenous democracies in North America—like the Haudenosaunee—(Barreiro, 1992; Dunbar-Ortiz, 2014; Grinde & Johansen, 1991; Lyons & Mohawk, 1992) and what colonial leaders like Benjamin Franklin learned about democracy from them and their Great Law of Peace [a document of Haudenosaunee world-view, cosmology, history, and government organization recorded on wampum belts].

Dr. King: Yes, there's both a Haudenosaunee influence on democracy and an African influence. Master scripts also leave out the existence of democracies in Africa, so there's no way for students to see the connection between the experiences of African people with democratic governance at home and their pursuit of democracy in the Diaspora. We plan to provide information about African democratic practices that are communal—that consider the needs and interests of the whole society, not only some or a majority of it—and how that idea of democracy was brought to the Americas and advocated for by African people [see Chapter 4 in this volume]. Learning what is African about the pursuit of democracy in this country gives us a way to see agreed-upon knowledge for what it is—an outside view that "tells" teachers and students what to think about democracy and who had it and who didn't. In another example of telling us what to think, standard instructional materials describe segregation as separating groups based on race (Berson et al., 2012; Boyd et al., 2011b). Segregation is presented as inevitable during a time when Black people "lost" rights. As these sanitized accounts go, White Southerners were trying to take back control that was taken away from them during Reconstruction, which omits the well-documented violence and terrorism they used to intimidate Black people during and after Reconstruction.

Ms. Singleton: Textbooks don't name segregation as violent and dehumanizing, and they definitely don't call it antidemocratic or include anything about the effects of segregation on whole communities, including Black and White people. Recent textbooks might suggest that "separate but equal" didn't work and that it was never equal, but they quickly move to show how progress was made toward ending segregation by including information about individuals who broke the "color barrier," like Jackie Robinson. Ending segregation was not about individuals being "firsts" . . . And textbooks certainly don't help us understand the white backlash that is happening in our society today. I just can't . . . I refuse to use these textbooks.

Dr. King: I hear you . . . and as for segregation, being separate was not the problem and individuals breaking the "color barrier" or being "firsts" was not how segregation ended. What these treatments fail to do is explain that maintaining white control through unjust laws, terrorism, and other illegal means was the problem, because it trampled on democracy, justice, and the humanity of everyone. As James Baldwin once said, "White is a metaphor for power" (Peck, 2017, p. 107).

I'm thinking about W.E.B. Du Bois, who had a conception of life as communal and reciprocal, which—if you look at the historical record—is African, not European. In education, he advocated for an end to segregation and viewed equally educating all children as everyone's responsibility, which is an expression of an African cultural concept—*protecting childhood as a collective responsibility [each child is everyone's child]*. Du Bois (1935) understood segregation as antithetical to the well-being of communities. Having this information about him can replace the agreed-upon view of segregation that we still get in instructional materials—the one that "tells" students and teachers to accept segregation as just the way it was back then. Du Bois's way of thinking about segregation allows us to step outside of this master script that standard school knowledge still perpetuates. By using a number of African cultural concepts, we can explain why Black people, including children, understood segregation as unethical and resisted it.

Ms. Singleton: More educators seem to know that we don't have enough information about African American history and culture—actually about all underrepresented or misrepresented groups—and even publishers are responding with more inclusion. But what troubles me is that making progress in connecting culture to learning isn't going to happen if too many teachers are satisfied with this tokenism in textbooks and other materials. I think that a "little more" inclusion actually makes things worse; it's an illusion of progress, not a real step forward. It doesn't help students to think critically about the past and connect the past to what's going on in the present.

Dr. King: So true . . . more inclusive master scripts are still master scripts and won't fix anything. They exist to preserve the status quo . . . or the illusion of one.

Ms. Singleton: I've noticed that a few recent U.S. social studies textbooks include brief information about West African empires [Ghana, Mali, and Songhoy], which some educators might see as positive. However, these empires—which I know were highly complex, organized civilizations—are only referred to as trading kingdoms or trading empires; and their trade, governance practices, leaders, scholars, and religious practices are presented as the outcome of Islamic influence, as if outside influence was responsible for these developments. What they omit are the ways in which African civilizations remained African while incorporating external influences, such as Islam. And there were and are many other civilizations throughout the African continent [e.g., Kanem Bornu, Benin, Asante, Nok, Kongo, Kush, Kemet, Aksum, Zimbabwe, Zulu] but there's no

information about them in the curriculum. So, over 12 or r._
years of schooling, students experience curricula and instructional materials about European civilizations—about their organization, what they accomplished, and how their civilizations
influenced developments all around the world. But there is nothing similar about African civilizations and their accomplishments
that influenced the world and came much earlier than those in
Europe.

Dr. King: And failing to include similar knowledge about African civilizations—
knowledge that is well researched and available—continues to reinforce false assumptions, such as Europeans planned and organized
civilizations and Africans did not; African social, political, and
cultural developments were the result of outside influences rather
than African achievements; and that there is no cultural continuity between Africa and the Diaspora. Through omission or very
minimal and distorted inclusions, we have been taught—and continue to teach—that Europe is the standard-bearer of civilization.

Ms. Singleton: This makes me think of what Dr. John Henrik Clarke said about
the importance of finding yourself on the "map of human geography." Children don't know that this removal or distortion of
what people of African ancestry have developed and accomplished
over centuries has been done purposefully to maintain white
supremacy—but they are experiencing its effects every day.

Dr. King: That's why curriculum and pedagogy are so important. We plan
to provide examples of African civilizational accomplishments by
including information about Songhoy civilization [West Africa],
the language connections that exist between Kemet [East Africa]
and Songhoy [West Africa] civilizations, and how we can use an
African language pedagogically to decipher important aspects of
the African American experience [see Chapter 3, "Teaching African Language for Historical Consciousness, Recovering Group
Memory and Identity"]. So much heritage knowledge or group
memory is embedded in African languages, and these languages
are mostly unknown by people of African ancestry in the Diaspora or any other groups for that matter. Teaching *Songhoy-senni*,
which was the language spoken in the Songhoy civilization of the
sixteenth century and earlier—and is still spoken today in Mali and
other neighboring West African countries—is a way to learn about
African/African American heritage *through* language. Students of
African ancestry experience a connection to their heritage, and all
students learn that the meanings of words and concepts are shaped
by the cultural contexts from which they come. Teachers will be
able to use the culturally informed content in this chapter to teach

about African civilizations and the African American experience more accurately and authentically.

Ms. Singleton: This knowledge is extremely important for all students. Not only does it put people of African ancestry on the map of human geography, as Dr. Clarke says, but knowing about the history and heritage of your ancestors is a solid foundation for early identity development, a way to experience belonging, and a solid ground to stand on when relating to others.

Dr. King: While this is so obvious and logical, a major stumbling block is that state ed departments and publishers—as well as most educators— are only functioning within a European worldview, so they have limited or no knowledge about the histories, cultures, and world-views of other world regions. And for educators, editors, authors, and administrators of Africa, indigenous, and Asian ancestry, they often have limited experience with using their history and heritage knowledge to shape their practice. So, a European worldview and cultural concepts are at the foundation of most educational materials and practices. This includes ontological orientations or ways of being like, Competition, Individualism, Difference [as deficit], and Survival of the Fittest; epistemologies or ways of knowing, like authority and the scientific method; and values, like a hierarchy of human worth and individual mindedness. You can see these worldview elements in concepts that influence what teachers do. So, as we explained in our last text [Chapter 5 in King & Swartz, 2016], if your worldview includes Individualism, Competition, Difference, and Survival of the Fittest, you are likely to view *achievement as excelling above others* and agree with the eurocratic concept of *expecting and accepting a certain amount of student failure.* And if authority and the scientific method are primary ways of knowing for you, then teaching as "telling"—*the transmission of agreed-upon information* assessed through standardized testing—is probably a comfortable pedagogy for you. In other words, European worldview and cultural concepts shape not only what educators know and value, but what they do in classrooms.

Ms. Singleton: A lot of teachers do accept a culturally limited curriculum, encourage competition, and expect and accept that some students will fail. And many tell students what they should know so they can give it back on all kinds of recall tests, rather than teach them to think for themselves. While these practices seem "normal" within a European worldview and have become standard, they aren't inevitable. So we should be able to change them.

Dr. King: Yes, we can change them by having access to other worldviews and cultural concepts. We are developing this idea for another chapter

[Chapter 5, "White Progressive Education, African Worldview, and Democratic Practice"]. During the early twentieth century, White progressive child-centered philosophers and educators like John Dewey, George Counts, and William Heard Kilpatrick advocated that schools become sites of democratic practice. However, their worldview and adherence to a racial hierarchy trumped their rhetoric and blocked them from acknowledging and learning from Black scholars who were working at the same time—scholars such as W.E.B. DuBois, Carter G. Woodson, Anna Julia Cooper, Alaine Locke, and Horace Mann Bond. These Black philosophers and educators were developing theoretical constructs to support their efforts to end systemic forms of oppression and educational inequalities so that all groups could experience the benefits of democracy, not only some. So, even though White child-centered educators advocated ideas and practices that challenged some aspects of a European worldview, they accepted and participated in practices of white supremacy like segregation. Their support of racial inequalities shows that their ideas of child centering did not include Black children; and by ignoring Black scholarship, they disconnected themselves from a cultural episteme that was actually more compatible with the ideas they claimed to value.

Ms. Singleton: Over my career I've seen the district try different versions of progressive ideas, but they never stick. Teachers show initial enthusiasm for these child-centered approaches, but if they don't see results fairly soon they typically go back to what they used to do—what seems familiar even though it hasn't been working.

Dr. King: Yes, and we can expect that because they are teaching in a society where the dominant worldview supports "what they used to do," not the new [to them] child-centered practices they are trying to do. We have the same problem with helping teachers move beyond agreed-upon historiography that decenters so many of our students. Actually, if we want to locate *all* students at the center of instruction, then we need a worldview and cultural concepts and practices that can do that.

Ms. Singleton: This "agreed-upon historiography" is like the grand narratives you wrote about in your last book where you gave some examples of the grand narratives that have shaped the social studies curriculum. I know that these narratives are in the heads of most teachers who were exposed to them every year in school since kindergarten.

Dr. King: And since these narratives are not based on accurate scholarship, they obscure the cultural assets of our students by obscuring the cultural assets of their ancestors and their families. Take the grand narrative of slavery [see page 66 in *The Afrocentric Praxis of Teaching* for *Freedom*, King & Swartz, 2016], which is an explanation of slavery agreed-upon by eurocratic authorities or "experts" in each generation. This grand narrative is an outcome of European worldview elements, such as Difference as deficit and Survival of the Fittest [ontological orientations], excessive use of authority [an epistemological orientation], and a hierarchy of human worth and "might makes right" [values]. The narrative describes chattel slavery through the self-serving lies of the plantocracy, which means that it represents how enslavers claimed to have more human worth than those they enslaved; and since enslavers used "might" to enslave others, they saw themselves as the "fittest," which in their Darwinian view of the world made them "right." And this grand narrative of slavery is maintained by the master scripts found in textbooks, standards, and curricula today. These distorted accounts of enslavement suggest that Africans and Europeans are both to blame for the European slavery enterprise and consistently omit the heritage and cultural assets that African people brought with them to the Americas. So when teachers use master scripts based on the grand narrative of slavery—with its omissions and lies about the history and heritage of African people—it makes it less likely that they can see the cultural assets of African people's descendants who are their students. And the lies continue over the decades, even when there are some slight revisions in master scripts to fit with the current sensibilities of each era. So, today U.S. textbooks don't use racial slurs and overtly ridicule African Diasporan people like they did in the past, and as we said, they include more "famous" Black people. But grand narratives stay basically the same because they reflect the dominant or European worldview that has remained quite stable over the past several hundred years.

Ms. Singleton: And some of the same European worldview elements you just mentioned [Difference as deficit, excessive use of authority, a hierarchy of human worth, and "might makes right"] explain why it took so much effort to end de jure segregation and why de facto segregation still exists and why Black lives don't matter. So, then, the problem with grand narratives is that they mirror the dominant worldview that informed the original events they are now "explaining." And this means that the grand narrative remains the same even if you remove racial slurs and are more inclusive.

Dr. King: Exactly, and there are cultural concepts through which these European worldview elements play out. Take concepts like *viewing cultural sovereignty as only the right of "advanced" cultures* and *distributing resources by status or rank* that express a hierarchy of human worth and excessive use of authority. These concepts supported chattel slavery, Jim

Crow—the old and the "new" one—and the devaluing of Black life
we still see today (Alexander, 2012; Glaude, 2016); and these same
concepts shape grand narratives about colonialism and imperialism
that tell students how to think. Euro-American powers have acted
and continue to act on these concepts as if it's a given that only they
have the right to maintain their cultures and have more material
benefits based on their "advanced" position. So in addition to telling students how to think, grand narratives teach that dominance is
inevitable, which explains why we need to replace these narratives,
not only objectionable words, phrases, and omissions.

Ms. Singleton: I'm thinking about what a narrative of enslavement would look
like if it was shaped by an African worldview [pointing to Figure 1.1], including Collectivity and Interdependence [ontological
orientations], relational knowing, mutuality, and empathy [episte-
mological orientations], right action and community-mindedness
[values], Truth and Justice [*Maatian* Cardinal Virtues], and Unity
and Self-Determination [Kwanzaa Principles].

Dr. King: And with those worldview elements we could frame that narrative
with African cultural concepts, like *the inherent worth of all people,
knowing that cultural sovereignty is a common right of all Peoples,* and
sharing responsibility for communal well-being and belonging. This part
of our conversation is relevant to another chapter we are considering [Chapter 6, "A Call for a Reparatory Justice Curriculum
for Human Freedom: Rewriting the Story of Our Dispossession
and the Debt Owed"]. We want to propose that an emancipatory
education component become part of international movements
for reparations. These movements, which date to the abolition
of legal slavery in the Americas [from Haiti in 1793 to Brazil in
1888], continue to seek an honest response from governments and
public and private institutions in Europe and the African Diaspora
that perpetrated and greatly benefit from the holocaust of centuries of enslavement and its Jim Crow aftermath—which has only
changed forms, not ended. An educational component is needed
because the ongoing denial of responsibility for these injuries is
kept alive in school knowledge with psychologically damaging and
false narratives and scripts about the history and culture of African
Diasporan Peoples. Critiquing and replacing these narratives are
an essential part of the remedy for these crimes against humanity
that have obstructed human freedom for all of us up to the present
day. In an African understanding, no one is free unless everyone
is free. So we want to place the educational work we are doing in
the context of public movements that are seeking more accurate
accounts about people of African ancestry. Acknowledging that

accounts of the past have been distorted is part of a restorative process that needs to occur, since governments and institutions in Europe and its colonial outposts reaped huge financial benefits—at great human cost—from the systems of slavery and colonial rule in the Americas . . . and still do.

Ms. Singleton: From what I've heard, a lot of people don't understand reparations. By connecting an educational component to this movement, educators would have a way to see how our work with students and families is essential to repairing injuries that stem from enslavement and its lingering effects (Leary, 2005).

Dr. King: And what we learn as we repair those injuries and recover more accurate narratives we can give back to our students, families, and communities. We're thinking about developing this idea of returning what we learn in our last chapter [Chapter 7, "Returning What We Learn to the People"]. An African epistemic foundation has shaped scholarly integrity in the Black intellectual tradition, which has given us an ethically and culturally grounded vision of human freedom and defined our responsibility as educators. We want to bring together the book's major themes by merging personal, professional, and political actions that draw upon this vision. These actions would show how students, teachers, scholars, and parents/families can participate in creating knowledge on behalf of advancing human freedom and sustainability for the world. As we teach, conduct research, and act to replace distorted narratives and societal myths about all groups of people, we are responsible to reciprocally engage with families and communities. We are all sites of memory, and can return what we have learned to nourish each other and our communities. That's how we view what you and Ms. Hart are doing in your school. For example, the Benjamin Banneker materials we provide and the lessons you develop can become part of a restorative educational process that is an essential component of reparations. This is one way we can give back what we have learned to students, families, and communities.

Ms. Singleton: I'll speak with Ms. Hart about this. I would be pleased to participate, and I'm pretty sure she will, too.

Dr. King: We really appreciate your interest in continuing to work with us. We'll be reviewing the recording of this conversation, and from what I've just experienced in talking with you, I'm sure it will help us to refine our thinking as we continue writing.

Ms. Singleton: There's so much potential here to present knowledge that shows students and families that they, too, can act with agency to make a difference in their communities like their ancestors did. I wouldn't miss this for anything!

References

Alexander, M. (2012). *The new Jim Crow: Mass incarceration in the age of color blindness.* New York: New Press.

Barreiro, J. (Ed.). (1992). *Indian roots of American democracy.* Ithaca, NY: Akwe: Kon Press.

Berson, M. J., Howard, T. C., & Salinas, C. (2012). *The United States: Making a new nation.* Boston: Houghton Mifflin Harcourt.

Bogado, A. (2016). *Meet the activist getting sued for complaining about a coal-ash dump.* Retrieved from http://readersupportednews.org/news-section2/318-66/37530-meet-the-activist-getting-sued-for-complaining-about-a-coal-ash-dump

Boyd, C. D., Gay, G., Geiger, R., Kracht, J. B., Ooka Pang, V., Risinger, C. F., & Sanchez, S. M. (2011a). *The United States.* Boston, MA: Pearson.

Boyd, C. D., Gay, G., Geiger, R., Kracht, J. B., Ooka Pang, V., Risinger, C. F., & Sanchez, S. M. (2011b). *People and places.* Boston, MA: Pearson.

Boyd-Thacher, J. (1903–1904). *Christopher Columbus, his life, his work, his remains* (Vol. 2). New York: G.P. Putnam's Sons.

Carruthers, J. (1995). *Mdw Ntr—Divine speech: A historiographical reflection of African deep thought from the time of the Pharaohs to the present.* London: Karnak House/Lawrenceville, NJ: Red Sea Press.

Clarke, J. H. (1992). *Christopher Columbus and the Afrikan holocaust: Slavery and the rise of European capitalism.* Brooklyn, NY: A & B Books.

Du Bois, W.E.B. (1935). Does the Negro need separate schools? *Journal of Negro Education, 4*, 329–335.

Dunbar-Ortiz, R. (2014). *An indigenous peoples' history of the United States.* Boston, MA: Beacon Press.

Glaude, E. S., Jr. (2016). *Democracy in Black: How race still enslaves the American soul.* New York, NY: Crown.

Grinde, D. A., Jr., & Johansen, B. E. (1991). *Exemplar of liberty: Native America and the evolution of democracy.* Los Angeles: American Indian Studies Center, University of California.

Hilliard, A. G. III (1997). *SBA: The reawakening of the African mind.* Gainesville, FL: Makare.

Karenga, M. (1998). *Kwanzaa: A celebration of family, community, and culture.* Los Angeles: University of Sankore Press.

Karenga, M. (2006). Philosophy in the African tradition of resistance: Issues of human freedom and human flourishing. In Lewis R. Gordon & Jane Anna Gordon (Eds.), *Not only the master's tools: African American studies in theory and practice* (pp. 243–271). Boulder, CO: Paradigm.

King, J. E., & Swartz, E. E. (2016). *The Afrocentric praxis of teaching for freedom: Connecting culture to learning.* New York, NY: Routledge.

King, J. E., Swartz, E. E., Campbell, L., Lemons-Smith, S., & López, E. (2014). *"Remembering" history in student and teacher learning: An Afrocentric culturally informed praxis.* New York, NY: Routledge.

Lawrence, H. G. (Kofi Wangara) (2007/1992). Mandinga voyages across the Atlantic. In I. Van Sertima (Ed.), *African presence in early America.* New Brunswick, NJ: Transaction.

Leary, J. D. (2005). *Post traumatic slave syndrome: America's legacy of enduring injury and healing.* Portland, OR: Joy DeGruy.

Lumpkin, B. (2007/1992). Pyramids—American and African: A comparison. In I. Van Sertima (Ed.), *African presence in early America* (pp. 136–154). New Brunswick, NJ: Transaction.

Lyons, O., & Mohawk, J. (Eds.). (1992). *Exiled in the land of the free: Democracy, Indian nations, and the U.S. Constitution.* Santa Fe, NM: Clear Light.

Painter, N. I. (2011). *The history of white people.* New York: W.W. Norton.

Peck, R. (2017). *I am not your Negro.* New York, NY: Vintage International.

Sullivan, S., & Tuana, N. (Eds.). (2007). *Races and epistemologies of ignorance.* Albany: SUNY Press.

Swartz, E. E. (2013). *Black community building: The African tradition of collective work and responsibility.* Rochester, NY: Omnicentric Press.

Van Sertima, I. (1976). *They came before Columbus: The African presence in ancient America.* New York: Random House.

Von Wuthenau, A. (1975). *Unexpected faces in ancient America: The historical testimony of the pre-Columbian artist.* New York, NY: Crown.

Von Wuthenau, A. (2007/1992). Unexpected African faces in pre-Columbian America. In I. Van Sertima (Ed.), *African presence in early America* (pp. 82–101). New Brunswick, NJ: Journal of African Civilizations.

Willis, B. (1998). *Adinkra dictionary: A visual primer on the language of Adinkra.* Washington, DC: Pyramid Complex.

2

LOCATING DEMOCRACY AND BENJAMIN BANNEKER

Theory and Practice

Ellen E. Swartz

This, Sir, was a time in which you clearly saw into the injustice of a state of slavery, and in which you had just apprehensions of the horrors of its condition. It was now, Sir, that your abhorrence thereof was so excited, that you publicly held forth this true and invaluable doctrine, which is worthy to be recorded and remembered in all succeeding ages. "We hold these truths to be self-evident, that all men are created equal; that they are endowed by their creator with certain unalienable rights, and that among these are life, liberty, and the pursuit of happiness."

Here was a time in which your tender feelings for your selves had engaged you thus to declare, you were then impressed with proper ideas of the great violation of liberty, and the free possession of those blessings, to which you were entitled by nature; but Sir how pitiable is it to reflect, that although you were so fully convinced of the benevolence of the Father of Mankind, and of his equal and impartial distribution of those rights and privileges, which he had conferred upon them, that you should at the same time counteract his mercies, in detaining by fraud and violence so numerous a part of my brethren, under groaning captivity and cruel oppression, that you should at the same time be found guilty of that most criminal act, which you professedly detested in others, with respect to yourselves.

Excerpt of letter written by Benjamin Banneker to
Thomas Jefferson (August 19, 1791)

What would history look like if we "re-membered" or put back together narratives of eras, movements, or events that more accurately represented the actions of those cultural groups that shaped them? And how would our understanding of that "re-membered" history be enhanced if we knew about the worldviews and cultural concepts that informed those "re-membered" narratives? What we

v, and will demonstrate in this chapter, is that by gathering and applying
...owledge from typically unconsidered sources, we can replace eurocratic master
scripts that still teach dominant and distorted accounts to school children with
knowledge that is closer to what actually occurred in the past (Epstein, 2009;
Goodwin, 1998; King & Swartz, 2014, 2016; Swartz, 1992).

We draw the theoretical concepts and culturally informed principles needed
to produce "re-membered" knowledge from the paradigm and analytical stance
of Afrocentricity. This paradigm locates the worldview, cultural concepts, knowledge, and actions of African Diasporan Peoples at the center of phenomena, not
on the margins to be defined by others (Asante, 1980/1988, 1987/1998, 2010;
Keto, 1995; Mazama, 2003a, 2003b). Using Afrocentric concepts and principles
makes it possible to develop more accurate and authentic curriculum for all
students as well as challenge current and dominant assumptions in all disciplines
when they omit, marginalize, or distort knowledge about Africa, African Peoples,
and their connections to the rest of the world (Asante, 2007; King & Swartz,
2014, 2016).

In this chapter we use Afrocentric theoretical concepts and culturally
informed principles to examine African Diasporan democratic practices and
to compare a "re-membered" account of Benjamin Banneker with one that
is master-scripted. We also conduct an observation of Ms. Singleton and
Ms. Hart teaching "re-membered" content about Banneker to their fifth-grade
students. This classroom demonstration exemplifies how the paradigm of
Afrocentricity, which is built on an African epistemic foundation, can guide
the retrieval and restoration of African Diasporan history and culture that
have long been silenced.

African Episteme and Afrocentricity

Afrocentricity is informed by an African episteme—that is, by ways of knowing
and conceptions of knowledge based on African worldview and the cultural
concepts that express that worldview. Standing on this African epistemic foundation, Afrocentricity sits within the academic discipline of Africology and provides
theories in many fields and disciplines (Asante, 2008; Bethel, 2003; Cokely, 2003;
Dove, 1998; Mazama, 2003a). One Afrocentric theory that is particularly useful
in education posits that locating Africa and African people at the center of
phenomena, not on the periphery to be described and defined by others, replaces
the universalized knowledge of the hierarchal European episteme with democratized knowledge through which all students benefit (Asante, 1980/1988, 2003a,
2003b, 2007; Karenga, 2003; Mazama, 2003a, 2003b). This human-centric theory
of representation views *all* people as normative subjects at the center of their
political, economic, and social experiences (Asante, 2007, 1991; Karenga, 2003).
We use this theory as a way of intervening in standard school knowledge that
continues to universalize what Europeans and their descendants have produced

and accomplished while omitting or failing to accurately depict the cultural productions and accomplishments of all other identity groups.

Afrocentric Theoretical Concepts

In the late nineteenth and early decades of the twentieth centuries, scholars in the Black intellectual tradition conducted research and wrote about ideas and practices that fostered self-determination, community uplift through service to others, standards of justice, and indigenous accounts of Black history (Du Bois, 1899, 1903, 1920, 1935/1972; Bond, 1934, 1935; Cooper, 1892/1969; Miller, 1908; Wells, 1892; Woodson, 1919a, 1919b, 1933; Work, 1916, 1919). This intellectual tradition is varied and extensive, including many other Diasporan scholars over two centuries (Crummel, 1898; Delany, 1852; Elliot, 1874; Fanon, 1963, 1965; Fontaine, 1940; Garnet, 1843/1972, 1859; Grant et al., 2016; Hilliard, 1978, 2003; King, 2004, 2015; Lynch, 1875; Mills, 1997; Walker, 1829/1965; Wynter, 1992, 2006). In the last few decades of the twentieth century, Afrocentricity built on the scholarship of the Black intellectual tradition—scholarship that locates African Diasporan people as historical agents who speak for, define, and name themselves (Alkebulan, 2007; Asante, 1980/1988, 1987/1998, 2011; Bankole, 1995, 2008; Karenga, 1999, 2003, 2006a; Kershaw, 1992, 2003; Mazama, 2003b). Table 2.1 provides brief definitions of several Afrocentric theoretical concepts that characterize the emancipatory intent of Afrocentricity. This table is reproduced from our 2014 text, *"Re-membering" History in Student and Teacher Learning: An Afrocentric Culturally Informed Praxis* (p. 38).

The foregoing theoretical concepts describe Africa and African people and events as locations or standing places for learning about the world. By using these concepts to frame the development of curriculum and instructional materials, we can "re-member" or draw back together knowledge that more accurately represents the past than standard school knowledge. For example, by framing a presentation of democracy's early origins and its development in North America with Centrality/Location and Reclamation of Cultural Heritage, African people— as well as Native Americans, particularly the Haudenosaunee—are locations or sites of memory (King, 1992) for learning about democratic practices of governance (Grinde, 1989, 1992; Grinde & Johansen, 1991; Gyekye, 1997; Lyons & Mohawk, 1992; Nyerere, 1965; Sithole, 1959). Likewise, the theoretical concepts of Collective Responsibility and Self-Determination "re-member" content about African Diasporan people working together for justice—not only for African people but for all people (Aptheker, 1951/1969; Bennett, 1968, 1975; Franklin, 1992; Gyekye, 1987; Hart, 1985/2002; Harding, 1990; Quarles, 1969). Further, when teaching about democratic practices in Africa the theoretical concept of Subjects with Agency can explain—and even predict—the ideas and actions of African people who brought knowledge about democracy with them into the Diaspora, where they consistently worked to expand democratic practices.

TABLE 2.1 Afrocentric Theoretical Concepts

- **Collective Consciousness**—This epistemology refers to the "retention of ancestral sensibilities" within and across generations (Nobles, 2005, p. 199). This way of knowing conveys the historic continuity of African essence, energy, and excellence; is sustained through relationships within the collective African family that make awareness, knowledge, and meaning possible; and elicits value for the human collective.

- **Collective Responsibility**—There are reciprocal and interconnected relationships among African people who together make and are made by the "best" practices within African culture. These "best" practices are emancipatory in that their collaborative enactment increases justice and right action for African people and the whole of humanity.

- **Centrality/Location**—Placing Africa and African people and experiences at the center of phenomena means that African knowledge, cultural ideals, values, and ways of knowing and being are a location or standing place from which the past and present can be viewed and understood.

- **Self-Determination**—African individuals make decisions, decide their fate, and control their lives within the context of considering the collective needs and interests of African people and maintaining the sovereignty of African and other cultures.

- **Subjects With Agency**—African people are subjects when and where they are present. They have the will and capacity to act in and on the world—not only as individuals but also as members of their cultural group.

- **Reclamation of Cultural Heritage**—The conscious recovery of African history, culture, and identity that is grounded in knowledge of African cosmology, ontology, epistemology, and axiology and presented with a culturally authentic lexicon is a model for reclaiming the heritage of diverse cultures and groups.

- **Anteriority of Classical African Civilizations**—Ancient Kemet and prior African civilizations developed and exhibited the earliest demonstrations of excellence in foundational disciplines such as philosophy, mathematics, science, medicine, the arts, and architecture.

This "re-membered" knowledge about democracy—which we discuss in greater detail in Chapter 4—is an outcome of using Afrocentric theoretical concepts to explain what is African about democratic ideas, actions, and practices; and it gives us a way to teach about democracy that is based on inclusive and multiply voiced scholarship.

The Epistemic Foundation of Afrocentric Theoretical Concepts

As described earlier, Afrocentric theoretical concepts were built on the ideas and practices of earlier scholars in the Black intellectual tradition who themselves were informed by a much older African epistemic foundation—one that has endured across time and geographic location. While cultural patterns and practices are situational, and differences exist across African cultures, there is an underlying and unifying episteme that is observable in the commonly held elements of African worldview and in African cultural concepts (Anyanwu, 1981; Gyekye, 1987, 1997; Idowu, 1973; Karenga, 2006a; Konadu, 2010; Mbiti, 1990; Nyang,

1980; Obenga, 1989; Tedla, 1995). (See Chapter 1 to review the elements of African worldview and the relationship between African worldview and African cultural concepts. Also, pages 112–133 in King & Swartz, 2016, that include a list and discussion of 18 African cultural concepts, many of which are presented throughout this and other chapters.) Scholars in the Black intellectual tradition, including Afrocentric scholars, have stood on this African epistemic foundation to develop concepts and practices such as the Afrocentric theoretical concepts described earlier in Table 2.1. Ahead we discuss how five of these theoretical concepts (in bold) are informed by an African episteme (African worldview elements and cultural concepts); and we explain how each theoretical concept can be used to frame knowledge about democracy in ways that include its African characteristics. If you are unfamiliar with knowledge about democracy in Africa and its continuation in the Diaspora, you may wish to read the section in Chapter 4 entitled "African Democracy: Continental and Diasporan" (see index for page number).

1. **Centrality/Location** is an Afrocentric theoretical concept informed by such African worldview elements as Collectivity (an ontological orientation), relational knowing (an epistemological orientation), community-mindedness (a value), Reciprocity (a *Maatian* Virtue), and the African cultural concept of *knowing as a communal experience in which everyone has something to contribute* (Akbar, 1984; Dixon, 1971; Fu-Kiau, 2001; Gyekye, 1987; Karenga, 2006b; Nkulu-N'Sengha, 2005; Nobles, 1976). In framing ideas about democracy, **Centrality/Location** describes the centering of all groups who have had experience with democracy as a source of knowledge and a standing place from which this topic can be viewed and understood. This theoretical concept explains that when Africa and African people are a source for learning about democracy, it is understood as a communal, relational, and reciprocal practice that views everyone as having something to contribute.

2. **Reclamation of Cultural Heritage** is an Afrocentric theoretical concept informed by African worldview elements such as Survival of the Group (an ontological orientation), intuition-reasoning—or way of knowing from heart-mind knowledge, which is linked, not separate (an epistemological orientation)—service to others and community-mindedness (values), Justice and Truth (*Maatian* Virtues), and the African cultural concept of *knowing that cultural sovereignty is a common right of all Peoples* (Césaire, 1955/2000; Karenga, 1996, 2006a; Nobles, 1976; Senghor, 1964; Sindima, 1995). As a theoretical concept, **Reclamation of Cultural Heritage** explains why acknowledging cultural sovereignty as a common right is necessary in order to explore varying conceptions and practices of democracy. Having access to African understandings and experiences of democracy allows us to identify and retrieve the service-oriented and communal characteristics of democracy that were brought from Africa to the Diaspora.

3. **Collective Responsibility** is an Afrocentric theoretical concept informed by African worldview elements such as Collaboration, Interdependence, and Collective Responsibility—a way of being in which everyone contributes to the well-being of the group (ontological orientations)—community-mindedness and right action (values), Reciprocity (a *Maatian* Virtue), Collective Work and Responsibility (an *Nguzo Saba* or *Kwanzaa* Principle), and the African cultural concept of *sharing responsibility for communal well-being and belonging* (Abímbólá, 1976; Fu-Kiau, 2001; Gyekye, 1987, 1997; Ikuenobe, 2006; Karenga, 1996, 2006b; Konadu, 2010; Nobles, 1976). Thus, in developing content about democracy, the Afrocentric theoretical concept of **Collective Responsibility**—with its collaborative, interdependent, and reciprocal characteristics—explains how African people viewed democratic forms of governance and ways of living and being together as a shared good and practice of belonging.
4. **Self-Determination** is an Afrocentric theoretical concept informed by African worldview elements such as Commonalities—a way of being that foremost identifies what people hold in common, not how they differ (an ontological orientation)—community-mindedness (a value), Justice (a *Maatian* Virtue), Self-Determination (an *Nguzo Saba* or *Kwanzaa* Principle), and the African cultural concept of *pursuing freedom and justice as communal responsibilities* (Akbar, 1984; Gyekye, 1997; Karenga, 1996; Konadu, 2010; Sindima, 1995). In framing content about democracy, **Self-Determination** explains that while African people understood freedom and justice as individuals making decisions, these decisions were made in the context of considering the collective needs of their communities. Once in the Diaspora, African people pursued freedom and justice as essential to the needs and common interests of their group as well as all groups of people seeking sovereignty over their lives.
5. **Subjects with Agency** is an Afrocentric theoretical concept informed by African worldview elements such as Collectivity (an ontological orientation), intuition-reasoning (an epistemological orientation), service to others (a value), Justice (a *Maatian* Virtue), Collective Work and Responsibility (an *Nguzo Saba* or *Kwanzaa* Principle), and the African cultural concept of *being responsible to bring good into the world through actions that are ethical, just, generous, compassionate, and peaceable* (Gyekye, 1987, 1997; Karenga, 1996, 1999, 2006a; Konadu, 2010; Nobles, 1976). The theoretical concept of **Subjects with Agency** explains that African people had the will and capacity to develop democratic systems of governance and ways of being together at home, and to pursue those same practices in the Diaspora as ways of engaging in ethical actions that bring good into the world and enhance human welfare (Du Bois, 1945; Franklin, 1992; Gyekye, 1987, 1997; Harding, 1990; Karenga, 2006a, 2006b).

To complement the foregoing narratives of how five Afrocentric theoretical concepts are informed by an African episteme, Figure 2.1 graphically depicts the connections between an African epistemic foundation (African worldview

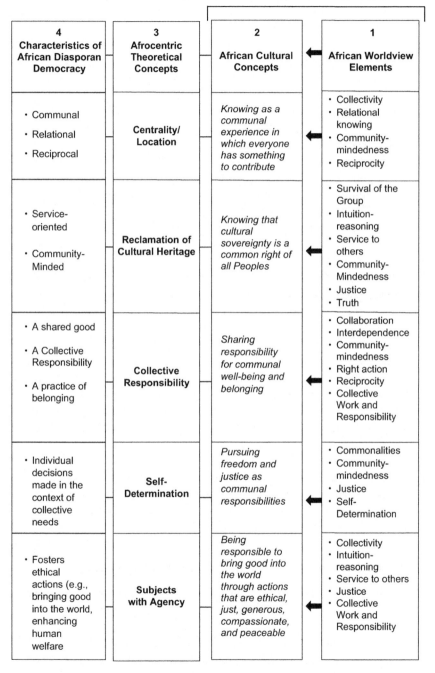

African Epistemic Foundation

4 Characteristics of African Diasporan Democracy	3 Afrocentric Theoretical Concepts	2 African Cultural Concepts	1 African Worldview Elements
• Communal • Relational • Reciprocal	Centrality/ Location	*Knowing as a communal experience in which everyone has something to contribute*	• Collectivity • Relational knowing • Community-mindedness • Reciprocity
• Service-oriented • Community-Minded	Reclamation of Cultural Heritage	*Knowing that cultural sovereignty is a common right of all Peoples*	• Survival of the Group • Intuition-reasoning • Service to others • Community-Mindedness • Justice • Truth
• A shared good • A Collective Responsibility • A practice of belonging	Collective Responsibility	*Sharing responsibility for communal well-being and belonging*	• Collaboration • Interdependence • Community-mindedness • Right action • Reciprocity • Collective Work and Responsibility
• Individual decisions made in the context of collective needs	Self-Determination	*Pursuing freedom and justice as communal responsibilities*	• Commonalities • Community-mindedness • Justice • Self-Determination
• Fosters ethical actions (e.g., bringing good into the world, enhancing human welfare	Subjects with Agency	*Being responsible to bring good into the world through actions that are ethical, just, generous, compassionate, and peaceable*	• Collectivity • Intuition-reasoning • Service to others • Justice • Collective Work and Responsibility

FIGURE 2.1 Epistemic Foundation of Afrocentric Theoretical Concepts and Characteristics of African Democracy

and cultural concepts), the five Afrocentric theoretical concepts just discussed, and how we use them to identify and explain the characteristics of African Diasporan democracy. Reading from right to left, African worldview elements (column 1, far right) can be seen in the cultural concepts that express them (column 2). Together they represent the African epistemic foundation that informs Afrocentric theoretical concepts (column 3), which make it possible to identify and explain the characteristics of African Diasporan democracy (column 4).

An African Diasporan understanding of democracy not only expands teachers' and students' knowledge but also counteracts eurocratic accounts that have effectively erased the African backstory to Black Peoples' ongoing pursuit of democracy in the Americas. This erasure is typical of the omissions and distortions that limit available knowledge about the social, political, economic, spiritual, and other institutional and cultural practices that African people brought with them into the Diaspora (Aptheker, 1951/1969; Carney, 2001; Gyekye, 1997; Hall, 2005; Nyerere, 1965; Piersen, 1993; Price, 1979; Sithole, 1959; Thompson, 1987; Walker, 2001). Using Afrocentric theoretical concepts to connect Diasporan people to the worldview, cultural concepts, and practices of their ancestors explains how African people brought and retained knowledge, concepts, ways of knowing and being, values, virtues, and practices—everything that makes up heritage—from one side of the Atlantic to the other. Failing to acknowledge this is an illogical and white supremacist assumption qua conclusion that continues to distort PK-12 curricular content and pedagogy. Such false conclusions—which are more common than not—explain why African American history is still presented as beginning with enslavement; colonial practices and enslavement are taught as exempt from ethical review; and individualistic, coercive, and punitive pedagogical practices are the norm. In sum, standard school knowledge and experiences continue to reproduce the *Maafa*'s disruption of ties between Diasporan people and their cultures of origin. Our task is to replace eurocratic content and pedagogy that sever these cultural connections with "re-membered" content and pedagogical practices that conceptualize and retrieve these connections. Along with Afrocentric theoretical concepts—and the African episteme that has informed them—let's turn to examining some compatible principles and pedagogies that can guide the writing and teaching of "re-membered" content.

Culturally Informed Principles and Emancipatory Pedagogies

Culturally informed principles (e.g., inclusion, representation, accurate scholarship, indigenous voice, critical thinking, collective humanity) are knowledge assertions that produce more accurate and comprehensive content by facilitating critical thinking and avoiding the privileging of some groups and the silencing of others. This effort to democratize knowledge builds on the educational ideas of scholars in the Black intellectual tradition (Asante, 1991; Bond, 1934; Du Bois, 1935; Hilliard, 2003; Karenga, 2003; King, 2015; Woodson, 1919b; Wynter, 1992).

These ideas were later taken up and studied by scholars in multicultural and culturally relevant/responsive education who put them into practice by critiquing instructional materials, conducting research, writing instructional materials, and designing professional development for educators (ANKN, 1999; Banks, 1973, 2004; CIBC, 1977; Gay, 1973, 2000; Goodwin & Swartz, 2008; Ladson-Billings, 1990, 2004; Sleeter & Grant, 1987; Swartz, 2012, 2013a, 2013b; Swartz & Bakari, 2005). Support for culturally informed principles is also found in Indigenous worldviews, cultural concepts, and ideas about education (Cajete, 1994; Grande, 2004; Lomawaima & McCarty, 2006; Simpson, 2014). Importantly, culturally informed principles stand on the same African epistemic foundation as Afrocentric theoretical concepts. Knowing this, we need pedagogies for teaching "re-membered" content that are aligned with those theoretical concepts and principles. We call these pedagogies emancipatory, which means that they

- center all students as normative and possessing cultural capital (Boykin, 1994; King & Swartz, 2014);
- build on what students know and who they are (Goodwin & Swartz, 2008);
- view students as active participants rather than passive receivers of knowledge transmitted to them (Freire, 1970; Gordon, 1986);
- stimulate critical thought and collaboration (Glaser, 1985; Gonzalez, 1997; Goodwin, 2004; Nelson, 1994); and
- foster caring and right relationship among teachers, students, and families (King & Swartz, 2016).

Figure 2.2 visualizes the relationship between the African epistemic foundation of worldview and cultural concepts, the Afrocentric theoretical concepts and culturally informed principles that have emerged from this foundation, and the compatible practices ("re-membered" content and emancipatory pedagogies) that this episteme produces.

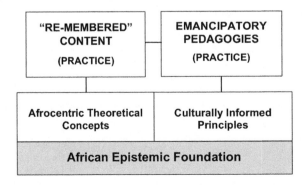

FIGURE 2.2 Relationships Between Concepts, Principles, and Practices

Earlier in this chapter we provided definitions of Afrocentric theoretical concepts in Table 2.1. In Table 2.2 we show the connections between Afrocentric theoretical concepts (left column), the culturally informed principles (middle column) used to identify or write "re-membered" content, and an emancipatory pedagogy (right column) that is congruent with these theoretical concepts and culturally informed principles. For example, look at culturally informed principle #4, indigenous voice (middle column). This principle refers to cultures and groups having agency—that is, speaking for, naming, and defining themselves. We use this principle to determine whether instructional materials exhibit indigenous voice, and if not, to write "re-membered" content in which cultures and groups speak for, name, and define themselves. Self-Determination and Subjects with Agency (left column) are the Afrocentric theoretical concepts that are the source or basis of indigenous voice as a culturally informed principle that can frame the ideas in "re-membered" content. Question-Driven Pedagogy (right column) is an emancipatory pedagogy that is congruent with indigenous voice because it invites students to use their voices by defining themselves and their ideas during instruction. After reviewing Table 2.2, can you see how Afrocentric theoretical concepts make it possible for teachers and students to experience each culturally informed principle through "re-membered" content *as well as during instruction?*

TABLE 2.2 Connecting Afrocentric Theoretical Concepts, Culturally Informed Principles and Emancipatory Pedagogies*

Afrocentric theoretical concepts ⟶	Culturally informed principles	Emancipatory pedagogies
• **Collective Responsibility** • **Subjects with Agency**	1. **Inclusion**—refers to all cultures and groups being the subjects of their own accounts. Inclusion asserts that when all cultures and groups are understood as substantive participants in human development, their presence is necessary, not expedient or token. This right action acknowledges the interconnectedness of humanity.	• **Eldering** refers to teachers being in right relationship with their students when they exhibit authentic authority based on knowledge, wisdom, and expertise. To develop relationships with all students, teachers build on who they are and what they know, ask critical questions, and collaborate with students and families. They understand that everyone is an essential participant and knowledge is a communal experience in which everyone has something to contribute.

Afrocentric theoretical concepts $\longrightarrow$	Culturally informed principles	Emancipatory pedagogies
• **Centrality/ Location** • **Collective Responsibility** • **Reclamation of Cultural Heritage**	2. **Representation**—refers to comprehensive portrayals of individuals and groups to avoid distortions and stereotypes. Representation asserts that when individuals and groups remain connected to their ancestral cultures, authentic portrayals are possible.	• **Locating Students** refers to teaching in ways that use students' normative cultural characteristics to center them. For example, if students' cultures are communally oriented, they will experience Representation when teachers structure learning opportunities that are collaborative and interdependent so that students can exchange ideas and learn together.
• **Reclamation of Cultural Heritage** • **Anteriority of Classical African Civilizations** • **Collective Responsibility**	3. **Accurate Scholarship**—refers to avoiding errors and omissions. It asserts that when relevant knowledge is present and when errors or omissions are avoided, curricular content becomes a reflection of the past rather than an appropriation of it.	• **Multiple Ways of Knowing** refers to teaching that taps into the epistemologies teachers have observed and studied about their students. Having this knowledge is a way for students to experience Accurate Scholarship during instruction. For example, if relational knowing is normative for students, teachers would organize activities that allow them to learn with and from each other.
• **Self- Determination** • **Subjects with Agency**	4. **Indigenous Voice**—refers to the portrayal of *all* cultures and groups through the experiences of their members and historical events through the voices and actions of those who were present. Indigenous Voice asserts that when cultures and groups speak for, name, and define themselves, their textual presence mirrors their agency in life.	• **Question-Driven Pedagogy** refers to teachers asking students thought-provoking questions that build on and expand what they know. Students experience Indigenous Voice during instruction when teaching and learning is a reciprocal and collective experience based on inquiry. By giving students opportunities to use their voices, they demonstrate agency by defining themselves and their ideas during instruction.

(Continued)

TABLE 2.2 (Continued)

Afrocentric theoretical concepts ⟶	Culturally informed principles	Emancipatory pedagogies
• **Collective Responsibility** • **Subjects with Agency**	5. **Critical Thinking—** refers to materials and curricula that provide broad content. Critical Thinking asserts that when content is broad, students can question, see connections and patterns, evaluate and synthesize information, identify areas of significance, and produce knowledge, rather than only recall and restate it.	• **Culturally Authentic Assessment Pedagogy** refers to (1) guiding students to produce knowledge and arrive at solutions through demonstration rather than being asked to give predetermined "right" answers; and (2) assessing students' learning using community-informed standards and expectations. Students experience Critical Thinking when they work with teachers and parents to complete and assess projects and performances that reflect imagination and bring benefit to the classroom and community.
• **Collective Consciousness** • **Collective Responsibility** • **Reclamation of Cultural Heritage**	6. **A Collective Humanity**—refers to the oneness of all humanity. It asserts that when there is no hierarchy of human worth that places some groups above others, all cultures and groups are presented as equally belonging to the human collective.	• **Communal Responsibility** is a pedagogy that invites students to act and make decisions that reflect the interests of the whole class, not only some or a majority of individuals. Students experience a Collective Humanity—a group unity and belonging—when they contribute to the group during cooperative learning, collaborative projects, and consensual decision making.

* Adapted from our 2016 text, *The Afrocentric Praxis of Teaching for Freedom* (pp. 16–17).

In the following section we use African worldview and cultural concepts (African epistemic foundation) and the Afrocentric theoretical concepts and culturally informed principles they support to compare two biographies of Benjamin Banneker written for students. One is a eurocratic account that typifies standard school knowledge and the other is a "re-membered" account that more accurately represents the life of Banneker, his African ancestors, and the time in which he lived. The epistemic foundation of each account is presented.

Benjamin Banneker: Eurocratized or "Re-membered"

The eurocratic biography of Benjamin Banneker comes from a fifth-grade textbook published by Scott Foresman (Boyd et al., 2011), and the "re-membered" biography comes from a fifth-grade text entitled *Freedom and Democracy, A Story Remembered* (Swartz, 2013a). The eurocratic account disconnects Banneker from his ancestral heritage, lacks indigenous voice, includes but distorts his advocacy for freedom, and has content that is too limited to stimulate critical thinking. The "re-membered" account includes and more comprehensively represents Banneker's accomplishments, keeps him connected to his ancestral heritage, and stimulates critical inquiry.

Benjamin Banneker: A Eurocratic Biography

In this textbook biography (Boyd et al., 2011), students learn that Benjamin Banneker "was an African American inventor and astronomer" (p. 367). The text explains that Banneker was born on a farm in Maryland and was an inventor who took apart and put back together a borrowed pocket watch and then made "the first wooden clock in colonial America" (p. 367). The biography goes on to explain that

> Banneker's intelligence and attention to detail impressed a neighbor, George Ellicott, a land surveyor. He lent Banneker books on mathematics and astronomy. In 1791, President George Washington appointed Andrew Ellicott [George's cousin], a surveyor and neighbor of Banneker [not at that time], to a team to help design the future District of Columbia. Banneker contributed to the project as an assistant to Ellicott.
>
> *(p. 367)*

Actually, Andrew Ellicott did not know Banneker, who was highly recommended to him by Andrew Ellicott's cousin George Ellicott.

This biography contains nothing about Banneker being African or any content that would connect his interest in studying the world around him to his African ancestry. The text also says that Banneker, who was free, spoke out against slavery, explaining this as a response to knowing the effects of slavery on "his father[,] who had been a slave." There is no information about the millions of his brothers and sisters who were enslaved. The biography also states that "When Banneker completed his first book he sent it to Secretary of State Thomas Jefferson and included a note asking Jefferson to help improve the treatment of African Americans" (p. 367). There is no information about this "book" being an almanac—the first of 28 known editions of a very popular yearly almanac he wrote over a six-year period as a self-taught astronomer; and the "note" was actually a several-page letter that did not ask for improved treatment, but made a thorough case for ending the system of slavery. In this letter that was published in Banneker's first almanac, he critiqued the system as cruel, criminal, fraudulent, and violent; and as a hypocritical and pitiable act by those, such as Jefferson, who were guilty of fighting for their own freedom from England but denying freedom to millions of African people (see epigraph at the beginning of this chapter and full letter; Banneker, 1791). Importantly, he reminded Jefferson that his words "all men are created equal" were applicable to all violations of freedom, not only some.

This eurocratic textbook account silences Benjamin Banneker's voice by ignoring his cultural identity and distorting his analysis of the system of slavery. This silence is further reinforced by the biography's placement in a chapter entitled "Washington as President" that focuses on Washington taking office, the development of two political parties, and developing the nation's capital in Washington, DC. Banneker's biography is presumably placed at the end of this chapter because of his participation on a team that surveyed the Federal Territory that became the nation's capital. This participation is mentioned toward the end of the chapter (prior to the biography), where it is implied that Banneker worked alongside the project's engineer Pierre L'Enfant in designing the capital. The textbook states, "The Map Adventure below [which shows the layout of streets and some buildings] gives you a chance to investigate the work of L'Enfant and Banneker" (p. 365). This portrayal of Banneker in relation to L'Enfant is incorrect as Banneker was not involved with the engineering aspects of the project. Further, it blurs the sociopolitical and racial hierarchy that defined the time in which both men lived by implying that the two men were working companions. In fact, Banneker lived by himself in the tent where he made his astronomical observations and monitored the various instruments needed for the project; and he ate at a separate table in the tent for dining (Bedini, 1999; Tyson, 1884). Also, the painting that illustrates Banneker in this biography is of a young man, whereas he was 60 years old with white hair when he undertook this project in 1791 (Bedini, 1999). What lines of inquiry might students be asked to consider if they knew that Banneker was an elder? These silences, distortions, and disconnections are typical of eurocratic content that concurrently includes information (often inaccurate, distorted, and/or exceptional) about people of African ancestry in ways that limit their agency and then uses that inclusion as a context, in this case, for sanitizing the country's early history.

European Epistemic Foundation

European worldview elements and cultural concepts form the epistemic foundation of most curricula in schools across the country (King & Swartz, 2016). Worldview elements such as Individuality, Independence, and a hierarchy of human worth are visible in European cultural concepts that typically inform school knowledge, such as *valorizing individual over group identity*; *knowledge as limited to what is agreed upon by experts*; *using hierarchies of race, class, and gender in determining access to freedom and justice*; and *self-determination as a way to achieve individual accomplishments* (Akbar, 1984; Boykin, 1983, 1986; Dixon, 1971; Fendler & Muzaffar, 2008; Kliewer & Fitzgerald, 2001; Nobles, 1976). Notice how this European episteme (worldview elements and cultural concepts) inform the foregoing account of Benjamin Banneker. While all biographies highlight the life and accomplishments of individuals, eurocratic biographies separate individuals of color from their People. They are great only as individuals, not as representatives of a People. Thus, Banneker was a great and accomplished individual mathematician, astronomer and inventor, but the African ancestral knowledge, traditions, and ways of knowing and being that were passed on to him are erased. His self-determination is presented only as a means to individual attainment, which also disconnects him from his 4 million enslaved brothers and sisters—even as he advocated for them. In this case, the obscured but identifiable backstory that is agreed upon by experts is the eighteenth-century white assumption of white racial supremacy in determining who had access to freedom and justice and who did not. This agreed-upon assumption is maintained in twenty-first-century texts informed by a European episteme.

Benjamin Banneker: A "Re-membered" Biography

The "re-membered" biography opens by presenting Banneker as a man of African ancestry:

> Benjamin Banneker followed in the tradition of African scholars. Some historians think that he was a descendent of the Dogon people of West Africa. Just like the Dogon, he was an observer of the natural world, a mathematician, and an astronomer.
>
> *(Swartz, 2013a, p. 22)*

Students learn how Banneker used his knowledge of astronomy to write almanacs that thousands of people used to learn about the weather and when to plant crops; and they read about Banneker the astronomer who was selected to be on the team that surveyed the new capital of Washington, DC. Students also learn that Banneker was a free man at a time when millions of his people were enslaved. The text explains that his African ancestors "understood that freedom was a natural right, and he knew this too. So he spoke to people about why slavery should end" (p. 23). There is content about the letter he wrote and sent to Secretary of State Thomas Jefferson along with his first almanac.

> He wrote on behalf of his people, including the millions of men, women, and children who were enslaved. In the letter, Banneker described the injustices of slavery. He reminded Jefferson that he had written "all men are created equal" in the Declaration of Independence. He asked Jefferson to be true to his own words and to work toward ending slavery.
>
> *(p. 23)*

This biography is at the end of a chapter entitled "African People in North America" that focuses first on West African people, in particular the Songhoy Nation—its organization, leadership, practices of freedom, universities, and other social conditions and accomplishments prior to the *Maafa* (European enslavement of African people). A description of chattel slavery follows, including its violence and cruelty, the contradiction of White colonists wanting freedom from England but taking away freedom from people of African descent, and the wealth made by White colonists and leaders who enslaved African people. There is also content in this chapter about the resistance of African men and women who "knew that freedom was the natural right of all people . . . [and] that they had never given up their right to be free" (Swartz, 2013a, p. 20). Thus, before reading the Banneker biography, students learn about African heritage prior to enslavement and the experience of enslavement, which together become the context for connecting Banneker to his African ancestry and describing his actions for freedom.

African Epistemic Foundation

There is an African epistemic foundation beneath the "re-membered" biography of Benjamin Banneker. This means that his African worldview—and the cultural concepts that can be seen in his actions—brings back together a wider range of knowledge compared to a eurocratic account. In terms of Banneker's worldview, you can see his Collective Responsibility, right action, Justice, and Reciprocity, which are visible in the cultural concepts that informed Banneker's actions, such as *pursuing freedom and justice as communal responsibilities, the inherent right of freedom, demonstrating concern for human welfare through actions based on community-mindedness and service to others,* and *exhibiting self-determination that considers the needs of the collective.*

By considering the African cultural foundation of knowledge about Benjamin Banneker, we were able to produce a biography that locates him as a subject with agency and keeps him connected to his cultural community. We use Afrocentric theoretical concepts such as Centrality/Location, Self-Determination,

Subjects with Agency, and the Reclamation of Cultural Heritage to frame this "re-membered" biography. Banneker is presented as African—a location from which his story can be viewed and understood. Content includes but is not limited to Banneker's accomplishments in math, science, invention, and astronomy. In seeking freedom and justice he thinks and acts upon the world as both an individual and a member of his cultural group, with his African heritage knowledge informing his actions that considered the collective needs of his people. In this way, the "re-membered" text consciously recovers a piece of African history and culture.

In terms of practice, this "re-membered" text is written with all six culturally informed principles: (1) Inclusion: Banneker is included as a subject of his own account not as an object of outsiders' accounts about him; (2) Representation: he remains connected to his African ancestors as a normative subject of his own experiences; (3) Accurate Scholarship: the content includes enough relevant information to characterize the time in which he lived; (4) Indigenous Voice: Banneker's voice is present in his view of freedom and in the letter he wrote to Jefferson; (5) Critical Thinking: the text is broad enough to allow students to critically explore Banneker's life experiences and the world around him; and (6) A Collective Humanity: Banneker's ideas and actions for human freedom communicate to students that freedom is inherent and that there is no hierarchy of human worth. Thus, in theory and practice, this "re-membered" biography teaches students what it is about Banneker's *being* African that informed his life. This is seen in his concern for his community, his interconnectedness to the natural world, and his pursuit of justice and human freedom—understood as inherent and present even though denied. Knowing how being African is relevant to who Banneker was retains a connection between Africa and the Diaspora. When instructional materials affirm the heritage knowledge of all students, they can experience themselves in the past and how that past is connected to the present.

Classroom Observation: Teaching About Benjamin Banneker

In Chapter 1, Ms. Singleton said that she would be interested in teaching "re-membered" content about Benjamin Banneker, and thought that it would be possible to link content about him to students' lives today. Vignette 2.1 shows Ms. Singleton and her colleague Ms. Hart team-teaching an excerpt from a lesson in which they engage students in a discussion that identifies Benjamin Banneker's character qualities. The class explores how his African heritage—which was passed on from one generation to the next—was part of shaping his character. After identifying character traits within themselves that are similar to Banneker's, students decide how they can use those traits to respond to a current issue in their community.

VIGNETTE 2.1 BENJAMIN BANNEKER: LESSON EXCERPT

Ms. Singleton

Class, I'd like to introduce our two guests, Dr. King and Dr. Swartz. Ms. Hart and I asked them to join us today to observe our lesson on Benjamin Banneker. Please welcome them.

Class

[in unison] Good morning, Dr. King and Dr. Swartz.

Dr. King

Good morning! It's a pleasure to be here. We have been looking forward to today's lesson!

Ms. Hart

Good morning. To catch you up, Drs. King and Swartz, we've read and discussed a biography of Benjamin Banneker, and today we are going to talk about his character, since the many things he accomplished were influenced by the traits or qualities of his character.

Ms. Singleton

Yes, and we've already discussed how Banneker is known for studying the world around him, and how doing that was a part of him being an inventor, astronomer, surveyor, and author of almanacs. He also wrote a letter to Thomas Jefferson explaining why the system of slavery was wrong and should be ended. [Turning to the class] In order to do all of this, what kind of character traits or qualities do you think Mr. Banneker had?

Clianda

I think that he was strong and he had a lot of confidence.

Ms. Singleton

Clianda, can you say a little more about what you mean?

Clianda

Well, he did all these things when there was slavery. He was free, but we talked about how even free Black people didn't have the same chances as White people so you had to be strong and confident to do things.

Jerome

And he worked hard. He had to teach himself how to do things. He was smart.

Ms. Hart

Yes, there's no doubt that he was smart—a scholar like his African ancestors, and that he was determined to learn. He seemed confident that he could do whatever he put his mind to—so I agree with Clianda and Jerome. And he was determined that everyone should be free and there should be justice, which means that he cared about others.

Akili

He helped others too, which is the right thing to do. I mean that the almanacs helped people know when to plant and things about the weather. He also helped to plan the new capital. And he tried to explain to Thomas Jefferson why he should do something to end slavery.

Elena

I thought he was curious and confident too. It's like he knew that everyone has something they can do to be helpful, and he figured out what he could do.

Ms. Singleton

What I'm thinking about as I listen to all your ideas is that Benjamin Banneker was community-minded—and like Akili said, he did right things, which we call "right action." He knew that everyone was responsible to contribute to the well-being of the whole community. [Pointing to the chart paper] I've written down what we've come up with about Benjamin Banneker's character [strong, hardworking, smart, scholarly, determined, just, confident, caring, helped others, curious, ethical as seen in his right actions, community-minded, responsible].

Ms. Hart

Okay, so we know that Banneker was African, which means that many of his character qualities were shaped by the knowledge passed on to him from his African family and ancestors. Every person's thoughts and actions are shaped by their cultural heritage, so let's look at a few examples of concepts in African heritage that were part of shaping some of Banneker's character.

Ms. Singleton

[Showing a PowerPoint slide] Here are two African cultural concepts that scholars tell us are present in many African communities, not only in Africa, but in other places in the world where people of African ancestry live. Let's read them together.

1. *being responsible to bring good into the world through actions that are ethical, just, generous, compassionate, and peaceable*
2. *exhibiting self-determination that considers the needs of the collective*

Ms. Hart

I'm printing out some copies of these two concepts and the list of 13 character qualities that we came up with for Banneker. Elena, can you pass these out? Let's look at the first concept that was part of Banneker's African heritage. How did the idea of being responsible to bring good into the world shape some of the qualities we see in him?

Janet

He was free, but he wrote that letter to Thomas Jefferson. That shows that he thought that everyone should be free. So [pointing to the list of character qualities] I think he brought good by being determined, caring, and responsible.

Bryon

He cared about others, not just himself, and wanted justice.

Ms. Singleton

Yes. So knowing that bringing good into the world was something one should do was part of shaping Banneker's character. What about concept 2?

Clianda

What about those almanacs he wrote and how he had to teach himself math and astronomy to write them? Lots of farmers used his almanacs. So I'm picking smart, determined, and helpful from the list.

Alejandro

And he was community-minded because he thought about what other people needed.

Ms. Hart

I'm impressed! You're showing that you get the connection between a person's heritage and a person's character. Heritage is passed on from one generation to another through families. So, our character traits are shaped by many things, and heritage is one of them.

Ms. Singleton

I'm impressed too! Now I'm wondering about each of us. What character traits do you see in yourself that might be like Benjamin Banneker's traits? Turn to a partner and talk about which of Banneker's character qualities you see in yourself. Explain to your partner why you think so, and then write your character qualities or traits on the smartboard.

Ms. Hart

[After students complete and make a list of their characteristics that are like Banneker's] Okay, Jelise, can you cross out all the duplicates and then erase them so there is an unduplicated list of students' characteristics? [The remaining list includes just, hardworking, smart, determined, caring, helping others, curious, community-minded, and responsible.]

Ms. Singleton

I'm thinking about how we can use the character qualities of students in our class—which were passed on to us from our families and from ancestors like Benjamin Banneker—to make some changes in our community. Last week we read and talked about how people in the Black Lives Matter movement are trying to change the policies and practices of police abuses in Black communities, including the killing of Black men, women, and children across the country. How can we contribute to that effort?

James

Well, I said I was curious and smart, so I could look into what the police are doing in this city so we know what's going on and if there's something we can do.

Raymond

I said I was hardworking and that I like to help others, so I could work with James.

Amaya

I'm determined and my gramma says I'm responsible, so I could do some research to see how the police act toward different groups of people.

Ms. Hart

Anyone else?

Sholanda

I could use the information Amaya comes up with and write a letter to the editor because I'm determined too and I care about the community and I think there should be justice. I know a lot of Black and Puerto Rican people who say they're not treated right by the police.

Dwayne

I could write a speech about how I think that the police could do things differently and enter the school-wide oratory contest we're having next month. I said I was determined, but I don't like to speak in front of people. I'm not too confident, but I know that when I set my mind to something I do it. If I make a speech in the contest I might get more confident.

Kwanjai

I like to help others and my mind thinks about having a community where everyone gets along. So maybe we could paint a mural that shows what a community looks like when people get along and the police respect everyone and are part of making this community a good place to live.

Ms. Singleton

These are all really good ideas and I know there are more! How should we proceed?

José

I think we should talk about whether each person should do their own idea or if there's a way to decide which ones to work on as a class.

Victoria

I say we need a plan. If we agree on a plan that includes at least something from all of our ideas then we'll be like a community that gets along, and is trying to help the whole city.

Ms. Hart

That sounds good to me. Before the end of the day, if each of you type your idea on the computer and send it to me, I'll put all our ideas together and tomorrow we'll talk about and decide how to go forward. For homework, I want you to tell your parents or family members what we're working on and to ask them for their ideas about how to change harmful police practices. We'll begin tomorrow's class with sharing what you learned at home.

Ms. Singleton

Yes, and we'll use consensus, like we often do. Then we can agree on what ideas to include. I think our ancestor Benjamin Banneker is going to be very proud of us.

Educators Talking

After students were dismissed for the day, educators Singleton, Hart, King, and Swartz talked briefly about the class.

Dr. King: What an excellent demonstration of merging theory and practice!

Dr. Swartz: Yes! I wish we had thought to videotape it.

Ms. Hart: I agree that it went well. The students have been very engaged in learning about Benjamin Banneker from the text you provided, and there are so many extensions we saw that we can make to connect learning about Banneker to the present day and to students themselves.

Ms. Singleton: The text has helped us to focus on connecting the heritage of an historical figure to his accomplishments, which we often don't do when we teach biographies. By making the heritage knowledge connection—to Banneker's agency and self-determination in service to community well-being—students can identify and use aspects of their own cultural background and heritage knowledge in response to current issues that affect them and their families. As you saw, this is where we are going next.

Dr. Swartz: Yes, and I liked that last touch when you said that you thought our ancestor Benjamin Banneker is going to be very proud of us!

Ms. Singleton: Thank you . . . and it's true.

Ms. Hart: And about making connections with families, we've been working more with parents and families this year, trying to connect what they know and think to what we are teaching about. My sense is that students will bring in some ideas tomorrow from home that we will be able to incorporate in this project. Many of our parents work, but we'll see if some can come in and be part of whatever project the class decides upon. When a parent or family member comes to class and is a part of our learning, even if it's someone else's parent, the environment seems to change for everyone; it feels more like family.

Dr. King: You may have already done this, but you might be able to involve parents providing feedback about students' work that they bring home or in being audiences for student performances and presentations where families can offer feedback.

Ms. Hart: We've done some of that, but we need to do more, and we can with this current project.

Dr. Swartz: One thing that stood out for me was the range of emancipatory pedagogies that you both used. You built on what students knew, used question-driven pedagogy, multiple ways of knowing, and I observed you both using eldering. Your authority was based on your knowledge and students responded so well to this. They seemed to draw confidence from you because your authority was authentic. It wasn't that kind of authority that's about control and compliance.

Dr. King: Yes. You guided students and you invited them to express their own ideas and then built on those ideas, like when one student said that Banneker was smart and you confirmed that and added that he was a scholar like his African ancestors. Then you linked being African, smart, and a scholar to Banneker knowing that everyone should be free and have justice. I kept thinking about how both you and the students were building the curriculum together.

Ms. Hart: That's good to hear because I've been seeing how much more engagement and learning occur when I see the students as necessary to teaching, not just there to "get" what I have to teach, but there to produce some knowledge with my guidance. It's a whole different way of thinking about teaching and I'm seeing how it produces real learning.

Ms. Singleton: What strikes me about all this is the importance of content. If we are going to connect students' history and heritage to their lives, we must have what you call "re-membered" content like this Banneker biography. As you know from our last conversation, Dr. King, we've started a program in our school that draws upon the heritage knowledge of our students in an effort to replace the more limited eurocratic curriculum that is so pervasive. So Ms. Hart and I—and several colleagues—would be open to using more of this content and to trying our hand at writing some content and the lessons to go with it. We have a working group and hope you can join us from time to time as our critical friends.

Dr. King: We'd be glad to be critical friends.

Dr. Swartz: Yes, certainly. And we do have more grade-level content to share with you.

Dr. King: It's becoming so clear to me that as academics we can visualize and theorize about teaching and learning, but it is PK-12 teachers who create the praxis that brings it all together.

   As the four educators say good-bye, they thank each other and agree to be in touch soon.

References

Abímbólá, W. (1976). *Ifá will mend our broken world: Thoughts on Yoruba religion and culture in Africa and the Diaspora.* Roxbury, MA: Aim Books.

Akbar, N. (1984). Africentric social sciences for human liberation. *Journal of Black Studies, 14*(4), 395–414.

Alkebulan, A. A. (2007). Defending the paradigm. *Journal of Black Studies, 37,* 410–427.

ANKN (Alaska Native Knowledge Network). (1999). *Guidelines for preparing culturally responsive teachers for Alaska's schools.* Retrieved from www.ankn.uaf.edu/publications/teachers.html

Anyanwu, K. C. (1981). The African world-view and theory knowledge. In E. A. Ruch & K. C. Anyanwu (authors), *African philosophy: An introduction to the main philosophical trends in contemporary Africa* (pp. 77–99). Rome: Catholic Book Agency.

Aptheker, H. (1951/1969). *A documentary history of the Negro people in the United States: From colonial times through the Civil War* (Vol. 1). New York: The Citadel Press.

Asante, M. K. (1980/1988). *Afrocentricity.* Trenton, NJ: Africa World Press.

Asante, M. K. (1987/1998). *The Afrocentric idea.* Philadelphia, PA: Temple University Press.

Asante, M. K. (1991). The Afrocentric idea in education. *Journal of Negro Education, 60*(2), 170–180.

Asante, M. K. (2003a). Locating a text: Implications of Afrocentric theory. In A. Mazama (Ed.), *The Afrocentric paradigm* (pp. 235–244). Trenton, NJ: Africa World Press.

Asante, M. K. (2003b). African American studies: The future of the discipline. In A. Mazama (Ed.), *The Afrocentric paradigm* (pp. 97–108). Trenton, NJ: Africa World Press.

Asante, M. K. (2007). *An Afrocentric manifesto.* Malden, MA: Polity Press.

Asante, M. K. (2008). Africology: Making a long story short in the age of intellectual confusion. *International Journal of Africana Studies, 14*(2), 352–369.

Asante, M. K. (2010). *Afrocentricity: The theory of social change.* Retrieved from http://multiworldindia.org/wp-content/uploads/2010/05/Afrocentricity.pdf

Asante, M. K. (2011). *Maat and human communication: Supporting identity, culture, and history without global domination.* Retrieved from www.asante.net/articles/47/maat-and-human-communication-supporting-identity-culture-and-history-without-global-domination/

Bankole, K. K. (1995). *Afrocentric guide to selected Black studies terms and concepts: An annotated index for students.* Oceanside, NY: Whittier.

Bankole, K. K. (2008). *Africalogical perspectives: Historical and contemporary analysis of race and Africana studies.* Bloomington, IN: iUniverse.

Banks, J. A. (Ed.). (1973). *Teaching ethnic studies: Concepts and strategies (43rd Yearbook).* Washington, DC: National Council for the Social Studies.

Banks, J. A. (2004). Multicultural education: Historical development, dimension, and practice. In J. A. Banks & C. A. McGee Banks (Eds.), *Handbook of research on multicultural education* (2nd ed., pp. 3–29). San Francisco, CA: Jossey-Bass.

Banneker, B. (1791, August). *Letter to Thomas Jefferson.* Retrieved from www.headlinesciencenow.com/wp-content/uploads/2015/02/Letter-from-Benjamin-Banneker-to-Thomas-Jefferson-Aug-1791.pdf

Bedini, S. A. (1999). *The life of Benjamin Banneker: The first African American man of science* (2nd ed.). Baltimore, MD: Maryland Historical Society.

Bennett, L., Jr. (1968). *Pioneers in protest.* Chicago, IL: Johnson.

Bennett, L., Jr. (1975). *The shaping of Black America.* Chicago: Johnson.

Bethel, K. E. (2003). Afrocentricity and the arrangement of knowledge. In J. L. Conyers, Jr. (Ed.), *Afrocentricity and the academy: Essays on theory and practice* (pp. 50–65). Jefferson, NC: McFarland.

Bond, H. M. (1934). *The education of the Negro in the American social order.* New York, NY: Octagon Books.

Bond, H. M. (1935). The curriculum and the Negro child. *The Journal of Negro Education, 4*(2), 159–168.

Boyd, C. D., Gay, G., Geiger, R., Kracht, J. B., Ooka Pang, V., Risinger, C. F., & Sanchez, S. M. (2011). *The United States* (fifth grade). Boston, MA: Pearson.

Boykin, A. W. (1983). The academic performance of Afro-American children. In J. Spence (Ed.), *Achievement and achievement motives* (pp. 321–371). San Francisco: W. Freeman.

Boykin, A. W. (1986). The triple quandary and the schooling of Afro-American children. In U. Neisser (Ed.), *The school achievement of minority children* (pp. 57–92). Hillsdale, NJ: Lawrence Erlbaum.

Boykin, A. W. (1994). Afrocultural expression and its implications for schooling. In E. R. Hollins, J. E. King, & W. C. Hayman (Eds.), *Teaching diverse populations: Formulating a knowledge base* (pp. 243–273). Albany: State University of New York Press.

Cajete, G. (1994). *Look to the mountain: An ecology of Indigenous education.* Durango, CO: Kivaki Press.

Carney, J. A. (2001). *Black rice: The African origins of rice cultivation in the Americas.* Cambridge, MA: Harvard University Press.

Césaire, A. (1955/2000). *Discourse on colonialism.* New York: Monthly Review Press. (Original work published 1955, Présence Africaine)

CIBC (The Council on Interracial Books for Children). (1977). *Stereotypes, distortions, and omissions in U.S. history textbooks.* New York, NY: CIBC.

Cokely, K. (2003). Afrocentricity and African psychology. In J. L. Conyers, Jr. (Ed.), *Afrocentricity and the academy: Essays on theory and practice* (pp. 141–162). Jefferson, NC: McFarland.

Cooper, A. J. (Haywood) (1892/1969). *A voice from the South, by a black woman of the South.* New York, NY: Negro Universities Press.

Crummel, A. (1898). Attitude of the American mind toward the Negro intellect. *Occasional Papers, American Negro Academy, 3,* 8–19.

Delany, M. R. (1852). *The condition, elevation, emigration, and destiny of the Colored people of the United States.* Retrieved from www.gutenberg.org/files/17154/17154-h/17154-h. htm

Dixon, V. J. (1971). African-oriented and Euro-American-oriented world views: Research methodologies and economics. *The Review of Black Political Economy, 7*(2), 119–156.

Dove, N. (1998). African womanism: An Afrocentric theory. *Journal of Black Studies, 28*(5), 515–539.

Du Bois, W.E.B. (1899). *The Philadelphia Negro: A social study.* New York: Schocken Books.

Du Bois, W.E.B. (1903). The talented tenth. In B. T. Washington (Ed.), *The Negro Problem: A series of articles by representative American Negroes of today* (pp. 33–75). New York, NY: James Pott.

Du Bois, W.E.B. (1920, February 18). On being Black. *New Republic, 21,* 338–341.

Du Bois, W.E.B. (1935). Does the Negro need separate schools? *Journal of Negro Education, 4,* 329–335.

Du Bois, W.E.B. (1935/1972). *Black reconstruction in America.* New York, NY: Atheneum.

Du Bois, W.E.B. (1945). *Color and democracy.* New York, NY: Harcourt, Brace.

Elliott, R. B. (1874, January 6). Speech in the House of Representatives addressing the Civil Rights Bill of 1875. *Congressional Record.* (Extracts printed in 1914 in *Masterpieces of Negro Eloquence* edited by Alice Moore Dunbar; reprinted in 1997 by G. K. Hall/ Simon & Schuster Macmillan)

Epstein, T. (2009). *Interpreting national history: Race, identity, and pedagogy in classrooms and communities.* New York, NY: Routledge.

Fanon, F. (1963). *The wretched of the earth.* New York, NY: Grove Press.

Fanon, F. (1965). *A dying colonialism.* New York, NY: Grove Press.

Fendler, L., & Muzaffar, I. (2008). The history of the bell curve: Sorting and the idea of normal. *Educational Theory, 58*(1), 63–82.

Fontaine, W. T. (1940). An interpretation of contemporary Negro thought from the standpoint of the sociology of knowledge. *Journal of Negro History, 25*(1), 6–13.

Franklin, V. P. (1992). *Black self-determination: A cultural history of African American resistance.* Chicago, IL: Lawrence Hill Books.

Freire, P. (1970). *Pedagogy of the oppressed.* New York: The Seabury Press.

Fu-Kiau, K. K. B. (2001). *African cosmology of the Bântu-Kôngo, tying the spiritual knot: Principles of life and living.* New York, NY: Athelia Henrietta Press.

Garnet, H. H. (1843/1972). Address to the slaves of the United States of America (Rejected by the National Convention held in Buffalo, NY, 1843). In S. Stuckey (Ed.), *The ideological origins of Black nationalism* (pp. 168–170). Boston: Beacon Press.

Garnet, H. H. (1859, September 17). Speech to the Colored citizens of Boston, 1859. *The Weekly Anglo African*, 1(9).

Gay, G. (1973). Racism in America: Imperatives for teaching ethnic studies. In J. A. Banks (Ed.), *Teaching ethnic studies: Concepts and strategies* (pp. 31–34). Washington, DC: National Council for the Social Studies.

Gay, G. (2000). *Culturally responsive teaching: Theory, research, and practice*. New York, NY: Teachers College Press.

Giroux, H. A. (1986). Radical pedagogy and the politics of student voice. *Interchange*, 17(1), 48–67. The Ontario Institute for Studies in Education.

Glaser, E. M. (1985). Critical thinking: Educating for responsible citizenship in a democracy. *National Forum*, 65, 24–27.

Gonzalez, V. (1997). Using critical thinking to stimulate in-service teachers' cognitive growth in multicultural education. *NYSABE Journal*, 92–120.

Goodwin, S. (1996). Teaching students of color. *Raising Standards: Journal of the Rochester Teachers Association*, 4(1), 23–35.

Goodwin, S. (1998). Sankofan education and emancipatory practices. *Raising Standards: Journal of the Rochester Teachers Association*, 6(1), 20–30.

Goodwin, S. (2004). Emancipatory pedagogy. In S. Goodwin & E. E. Swartz (Eds.), *Teaching children of color: Seven constructs of effective teaching in urban schools* (pp. 37–48). Rochester, NY: RTA Press.

Goodwin, S., & Swartz, E. E. (2008). *Culturally responsive practice: Lesson planning and construction*. Rochester, NY: RTA Press.

Gordon, B. M. (1986). The use of emancipatory pedagogy in teacher education. *Journal of Educational Thought*, 20(2), 59–66.

Grande, S. (2004). *Red pedagogy: Native American social and political thought*. Lanham, MD: Rowman & Littlefield.

Grant, C. A., Brown, K. D., & Brown, A. L. (2016). *Black intellectual thought in education: The missing traditions of Anna Julia Cooper, Carter G. Woodson, and Alain LeRoy Locke*. New York, NY: Routledge.

Grinde, D. A., Jr. (1989, Winter). Iroquoian political concept and the genesis of American government. *Northeast Indian Quarterly*, 6(4), 10–21.

Grinde, D. A., Jr. (1992). Iroquois political theory and the roots of American democracy. In O. Lyons & J. Mohawk (Eds.), *Exiled in the land of the free: Democracy, Indian nations, and the U.S. constitution* (pp. 228–280). Santa Fe, NM: Clear Light.

Grinde, D. A., Jr., & Johansen, B. E. (1991). *Exemplar of liberty: Native America and the evolution of democracy*. Los Angeles: American Indian Studies Center, University of California.

Gyekye, K. (1987). *An essay on African philosophical thought: The Akan conceptual scheme*. Cambridge: Cambridge University Press.

Gyekye, K. (1997). *Tradition and modernity: Philosophical reflections on the African experience*. New York: Oxford University Press.

Hall, G. M. (2005). *Slavery and African ethnicities in the Americas: Restoring the links*. Chapel Hill: University of North Carolina Press.

Harding, V. (1990). *Hope and history*. New York, NY: Orbis Books.

Hart, R. (1985/2002). *Slaves who abolished slavery: Blacks in rebellion*. Kingston, Jamaica: University of the West Indies Press.

Hilliard, A. G. III (1978). *Free your mind, return to the source: The African origin of civilization.* San Francisco: Urban Institute for Human Services.

Hilliard, A. G. III (2003). No mystery: Closing the achievement gap between Africans and excellence. In T. Perry, C. Steele, & A. Hilliard, III (Eds.), *Young, gifted, and Black: Promoting high achievement among African American students* (pp. 131–165). Boston, MA: Beacon Press.

Idowu, E. B. (1973). *African traditional religion: A definition.* London: SCM Press.

Ikuenobe, P. (2006). *Philosophical perspectives on communalism and morality in African traditions.* Lanham, MD: Lexington Books.

Karenga, M. (1996). The Nguzo Saba (the seven principles). In M. K. Asante & A. S. Abarry (Eds.), *African intellectual heritage: A book of sources* (pp. 543–554). Philadelphia, PA: Temple University.

Karenga, M. (1999). *Odù Ifá: The ethical teachings.* Los Angeles, CA: University of Sankore Press.

Karenga, M. (2003). Afrocentricity and multicultural education: Concept, challenge and contribution. In A. Mazama (Ed.), *The Afrocentric paradigm* (pp. 73–94). Trenton, NJ: Africa World Press.

Karenga, M. (2006a). Philosophy in the African tradition of resistance: Issues of human freedom and human flourishing. In L. R. Gordon & J. A. Gordon (Eds.), *Not only the master's tools: African American studies in theory and practice* (pp. 243–271). Boulder, CO: Paradigm.

Karenga, M. (2006b). *Maat, the moral ideal of ancient Egypt: A study in classical African ethics.* New York, NY: Routledge.

Kershaw, T. (1992). Afrocentrism and the Afrocentric method. *The Western Journal of Black Studies, 16*(3), 160–168.

Kershaw, T. (2003). The Black studies paradigm: The making of scholar activists. In J. L. Conyers, Jr. (Ed.), *Afrocentricity and the academy: Essays on theory and practice* (pp. 27–36). Jefferson, NC: McFarland.

Keto, C. T. (1995). *Vision, identity, and time: The Afrocentric paradigm and the study of the past.* Dubuque, IA: Kendall/Hunt.

King, J. E. (1992). Diaspora literacy and consciousness in the struggle against miseducation in the Black community. *Journal of Negro Education, 61*(3), 317–340.

King, J. E. (2004). Culture-centered knowledge: Black studies, curriculum transformation, and social action. In J. A. Banks & C. A. McGee Banks (Eds.), *Handbook of research on multicultural education* (2nd ed., pp. 349–378). San Francisco, CA: Jossey-Bass.

King, J. E. (2015). *Dysconscious racism, Afrocentric praxis, and education for human freedom: Through the years I keep on toiling, the selected works of Joyce E. King.* New York, NY: Routledge.

King, J. E., & Swartz, E. E. (2016). *The Afrocentric praxis of teaching for freedom: Connecting culture to learning.* New York: NY: Routledge.

King, J. E., Swartz, E. E., Campbell, L., Lemons-Smith, S., & López, E. (2014). *"Remembering" history in student and teacher learning: An Afrocentric culturally informed praxis.* New York, NY: Routledge.

Kliewer, C., & Fitzgerald, L. M. (2001). Disability, schooling, and the artifacts of colonialism. *Teachers College Record, 103*(3), 450–470.

Konadu, K. (2010). *The Akan diaspora in the Americas.* New York, NY: Oxford University Press.

Ladson-Billings, G. (1990). Culturally relevant teaching, effective instruction for Black students. *The College Board Review, 155*, 20–25.

Ladson-Billings, G. (2004). New directions in multicultural education: Complexities, boundaries, and critical race theory. In J. A. Banks & C. A. McGee Banks (Eds.), *Handbook of research on multicultural education* (2nd ed., pp. 50–65). San Francisco, CA: Jossey-Bass.

Lomawaima, K. T., & McCarty, T. L. (2006). *To remain an Indian: Lessons in democracy from a century of Native American education.* New York, NY: Teachers College Press.

Lynch, J. R. (1875, February 3). Civil rights and social equality: Speech in the House of Representatives. *Congressional Record.* (Extracts printed in 1914 in *Masterpieces of Negro Eloquence* edited by A. Moore Dunbar; reprinted in 1997 by G. K. Hall/Simon & Schuster Macmillan)

Lyons, O., & Mohawk, J. (Eds.). (1992). *Exiled in the land of the free: Democracy, Indian nations, and the U.S. constitution.* Santa Fe, NM: Clear Light.

Mazama, A. (2003a). *The Afrocentric paradigm.* Trenton, NJ: Africa World Press.

Mazama, A. (2003b). The Afrocentric paradigm, an introduction. In A. Mazama (Ed.), *The Afrocentric paradigm* (pp. 3–34). Trenton, NJ: Africa World Press.

Mbiti, J. S. (1990). *African religions and philosophy* (2nd ed.). Portsmouth, NH: Heinemann Educational Books.

Miller, K. (1908). *Race adjustment: Essays on the Negro in America.* New York, NY: Neale.

Mills, C. W. (1997). *The racial contract.* Ithaca, NY: Cornell University Press.

Nelson, C. E. (1994). Critical thinking and collaborative learning. In K. Bosworth & S. J. Hamilton (Eds.), *Collaborative learning: Underlying processes and effective techniques* (pp. 45–58). San Francisco, CA: Jossey-Bass.

Nkulu-N'Sengha, M. (2005). African epistemology. In M. K. Asante & A. Mazama (Eds.), *Encyclopedia of Black studies* (pp. 39–44). Thousand Oaks, CA: SAGE.

Nobles, W. W. (1976). Extended self: Rethinking the so-called Negro self-concept. *The Journal of Black Psychology, 2*(2), 15–24.

Nobles, W. W. (2005). Consciousness. In M. K. Asante & A. Mazama (Eds.), *Encyclopedia of Black studies* (pp. 197–200). Thousand Oaks, CA: SAGE.

Nyang, S. S. (1980). Reflections on traditional African cosmology. *New Directions: The Howard University Magazine, 7,* 28–32.

Nyerere, J. (1965). Democracy and the party system. In R. Emerson & M. Kilson (Eds.), *The political awakening of Africa* (pp. 122–128). Englewood Cliffs, NJ: Prentice-Hall.

Obenga, T. (1989). African philosophy of the Pharaonic period (2780–330 B.C.) (Excerpt from a work in translation). In I. Van Sertima (Ed.), *Egypt revisited* (2nd ed., pp. 286–324). New Brunswick, NJ: Transaction.

Piersen, W. D. (1993). *Black legacy: America's hidden heritage.* Amherst: University of Massachusetts Press.

Price, R. (Ed.). (1979). *Maroon societies: Rebel slave communities in the Americas* (2nd ed.). Baltimore, MD: The Johns Hopkins University Press.

Quarles, B. (1969). *Black abolitionists.* New York, NY: Oxford University Press.

Senghor, L. S. (1964). *On African socialism.* (M. Cook, Trans.). New York, NY: Frederick A. Praeger. (Original work published 1961)

Simpson, L. B. (2014). Land as pedagogy: Nishnaabeg intelligence and rebellious transformation. *Decolonization: Indigeneity, Education & Society, 3*(3), 1–25.

Sindima, H. (1995). *Africa's agenda: The legacy of liberalism and colonialism in the crisis of African values.* Westport, CT: Greenwood.

Sithole, N. (1959). *African nationalism.* London: Oxford University Press.

Sleeter, C. E., & Grant, C. A. (1987, November). An analysis of multicultural education in the United States. *Harvard Educational Review, 57*(4), 421–444.

Swartz, E. E. (1992). Emancipatory narratives: Rewriting the master script in the school curriculum. *The Journal of Negro Education, 61*, 341–355.

Swartz, E. E. (2012). *Remembering our ancestors.* Rochester, NY: Rochester City School District.

Swartz, E. E. (2013a). *Freedom and democracy: A Story Remembered.* Rochester, NY: Omnicentric Press.

Swartz, E. E. (2013b). *Black community building: The African tradition of collective work and responsibility.* Rochester, NY: Omnicentric Press.

Swartz, E. E., & Bakari, R. (2005). Development of the teaching in urban schools scale. *Teaching and Teacher Education, 21*(7), 829–841.

Tedla, E. (1995). *Sankofa: African thought and education.* New York, NY: Peter Lang.

Thompson, V. B. (1987). *The making of the African diaspora in the Americas 1441–1900.* New York, NY: Longman.

Tyson, M. E. (1884). *Banneker, the Afric-American astronomer: From the posthumous papers of Martha E. Tyson, edited by her daughter [Anne T. Kirk].* Philadelphia, PA: Friends' Book Association.

Walker, D. (1829/1965). *David Walker's appeal.* C. M. Wiltse (Ed.). New York, NY: Hill and Wang.

Walker, S. S. (Ed.). (2001). *African roots/American cultures: Africa in the creation of the Americas.* Lanham, MD: Rowman & Littlefield.

Wells, I. B. (1892). *Southern horrors: Lynch law in all its phases.* New York, NY: The New York Age Print.

Woodson, C. G. (1919a). *The education of the Negro prior to 1861: A history of the education of the Colored people of the United States from the beginning of slavery to the Civil War* (2nd ed.). Washington, DC: Associated.

Woodson, C. G. (1919b). Negro life and history as presented in the schools. *The Journal of Negro History, 4*, 273–280.

Woodson, C. G. (1933). *The mis-education of the Negro.* Washington, DC: Associated.

Work, M. N. (1916). The passing tradition and the African civilization. *Journal of Negro History, 1*(1). Retrieved from www.gutenberg.org/files/13642/13642-h/13642-h.htm#a1-3

Work, M. N. (1919). The life of Charles B. Ray. *Journal of Negro History, 4*(4), 361–371.

Wynter, S. (1992). *Do not call us "Negroes": How multicultural textbooks perpetuate racism.* San Francisco, CA: Aspire Books.

Wynter, S. (2006). On how we mistook the map for the territory, and re-imprisoned ourselves in our unbearable wrongness of being, of Désêtre: Black studies toward the human project. In L. R. Gordon & J. A. Gordon (Eds.), *Not only the master's tools: African American studies in theory and practice* (pp. 107–169). Boulder, CO: Paradigm.

3

TEACHING AFRICAN LANGUAGE FOR HISTORICAL CONSCIOUSNESS

Recovering Group Memory and Identity

Joyce E. King and Hassimi O. Maïga

Language, any language, has a dual character: it is both a means of communication and a carrier of culture.

(Ngũgĩ Wa Thiong'o, 1981)

"Ni boŋ bay, za borey mana ni bay!"

Know yourself before other people know you!

(Songhoy proverb)

I concluded that I did not know so much as I might about my own people.
—W.E.B. DuBois, *The Autobiography of W.E.B. DuBois*

Contrary to what many people believe, the lives of African Americans continue to be shaped and informed by African epistemology. People and scholars mistakenly believe that African Americans have no distinct cultural heritage intact as a foundation for excellence and resilience.
—Joyce E. King, 2015 AERA Presidential Address

Introduction

Songhoy (or *Soŋay, Songhai,* or *Songhay*), which eclipsed the Kingdom of Ghana and the Empire of Mali, was West Africa's last great classical civilization. *Songhoy-senni,* which was the lingua franca of the Songhoy dynasties and the grand multiethnic civilization of the sixteenth century and earlier, is still spoken in Mali and other West African nations. Teaching and deciphering *Songhoy-senni* using an African epistemic framework are another way for students (and their parents and teachers) in the Diaspora to recover and experience the cultural continuity of Africa and the African Diaspora. Students of African ancestry studying this language today experience a connection to their heritage through the cultural values and practices embodied within this language. While students of African ancestry experience a connection to their heritage, all students learn that the meanings of words and concepts are shaped by the cultural contexts from which they come.

We begin this chapter by recalling two classroom encounters we had with *Songhoy-senni* (the language) that affected us both so profoundly that we were thrust quite unknowingly upon what has become a near 30-year journey of collective work and responsibility, including the use of this language to contribute to our historical consciousness and the recovery of our memory of our identity— that we belong to one big African family. Thus, rather than merely an academic exercise, this chapter recounts our stories of personal and shared struggle to know ourselves better—that is, to recognize and affirm the cultural continuity that exists between Africa and its Diaspora, and to resist threats to our existence as a people—in particular the nihilating erasure of epistemic curriculum violence (King, 2017, see also Chapter 6).

This has been and continues to be a momentous journey of discovery for both of us. Along the way we discovered a method of teaching *Songhoy-senni* for historical consciousness and cultural recovery (King et al., 2014). This method entails a deciphering analysis of *Songhoy-senni* within an African epistemic framework that reveals the values, cultural expressions, and communal consciousness that African people share. This analytical approach permits us to use this language as a site of memory to recover our group identity despite the historical ruptures that have caused us to be dispersed and separated from each other as well as societally imposed cultural amnesia and the myth that "Africans lost everything" they knew (King, 1992, p. 332). We discovered that this cultural recovery is made more possible when continental African and Diaspora Peoples can bring our recovered stories together like pieces of a puzzle (King, 2014; Nobles, 2005, 2015; Nobles et al., 2016).

Importantly, recovering these stories has been obstructed by the absence of African languages—and the civilizational concepts they embody—in school curricula. This has resulted in the orthodoxy of teaching Europe (and Mesopotamia rather than its predecessor Kemet) as the primary standard-bearer of human flourishing and civilization. Teachers can use the culturally informed content in this chapter to avoid this false assumption and to teach more accurately and authentically about Africana history, culture, and Diasporan connections.

Our Stories

Hassimi Maïga's story is a journey of retrieving certain aspects of his home language—*Songhoy-senni*—such as their indigenous words for the seven days of the week before Arab terms were adopted as well as an ancient written script that would otherwise have been completely forgotten (Maïga, 2010). In addition to retrieving *Songhoy-senni* concepts and cultural practices conveyed in this language, he has also connected the sociocultural identity of the imperial Songhoy state to the earlier African civilization of ancient Kemet (Maïga, 2016; Moumouni, 2008).

Joyce King's story is a journey of "re-membering," using Songhoy culture and language to create opportunities for young people, teachers, and parents to experience the connections that exist between the Diaspora and our African cultural background. Using emancipatory pedagogy such as Multiple Ways of Knowing and Communal Responsibility (Goodwin, 2004; King & Swartz, 2014)— for example, in after-school and Saturday school programs, the Songhoy Club and the Songhoy Princess Clubs, International, which double as pedagogical labs—African American adolescents, graduate student teaching assistants, and parents have experienced the indigenous voices and worldview of Songhoy people (King et al., 2014). Consider these two experiences we had with *Songhoy-senni* in two classroom encounters that set us on a journey toward healing, belonging, and wellness.

Classroom Encounter #1—Joyce's Story

In 1992 when we conducted a professional development workshop at Santa Clara University focused on cultural competency and diversity with teachers, I presented Robert B. Moore's (1976) analysis in *Racism in the English Language* for discussion using this excerpt from his "short play on black and white words":

> Some may blackly (angrily) accuse me of trying to blacken (defame) the English language, to give it a black eye (a mark of shame) by writing such black words (hostile). They may denigrate (to cast aspersions, to darken) me by accusing me of being black hearted (malevolent), of having a black outlook (pessimistic, dismal) on life, of being a blackguard (scoundrel)— which would certainly be a black mark (detrimental fact) against me. Some may black-brow (scowl at) me and hope that a black cat crosses in front of me because of his black deed. I may be a black sheep (one who causes shame or embarrassment because of deviation from the accepted standards), who will be black balled (ostracized) by being placed on a blacklist (list of undesirables in an attempt to blackmail (force or coerce into a particular action) me to retract my words.
>
> *(Moore, 1976, p. 5)*

When one of the teachers in the workshop asked Dr. Maïga if blackness is negative in his language as well, he said, "No." But observing him I could feel that there was more on his mind that he didn't say. During the break, I asked him what was going on when the teacher asked him that question about his language. His response absolutely stunned me. Pointing to the back of his hand, he said, "Never in all my life have I ever had the idea or the thought that there was something wrong with 'black' or with blackness." I said, "How could that possibly be the case?"—assuming that regarding black/blackness as negative as we do in American society is normal, natural, and virtually universal. He explained, "In my language black is always positive. In fact, it's extremely positive."

Then, it was my turn. I thought to myself, "Never in all my life could I ever have imagined this idea—that there was somewhere where blackness was only positive." This thought had never occurred to me. We had both learned something quite profound that day that neither of us had ever imagined and this discovery led us to develop the first *Songhoy-senni* course that Hassimi Maïga taught a few years later at the University of New Orleans, using the Songhoy-language textbook for English speakers that he wrote (Maïga, 1996/2003). Ahead are some examples of positive meanings associated with blackness in *Songhoy-senni* and Songhoy culture, which are discussed in this textbook:

- *Wayne bibi*—Black sun. When the sun is at its fullest expression at noon, the Songhoy people say, the sun is black.
- *Hari bibi*—Black water. When people are crossing the Niger River in a canoe, and they want to drink clean potable water, they ask for *hari bibi*, from the deepest part of the river.
- *Labu bibi*—Black earth. A Songhoy proverb says, "Do not plant your garden until the earth is black."

When we were in Mali sharing this experience with family members, one of Dr. Maïga's nephews reminded us to include the fundamental concept of Songhoy cosmology, *Ciini bibi*, which means "the Black Word." The Songhoy people say, "In the beginning was the Word and the Word was black and the black word has the power to make things move."

Since then, I have shared this story of our journey of discovery and "re-membering" many times in workshops and presentations on cultural diversity and urban education with teachers, parents, and young people in various cities in the United States, Brazil, Canada, the UK, and other Diaspora communities. Wherever I have shared our story, African people express the same astonishment and appreciation. Indeed, they often express that having this knowledge is healing. With this in mind, one of the workshop titles I have used is *"Naarumey*—The Healing Journey Back Home."

Classroom Encounter #2: Hassimi's Story

In 2002, I accepted an invitation to teach a Saturday morning class, a *Songhoy-senni* course for adults, in Atlanta, Georgia. The class, which included community elders, parents, and younger working people, met at Morris Brown

College. It was a very congenial atmosphere and people were genuinely interested in learning the language and Songhoy culture. During the second meeting of the class, I presented the cultural practice of Songhoy women's and girls' hair beading—seven hairstyles that mark seven stages of socialization from puberty/adolescence to eldership in the Songhoy community (Maïga, 2002/2005). When I showed a photo of the intricately beaded hairstyle worn by Songhoy noble women—community leaders—someone asked, "What does it mean to be 'noble'?" Unaware of the way the class would react when a continental African discusses slavery, I said, "To explain what it means to be noble, first, I have to tell you what it means to be a slave." At the chalkboard I wrote these words:

> *Borciin*: a noble person in Songhoy society
> *Barnya*: *Bar*—to exchange/*Nya*—mother
> *Baanya*: *Baa*—does not even have/*Nya*—mother

I briefly explained the difference between "slavery," the various forms of domestic servitude that existed on the continent before the periods of Arab and European enslavement, and transatlantic chattel slavery in the African Diaspora, which, in Songhoy, began after the Moroccans, armed with gunpowder weapons and cannons supplied by the British, defeated the Songhoy Empire in 1591. Then, I explained the meaning of the two words that make up the compound word for "slave" in *Songhoy-senni*: "*bar*" means "to exchange" and "*baa*" means "does not even have."—"*nya*" a mother. *Barnya* refers to someone whose mother has been exchanged—that is, traded or sold. Also, anyone who was captured in war or who had committed a crime became a *baanya* and they, too, were without the protection of their lineage—that is, their mother's people—in traditional Songhoy society (Maïga, 2010, pp. 82–85).

Whenever we have told this story, we explain what Joyce observed that day. She was there taking notes. She noticed how abruptly the atmosphere shifted in the classroom as soon as I mentioned "slavery"; there was a kind of chill—a palpable tension that cut through the air. (African Americans would say: "People's jaws got tight.") I felt it, too, but at that time I didn't understand what was happening—that African Americans are very suspicious regarding the role continental Africans played in the enslavement of their ancestors. Then, as I proceeded with my lesson, just as suddenly when I said that "*nya*" means mother, the classroom atmosphere shifted again. This time some people in the class started to weep as they sang these words: "Sometimes I feel like a motherless child, a l-o-o-o-o-o-n-g way from home." I was even more perplexed. I wondered, what could I have said? Was it something offensive, even hurtful enough to make people cry? Given my formal pedagogical training and my professional experience as an educator, singing and crying in my classroom were just totally incomprehensible.

A Deciphering Analysis:
Songhoy Language and Concepts

Such classroom encounters with *Songhoy-senni* have pointed us toward an analysis that deciphers and deepens our knowledge and consciousness of our shared heritage and identity as Africans. For us in the Diaspora learning that the meanings associated with "black words" and blackness are positive in an African language is profoundly and immediately restorative beyond mere cognition but also touching the spirit and healing the soul (Nobles, 1978). With this knowledge the brain seems to just stop, halting within the limits of the dominant episteme of anti-blackness (Fanon, 2008). Also, discovering that there are words in *Songhoy-senni* that inspire Black people to weep in unuttered remembrance, expressing deep emotion in the African American spiritual tradition, is instructive on several levels.

First, why did our enslaved ancestors create a "sorrow song" of lament about being a "motherless child"? Why not a fatherless child? Is it because the meanings of *"barnya"* and *"baanya"* in *Songhoy-senni*—about the *mother* who has been exchanged or traded—those who do not even have a mother (due in this case to being kidnapped)—are remembered at some deeper level for which we actually do not even have the language to describe in English because there is no cultural practice in Western societies that requires such a term?

Second, what we have experienced while teaching this aspect of *Songhoy-senni* is consistent with contemporary scholarship within an African episteme that connects the communal consciousness and indigenous voice in the "slave songs" our ancestors created to their African heritage (Stuckey, 1987). While prevailing historiography has maintained incorrectly that the enslaved Africans "lost" all their culture, Levine's (1977) analysis of West African cultures embodied in the spirituals remains pertinent:

> Though they varied widely in language, institutions, gods, familial patterns, they shared a fundamental outlook toward the past, present and future and common means of cultural expression which could well have constituted the basis of a sense of common identity and world view capable of withstanding slavery.
>
> *(p. 4)*

Levine concluded:

> For all its horrors, slavery was never so complete a system of psychic assault that it prevented the slaves from carving out independent cultural forms. It never pervaded all of the interstices of their minds and their culture, and in those gaps, they were about to create an independent art form and a distinctive voice. If North American slavery eroded the Africans' linguistic and institutional life, it nevertheless allowed them to continue to develop

the patterns of verbal art which were so central to their past culture. Historians have not yet fully come to terms with what the continuance of the oral tradition meant to blacks in slavery.

(p. 30)

Third, Hassimi's story of his experiences teaching *Songhoy-senni* in the United States is particularly instructive with regard to the oral tradition and also in so far as the inadequacy of English-language words and concepts that are available to describe African Peoples' sociocultural reality and historical consciousness is concerned. For example, Dr. Maïga has pointed out that in *Songhoy-senni* there is no word for "prison," "orphanage," or "retirement" (Maïga, 2010, p. 89). These words do not exist in his language because the cultural practices associated with them did not exist. In Songhoy culture, no child was an orphan and elders always have a useful social role to play. Teaching indigenous language terms and concepts to refer to African people's communal consciousness and identity provides a way into perceiving Songhoy people's worldview and the logic of Songhoy cultural practices, such as the importance of familial bonds, relationships, and collective spirituality.

In our classes and workshops we have used a number of key words that are particularly indicative as well as proverbs that also illustrate Songhoy people's values and cultural practices. For example, the following words show the connection between the communal nature of spirituality and cultural practices in Songhoy societies:

- *Irkoy*—God (*Ir* = Our; *Koy* = God, Divinity) or "our God in us."
- *Boŋkoyno*—Chief (*Boŋ* = the head; *Koy* = God; *No* = the one anointed, chosen). Thus, a Songhoy chief is the one appointed by God to be the head of the people.
- *Koy ramarga*—Village (*Koy* = God; *Ra*= the place; *Marga* = assemble) is the place anointed by God where the people are to assemble or gather. (*Koyramarga* is also a female name in Songhoy.)

These words indicate that Songhoy people's relationship to God is both personal and communal; God belongs to the people as a group ("our God is in us") and in Songhoy culture God is also understood as within, not outside of, *each* of us; and God is essentially present in the central social structures and practices of everyday Songhoy life and culture. While it is beyond the scope of this chapter, it is worth mentioning that this communal comprehension of God that is expressed in Songhoy language is consistent with scholarly analyses of African American spirituality. Huggins's (1977) interpretation offers illuminating insights:

> Europeans used the word "Lord" to refer to the son of God, but the word has associations with feudal and magisterial authority. Black Christians called Jesus "Lord," of course, but the word also symbolically touched on

the lamb of God, the Spirit, themselves, and all godly manifestations. The prayers of black Christians were less likely to be supplications upward to authority than they were to be directed both outward and inward to establish the unity of spirit with self, to be one with the body of God.

(p. 75)

Finally, another important conceptualization that has informed our teaching of *Songhoy-senni* is the "journey of the Songhoy people" from east (ancient KMT or Kemet) to west—that is, from the Nile River Valley to the Niger River Valley, and further west to the African Diaspora. Scholarship documents the origins of *Songhoy-senni* in ancient Kemetic language (Moumouni, 2008; Maïga, 2016). Additional scholarship provides evidence of similarities between East and West African languages and scripts due to trade exchanges and migration over centuries (Johnson, 1983/2009; Winters, 1979). This scholarship—along with examples of Kemetic hieratic script (cursive form of Medu Neter or hieroglyphics) found in some indigenous languages of North America, and words from West African languages identified in indigenous languages of the Caribbean and Meso America (Lawrence, 1992; Van Sertima, 1976)—indicates how language is one way to document the connections among the civilizations of the Nile, Niger, and Diaspora. The relevance of Songhoy, West Africa's last great classical civilization, for the recovery of group memory and identity, discussed next, is that many in the Diaspora have family origins within the territory (ten modern African states)—that composed the imperial *Songhoy Ganda* (Songhoy land) from Lake Chad to the Atlantic coast (Gomez, 2005; Mann, 1996).

The Chronology of Songhoy Dynasties

Following the conceptual framework set forth by Dr. Edward Robinson and his co-authors in the text *The Journey of the Songhai People* (1992), we use imperial Songhoy, the grand multiethnic state that eclipsed Ghana and Mali, to situate Diaspora African Peoples "on the map of human geography" (Clarke, 1994, p. 104). What follows illustrates the recovery of Songhoy memory and identity from inaccurate, incomplete, or omitted scholarship (Maïga, 2010; Royster, 2017). This brief history of Songhoy has been as important for the African people we have taught in the Diaspora as it is for Africans on the continent, who also are not typically taught about their heritage. It is this content—and the content throughout this chapter—that informs our teaching and can inform school curriculum at all levels.

Songhoy Dynasties

In his books *Notes on Classical Songhoy Civilization* (2002/2005), which Asa Hilliard urged him to write, and the more comprehensive *Balancing Written History With Oral Tradition: The Legacy of the Songhoy People* (2010), Hassimi Maïga draws upon the Songhoy oral tradition to present the chronology of the first Songhoy dynasty for the first time in any history book. This dynasty represented 282 years of outstanding political life (Maïga, 2002/2005). Sixteen Songhoy chiefs ruled during the dynasty of the Koungourogossi. The period of each chief's reign is known—that is to say, it is remembered—as well as the accomplishments of each leader. For example, Imran Naaki-Songhoy, the last chief of the Koungourogossi, was the first chief to adopt the surname Maïga—which means the "owner of the land." This first dynasty lasted from the early foundation of Gao to AD 670, with the arrival of the Dia (pronounced "jah")—the next dynasty. The Dia Dynasty, which was formally recorded, included 31 kings who ruled from AD 670 to 1355. The Songhoy third dynasty, which consisted of 19 Sonni emperors, who ruled Songhoy from 1355 to 1493, conquered vast territories and absorbed the earlier dynasties of Ghana and Mali. The French explorer Félix DuBois, who wrote *Timbuctoo the Mysterious* (1896), recorded the following about Sonni Ali Ber ("Ali the Great"):

> A wonderful impulse was imparted to this country in the sixteenth century, and a marvellous civilisation appeared in the very heart of the black continent. This civilisation was not imposed by circumstances and force, as is so often the case, even in our own countries, but was spontaneously desired, evoked, and propagated by a man of the negro [Negro] races.
>
> *(p. 177)*

In 28 years after he ascended to the throne of leadership, Sonni Ali (also Sunni) turned the kingdom of Gao into the imperial Songhoy state or *Songhoy Ganda*, which stretched from the Niger in the east to Jenné in the west and from Timbuktu in the north to Hombori, the wide arch formed by the Northern Niger bend, in the south. Songhoy ultimately developed into the greatest of the Sudanic empires and, like Mali and Ghana, was strategically located along trans-Saharan trade routes. As known through oral tradition research, the Sonni Charter or constitution included the following provisions:

- Victory, never overcome, always victory, only victory: always victorious.
- The unification of the whole nation.
- To work for endogenous global development.
- To have a great capacity of anticipation and an appalling force of striking in any place and to receive everything from the empire.
- To make use of the effect of surprise in action.
- Never surrender or flee the combat because life is a combat. Rigor in the management of state affairs . . .
- To teach the virtues of work.
- To put one's people to work.
- To be envied, for having been happy.

- To have faith in our traditional values and civilization.
- To listen to each other.
- To implement solidarity and sharing values.
- Education: to have a solid physical, psychic, and intellectual training.
- To accomplish innovative creations by the contributions of trained scientists.
- To be curious and to have the taste of adventure.
- To be a Believer and do his prayers.

*(Oumar Yamadou Diallo, Researcher, Historian-Archaeologist-Curator,
Bamako-Mali, pers. comm. to Hassimi O. Maïga, May 2012)*

These provisions reflect African Peoples' values, ideals, and victorious consciousness, which are important aspects of African-centered philosophy, including unity, communal well-being and belonging, solidarity in achievement through work based on shared values and creativity, and the value of knowledge in being victorious.

The last Songhoy dynasty, the Askyas, building on the foundation established by Sonni Ali, was widely known for its administrative organization, foreign affairs, and flourishing scholarship that included three universities: Sankoré, Jenné, and Gao (Gomez, 1990). After the death of Sonni Ali, 11 Askyas ruled the Songhoy Empire from 1493 to 1593. In the administration of the first Askya—Askya Muhammad (1493–1528)—the business of scholarship, including organized academic work, international scholarly exchanges, and the production of manuscripts across the disciplines from the sciences to the humanities—a written tradition—reached its highest level of development. This written tradition has gained notoriety and has been identified with the "Manuscripts of Timbuktu," but there are also still uncatalogued manuscripts in Gao. Thus, as Leo Africanus observed, books were the most important items of commerce during the reign of Askya Muhammad. Among the disciplines in the syllabus taught at the University of Sankoré were genealogy, mathematics, logic, and traditions (Maïga, 2010). In this administration there was also a ministry called *Korei Farma*: "the minister in charge of white foreigners" (Cissoko, 1984, p. 198). Note that the term *korei (koorey/kaarey)*, which means "white" in *Songhoy-senni*, does not refer to a racial term, but at that time to foreigners of diverse backgrounds, who were not Africans and who spoke another language. These are some of the reasons imperial Songhoy, which encompassed more than ten modern African states and diverse nationalities, according to Ibrahima Baba Kake, is referred to as a civilization (Maïga, 2010). In a recent translation of the *Holy Qur'an* into *Songhoy-senni* edited by El Hadjj Dr. Hassimi Oumarou Maïga (2016), this language, the lingua franca of the Songhoy civilization, continues the unifying African written tradition.

Numerous inaccuracies regarding the history, heritage, and identities of African Peoples stem from the lack of Western/European and even African Peoples' knowledge and understanding of African languages and culture. One example is the misidentification of the heritage and identity of Songhoy emperor Askya Muhammad. First, following the French colonial administrator Maurice Delafosse's (1870–1926) inaccurate translation of and apparent confusion regarding two West African locations—Fouta Djallon (in Guinea Conakry) and Fouta Toro (in today's Senegal)—Askya Muhammad has been incorrectly identified in many historical texts with the Marka people, not as a person of Songhoy origin but as Askya Muhammad Touré (e.g., from "toro" or Touré of the Arma people). Second, even some African scholars have misidentified Emperor Askya Muhammad as Askya Muhammad Sylla—that is, as a person of Soninké/Marka origin. This would mean he was a Syllanche, belonging to a group of people from a region in today's southern Mali rather than Gao, in northern Mali, the cradle of the Songhoy Empire.

It appears that there is confusion regarding Emperor Askya's heritage and identity due to a lack of knowledge of the actual meaning of the word "*sylla*" in *Songhoy-senni*, which is the root word of "*syllanche*" in this language of northern Mali (today). In *Songhoy-senni*, "*sylla*" is a fundamental vocabulary word, meaning it has not been borrowed from any other language. "*Sylla*" refers to the place where the cows come to be milked in the evening in Songhoy territory, because this is where their calves are kept safely tied to a long rope. The calves are tethered to this rope with a cord around each of their necks. Both this cow-milking place and the rope to which the calves are tied are called "*hawiizey sylla*." "*Haw*" means cow. "*Izey*" means babies—that is, "baby cows" or calves in *Songhoy-senni*. In Songhoy territory, all the people involved in and associated with these domestic cattle raising activities and family-based dairy work are known as "*syllanche*." This information comes from conversations Dr. Hassimi Maïga has had with Songhoy language special- ists who are steeped in traditional Songhoy culture. Historically, the Songhoy are known as warriors, but Songhoy people have also been rice farmers, fisher- men, and sedentary cattle raisers who have tended to their cows in this tradi- tional way.

These examples illustrate the importance of the study of African languages and culture for the recovery of group memory and identity. We conclude this chapter in the next section with a focus on how we use African and African Diaspora orature, proverbs, and tales, in particular, to immerse students (educators and parents) in our African cultural background.

Songhoy-senni—African Language Teaching for All

Enabling African ancestry students to identify with their African heritage by recovering group memory and historical consciousness *through* the study of Songhoy civilization, culture, and language has also provided opportunities for other learners (youth and adults) of diverse backgrounds to benefit as well from the ways that we use emancipatory pedagogy to: (a) locate or center learners in authentic representations of Africa and Diaspora sociohistorical realities through accurate scholarship or indigenous orature and (b) to recognize and value multiple ways of knowing and epistemologies through indigenous voice. The instructional materials we have produced and incorporated into our teaching use Songhoy and Diaspora orature—proverbs, tales, and toasts—to support these examples of emancipatory pedagogy.

Locating Learners Within Songhoy Values and Mores

Here are several typical proverbs that we have included in workshop materials to locate or center learners in the "mind of Africa"—that is, to illustrate African people's humanity through examples of moral concerns and right conduct expressed in Songhoy proverbial wisdom:

> *Dabari futu si nga koyo hatta soko boro tana.*
> The evil that comes back upon evildoers may not miss innocent people.
> *Explanation*: When you are doing something evil to someone else, your actions may actually hurt you and your own loved ones. People also say, "What goes around comes around."

> *Boro si wanga jifa ka haro zuu.*
> If you can't eat the meat from a lamb because it hasn't been killed in the right way, don't ask for the soup.
> *Explanation*: We should avoid being inconsistent with our principles versus our actions. This proverb might also be understood to mean "Put your money where your mouth is."

> *Boro kul si bone bay ka too talka.*
> No one knows more about misery than a poor man.
> *Explanation*: This proverb is about people who think they know every-thing, even more than those who have personal experience with something. The proverb advises us to be more humble. For example, you might be the best gynecologist, but if you have never given birth to a baby yourself, you cannot really know what it feels like.

Another example of teaching materials that center students in authentic representations of Songhoy culture includes the online demonstration lessons that we created as part of the work of the American Educational Research Association's Commission on Research in Black Education (CORIBE) in 2000. On the CORIBE website, we created a colorful, animated, multimedia interactive online lesson titled "Black Is," which with a mouse click displays and calls out positive words associated with blackness (in the English language). Next, the learner is presented with the positive meanings associated with blackness in Songhoy culture and language discussed earlier—that is, black sun (*wayne bibi*), black water (*hari bibi*), and black earth (*labu bibi*). This latter conceptualization was illustrated using this Songhoy proverb:

> "*Saddiŋa labu si boori kala nd'a bibi.*"
> The soil in a garden is not good for planting unless it is black.
>
> *(Maïga, 2005, pp. 173–174)*

In addition, the website includes a lively folktale about a "choosey Hyena" that affirms Songhoy people's positive valuation of what blackness means. In this tale Hyena goes to see the shoemaker to ask him to make a leather box in which to put her amulet or charm (*gris-gris*). After choosing and rejecting various colors—bright red and green (which the shoemaker says will fade and turn dark), white (which will get stained with mud when she runs through water), and yellow (which in the long run will just turn black like all the others), Hyena says to the shoemaker, "Well, why didn't you just tell me I needed to choose black in the first place?"

The shoemaker said, "I couldn't tell you anything, because you started out being too choosy and so concerned about colors. That's why I didn't have a chance to tell you that black (*bibi*) is the only everlasting color." When Hyena finally chooses the color black for the leather box in which she will keep her gris-gris, the shoemaker says, "Aha . . . at last this is a wise choice" (Maïga, 1996/2003, pp. 19–20). This tale illustrates the wit and wisdom of Songhoy proverbial knowledge, which permit learners to experience Songhoy people's positive valuation of blackness.

Recognizing and Valuing Multiple Ways of Knowing/Epistemologies

While proverbs are understood as commonsense sayings or parables to guide behavior and for passing on values and morals, scholarship on the pedagogical uses of African orature in general and proverbs more specifically indicates the powerful epistemological contributions of this traditional medium of communication and instruction in African cultural contexts (Dei, 2016). As Dei (2015) explains,

> African indigenous philosophies conveyed in proverbs, fables, riddles, folklore, tales, cultural stories, and songs have historically assisted African peoples to interpret, understand, and exercise their agencies in resistance struggles. Proverbs offer a key to the past, present, and future . . . Proverbs play a role in setting the social code for acceptable and unacceptable behavior . . . Those who evoke proverbs in their speeches . . . are usually rewarded

through public approvals of their "charm," "wit," "intelligence," and "eloquence."

(Dei, p. 136)

In so far as wit and intelligence are concerned, Yankah (1989) describes proverb games in Akan culture in Ghana "where participants test each other's proverb knowledge (not necessarily competence) through proverb exchanges" (1989, p. 251). Stewart (1997) notes that proverbs are a genre of African literature that is "more plentiful than others" and "many African cultures assign great importance to proverbs" (p. ix). Indeed, "The ability to use proverbs effectively in speech and conversation is essential to attaining positions of leadership and respect in some African societies" (p. ix). Stewart cites this Yoruba proverb of Nigeria as an example: "A wise man who knows proverbs reconciles difficulties" (p. ix). Maïga (2010) describes Songhoy storytelling as character education:

> Story-telling not only demonstrates the love of a given person for their community but also shows what the community wants people to know and to remember . . . Songhoy stories . . . suggest morals or lessons that can strengthen not only values and traditions, but telling these stories can provide lessons that shape and nurture adult behavior and children's character to maintain balance and harmony in the community as a whole.

(p. 96)

So much heritage knowledge or group memory is embedded in African languages and lore, but because these languages and the forms of cultural expression they convey are mostly unknown by people of African ancestry in the Diaspora, we are not able to recognize possible African origins in our language practices—that is to say, in the "Black oral tradition" (and the broader Diaspora). This Diaspora oral tradition includes not only plantation proverbs ("You can hide the smoke, but what you gon' do about the fire?"), the quintessential trickster, "Brer Rabbit" (or "Buh Rabbit"), and other animal tales recorded in the Uncle Remus stories (in the United States), for example, but also analogous Afro-Latino animal tales, like *Tio y Conejo*, which Afro-Ecuadorian folklorist Juan Garcia Salazar collected in Esmeraldas (Belkin, 1993; see also Anderson, 2017; www.iaf.gov/resources/publications/grassroots-development-journal/2007-african-descendants-and-development/lessons-of-the-elders).

Senegalese historian Ibrahima Seck (2014) traces the African origins of various Louisiana tales. For example, he identifies the source of a Louisiana tale that involves the "rabbit/hare, the elephant, and the whale" in an identical tale recorded in Senegal, West Africa, which was the Motherland of many enslaved Africans in Louisiana: Bouki is "the same animal . . . found begging for the help of the elephant to pull an imaginary treasure from the bottom of the ocean" (p. 135). Likewise, Anansi the spider of Ghana tales can be recognized in stories about

"Aunt Nancy" in the Caribbean. Seck discusses African slave storytelling in North America and the Caribbean as both "entertainment" and "resistance."

Geneva Smitherman (2000) defines toasts as "rhyming epic-like Black folk stories, usually raw and racy, that celebrate Blacks" (p. 256). She explains:

> All of these folk narrative forms have as their overriding theme the coping ability, strength, endurance, trickeration capacity, and power of black people . . . The Toast is a variation on the trickster, bad nigguh theme done in poetic form. While the High John and Brer Rabbit stories are rural and older in time, the Toast is a modern urban continuance of this tradition. In contrast to the lack of profanities and sexual allusions in the older folk stories, Toasts are replete with funk in practically every rhymed couplet . . . . The hero is fearless, defiant, openly rebellious, and full of braggadocio about his masculinity, sexuality, fighting ability, and general badness. Narrated in first person, this epic folk style is a tribute—that is, a "toast"—to this superbad, omnipotent black hustler, pimp, playa, killer who is mean to the max.
>
> *(pp. 156–157)*

This genre of the Black oral tradition functioned almost like a rite of passage for urban youth, especially boys, in the United States through the 1950s and 1960s. On the street corners and in jail African American boys and men used to learn not just to recite but also to perform these long, complex poems like (Shine and the Sinking of the) "The Titanic," "Stackolee" (Jackson, 1974; also "Stagolee," Lester, 1969), "High John the Conqueror," and "The Signifying Monkey," among others. Stackolee is actually from a song about a real man. Here is how the version in Julius Lester's (1969) *Black Folktales* describes Stagolee:

> Stagolee was undoubtedly and without question, the baddest . . . [dude] that ever lived. Stagolee was so bad [meaning fearless and fear-inspiring] that the flies wouldn't even fly around his head in the summertime, and snow wouldn't fall on his house in the winter. He was bad.
>
> *(Lester, 1969, p. 113)*

However, Bruce Jackson notes that the "character Stagolee or Stackolee figures in ballad and prose narrative tradition as well as toast tradition":

> Negro bad man, who according to the ballad, shot and killed Billy Lyon . . . in a barroom brawl . . . for stealing his "Magic Stetson." Legend says . . . that this magic hat, for which Stakalee sold his soul to the Devil, enabled him to assume various shapes, from mountains to

varmints, to walk barefooted on hot slag, and to eat fire. When he got too ornery even for the Devil to stand, the latter caused him to lose his hat and his magic via Billy Lyon, and ultimately to burn in hell.

(p. 43)

"High John the Conqueror," a tale from slavery, recounts the heroic exploits of another "bad" Black man who was also unafraid and unbossed. According to Jackson,

> Toasts are not recited, they are acted; the teller does not just say a toast, he performs it. His voice changes for the various personae of the poem, and sometimes there is another voice for the narrator. There are differences in stress, in accent, in clarity of articulation for various characters. The toast is a kind of street theater, a theater involving only one performer at a time. People who can say the lines but cannot act them get little opportunity to perform, because they are boring.

> *(p. 5)*

Designing lessons for young people in the Songhoy Club (after-school heritage program), we made the connections explicit between the high regard accorded to proverb and storytelling performance, as forms of indigenous instruction in African cultural contexts, mastering the highly esteemed verbal art of (memorizing) and performing such toasts—the "poetic literature of the street" (Jackson, 1974, p. 3)—and the intellectual acuity and verbal dexterity of celebrated hip hop performances today (King et al., 2014). Producing such a lesson first required introducing to the Songhoy Club graduate student teaching assistant both a Songhoy folk tale, "The Hyena, the Monkey, and the Rabbit," *and* the "Signifying Monkey" toast, a recognized precursor to hip hop poetry. The veteran high school English teacher, who developed and taught this lesson, had never heard of African American toasts and tales narrative poetry nor was he familiar enough with African orature to use a Songhoy folktale pedagogically in relation to the Black oral tradition. Because of these multidimensional learning experiences, we describe the Songhoy Club (and the Songhoy Princess Clubs) as a pedagogical lab (King et al., 2014).

Importantly, this lesson introduced students (and the teacher) to what signifying means (what the Monkey does in this toast). The term refers to the performance of ritual insults. Smitherman (1977) offers these detailed explanations of "*signifyin*" or "*signification*":

> [It] refers to the verbal art of insult in which a speaker humorously puts down, talks about, needles—that is, signifies on—the listener. Sometimes signifyin (also siggin) is down to make a point, sometimes it's just for fun.

> This type of folk expression in the oral tradition has the status of a customary ritual that's accepted at face value . . . nobody who's signified on is supposed to take it to heart. It's a culturally approved method of talking about somebody—usually through verbal indirection. Since the signifier employs humor, it makes the put-down easier to swallow and gives the recipient a socially acceptable way out. That is, if they can't come back with no bad signification of they own, they can just laugh along with the group.
>
> *(pp. 118–119)*

Further, Smitherman (1994) notes that as "ritualized verbal art," *signifyin* "depends on double meaning and irony, exploits the unexpected, and uses quick verbal surprises and humor" (p. 260). Also *"siggin, sigon"* "can be used for playful commentary or serious social critique couched as play" (Smitherman, 2006, p. 43).

Clarence Major (1970) had previously described signifying as "'performance' talk; to berate someone" as in the "indigenous verbal folk game" that has many names, such as "joning," "capping," and the "Dozens." The latter, according to Major, is a

> A very elaborate verbal rhyming game traditionally played by black boys, in which the participants insult each other's relatives . . . especially their mothers. *The object of the game is to test emotional strengths. The first person to give in to anger is the loser.*
>
> *(p. 138, emphasis added)*

H. Rap Brown (1969), the eloquent political activist, and Henry Louis Gates, who proposed a vernacular theory of literary criticism based on the tale of the Signifying Monkey, are among those who note that "signifyin(g) . . . can be undertaken with equal facility and effect by women" (and girls) as well as men (Gates, 1998, p. 60). The role of the audience or listeners present is also crucial. As ritual insults are being traded back and forth between two persons, a listener who loses self-control and laughs too much, implicitly judging one person to have landed the winning barb, can easily become a target; hence the not-so-subtle warning "If you grin, you in" (the game).

Using the folktale in Figure 3.1 as an example of Songhoy culture, worldview, and language practice, the lesson allowed the students to also experience the epistemological lineage connecting African folktales to African American "street poetry" (toasts) as a bridge to urban hip hop, and also used lyrics from a popular Tupac Shakur poem ("The Rose That Grew From Concrete"), engaging the students in thinking critically about challenges many of them are negotiating in

The Hyena, the Monkey, and the Rabbit A Songhoy Folktale	An African American Folk Narrative A Toast to the Signifying Monkey
Hyena had fallen into a water-well and couldn't get out for days. When a Monkey came along, Hyena called out, "My friend, dear friend, get me out of here, out of this water well."	It was early in the morning one bright summer day, the Lion was comin' down the Monkey's way. The Monkey laid up in a tree and he thought up a scheme, and he thought he'd try one a his fantastic dreams.
The Monkey replied, "How can I do it?" Hyena said, "Drop your tail into the water-well and pull it back. I will hang onto it until I am out!" The Monkey agreed . . . and let the Hyena grab his tail and pulled until she was out of the water-well.	He say, "Hey, Brother Lion, a big rascal just went down the way, a whole lot of things I'm afraid to say. The way he talked about you and your father was a terrible sin, said you and your grandmother wasn't even no kin." Lion got mad, he bent back on his knees, He went through the jungle knockin' down coconut trees.
Once out of danger, Hyena said, "I cannot walk by myself. I will need your assistance to hold onto your shoulder until I get home." When the Monkey agreed again, this time to let Hyena hold onto his shoulder, she grabbed him tightly and said, "This time you will not escape from me. Don't you know that I spent days in this water-well without eating and you are just one of the finest dinners that I will ever eat!"	That's when he spotted the big rascal up under the tree, he say, "Hey, big bad dude, it's gonna be you and me!" The Elephant looked out the corner of his eyes, Said, "Why don't you find somebody to mess with more your size?" The Lion made a fancy pass, the Elephant stepped aside and kicked him dead in his ____* They fought all that night and they fought all the day, I don't see how in Heaven the Lion got away.
The Monkey started crying and crying until a Rabbit, who was just passing by, heard him. Rabbit stopped and asked, "What is the matter?" The monkey narrated the whole story to the Rabbit. The Rabbit replied, "I cannot believe what I'm hearing! How in the world it is possible for you to fall into a water-well and for this Monkey to pull Hyena? I do not see how this is even possible in the first place. I need to see the Hyena in the well again for me to witness what has happened. Please show me, Hyena, if this is true, how the Monkey pulled you out."	He come back through the jungle more dead than alive, that's when the Monkey started his jive. Say, "You left yesterday ringing like bells, and you come back this evenin' all whipped up like hell." . . . "Get out from under my tree before I swing out and slap you." The Monkey got happy and he jumped up and down, his two feet slipped but hit the ground. Like a bolt of lightnin' and a bushel of wheat, The Lion was on him with all four feet. "Say," he say, "I'm going to beat you down 'cause the Elephant beat me. I'm going to whip you for signifying."
As soon as Rabbit said it, Hyena jumped back into the well. Then Rabbit told the Monkey, "What are you waiting for, Judgment Day?" The Monkey went back to his trees and Hyena started crying when she understood that she had been tricked.	Monkey lay down there holding his head, he said, "Let me get up. I'll fight you like a natural man." The Lion jumped back, all squared off for a fight, that's when the Monkey jumped clean out of sight.
The moral of this story: *Not all good deeds are rewarded.* *Even if good deeds aren't rewarded, why should we continue to do good deeds toward each other?*	**The moral of this toast:** *Don't let someone goad you into a fight and for thewrong reason.* *Based on the toast, what do you think "signifying" means?"*
	* Age-inappropriate language was replaced in this edited version adapted from Jackson 1974, pp. 167-168.

FIGURE 3.1 A Songhoy Tale and an African American Folk Narrative Poem–Toast

their neighborhood and at school—in particular, fighting when they feel someone has "dissed" (disrespected) them. Fighting is one of the reasons Black students are overrepresented in school discipline and pushed into juvenile incarceration (Davis, 2016; Skiba & Williams, 2014; see also: http://keepschoolssafe.org/students/fighting.htm). In this regard Mississippi rap artist David Banner has made a pertinent observation: "Black kids kill Black kids for the same reason cops do. They see no value" (Banner, 2014).

The lesson demonstrated cultural continuity between Africa and the Diaspora and the classroom discussion focused on how African people have and continue to use language creatively to communicate moral lessons to guide behavior (Nobles, 1995, 2015). Thus, the lesson provided opportunities for critical thinking about making wise choices and right action in the context of African worldview, values, and the moral messages conveyed in tales and toasts (ahead) in both cultural contexts.

In conclusion, as Wade Nobles, Lesiba Baloyi, and Tholene Sodi (2016) astutely observe, "It is through the penetrating reinterpretation of the language and logic of our African ancestry that Africans (both Continental and Diasporan) will be able to rescue and remember our humanity, wholeness, and wellness" (p. 44). In the various venues where we have taught *Songhoy-senni*, we have incorporated African (Songhoy) and African American orature in forms of emancipatory pedagogy to enable students (teachers, parents, and other community adults) to make connections between our African cultural background—"what it means to be human and a person"—and Diaspora heritage knowledge. We have used African language, in the form of key words, greetings, proverbs, and tales, to decipher important indicators of the continuity of our African cultural background in the Diaspora to contribute to what Wade W. Nobles-Ifagbemi Sangodare Nana Kwaku Berko I (2015) refers to as the "the restoration of African mind" (p. 17) and in so doing to recover what Nobles et al. (2016) describe as our "Pan African humanness," a particular state of being, belonging, and becoming (p. 39). Retrieving the African episteme in teaching *Songhoy-senni* proverbial tales and African American toasts is a way to learn about and experience our shared African heritage *through* language. This is significant because "despite much damaging cultural loss . . . our lives continue to be shaped and informed by African epistemology, whether we are aware of the Africanity of these connections or not" (King, 2017, p. 218). Asa Hilliard understood the vital importance of scholarship and praxis that affirm this reality when he suggested that Hassimi Maïga should write what became his book *Notes on Classical Songhoy Education and Socialization* (2002/2005). In the preface Baba Asa Hilliard-Nana Baffour Amankwatia II wrote,

> In writing this book, Dr. Hassimi Maïga has managed a great feat. With great clarity, he has packed tightly, into a small book, choice details describing the traditional socialization of Songhoy culture in particular, and the

African culture in general. The "iron curtain" that has been drawn between contemporary Africans on the continent and in the Diaspora, between them and the vital memories of African ways, is pierced and a valuable view of our excellence tradition is revealed in this book.

(Hilliard, 2002/2005, p. iv)

Such knowledge of our heritage, which permits us to recover our historical and cultural consciousness, is essential to mastery of self, an important function of education (Ighodaro & Wiggan, 2010). Moreover, knowing self in order to be of service to others and knowing yourself before anyone else has to tell you who you are or to correct your behavior are an important function of education for cultural excellence. Hopefully, "our Ancestors are pleased" (Hilliard, 2002/2005, p. vii).

References

Anderson, M. (2017, August 23). Latino experience is in focus at African American History and Culture Museum. *Smithsonian Insider*. Retrieved from http://insider.si.edu/2017/08/latino-experience-focus-african-american-history-culture-museum/#.WbFXvPwffKQ.facebook

Banner, D. (2014, August 14). David Banner defends Tweets On CNN, explains why Black men are undervalued. *Stacks*. Retrieved from www.stacksmag.net/2014/08/david-banner-defends-tweets-cnn-why-black-men-undervalued.html

Belkin, A. (1993). *Collective memory: The African presence in Latin America: A study guide on the Maroon community of Esmeraldas, Ecuador*. Washington, DC: Network of Educators on the Americas (NECA). ERIC No. ED398131.

Brown, H. (1969). *Die nigger die!: A political autobiography*. Westport, CT: Lawrence Hill Books.

Cissoko, S. M. (1984). The Songhay from the 12th to the 16th century. In D. T. Niane (Ed.), *UNESCO general history of Africa, Volume IV: Africa from the twelfth to the sixteenth century* (pp. 186–210). Berkeley: University of California Press.

Clarke, J. H. (1994). *Christopher Columbus and the Afrikan holocaust: Slavery and the rise of European capitalism*. Brooklyn, NY: A & B.

Davis, S. (2016). *An empowering YPAR project: Black girls' examination of the educational pathway to STEM fields and school-based issues*. (Unpublished doctoral dissertation). Georgia State University, Atlanta, GA.

Dei, G. S. (2015). African proverbs as a form of epistemology. In M. J. Shujaa & K. J. Shujaa (Eds.), *The SAGE encyclopedia of African cultural heritage in North America* (Vol. 1, pp. 135–137). Thousand Oaks, CA: SAGE.

Dei, G. S. (2016). Integrating African proverbs in the education of young learners: The challenge of knowledge synthesis. In P. Sillitoe (Ed.), *Indigenous studies and engaged anthropology: The collaborative moment* (pp. 181–200). New York, NY: Routledge.

Du Bois, F. (1896). *Timbuctoo the mysterious*. (D. White, Trans.). New York, NY: Longmans, Green.

Fanon, F. (2008). *Black skins, white masks*. New York, NY: Grove Press.

Gates, H. L. (1998). *The signifying monkey: A theory of African-American literary criticism*. New York, NY: Oxford University Press.

Gomez, M. (1990). Timbuktu under imperial Songhay: A reconsideration of autonomy. *The Journal of African history, 31*(1), 5–24.

Gomez, M. (2005). *Reversing sail: A history of the African Diaspora.* New York, NY: Cambridge University Press.

Goodwin, S. (2004). Emancipatory pedagogy. In S. Goodwin & E. Swartz (Eds.), *Teaching children of color: Seven constructs of effective teaching in urban schools* (pp. 37–48). Rochester, NY: RTA Press.

Hilliard, A. (2002/2005). Preface. In H. O. Maïga, *Notes on classical Songhoy education and socialization: The world of women and child rearing practices in West Africa* (3rd ed., pp. iii–vii). Atlanta, GA: Murehm Books.

Huggins, N. (1977). *Black odyssey: The African-American ordeal in slavery.* New York, NY: Vintage Books.

Ighodaro, E., & Wiggan, G. (2010). *Curriculum violence: America's new civil rights issue.* New York, NY: Nova Science.

Jackson, B. (1974). *Get your ass in the water and swim like me: Narrative poetry from the Black oral tradition.* Cambridge, MA: Harvard University Press.

Johnson, W. R. (1983). The ancient Akan script, a review of *Sankofa* by Niangoran-Bouah. In I. Van Sertima (Ed.), *Blacks in science: Ancient and modern* (pp. 197–207). New Brunswick, NJ: Transaction Books.

King, J. E. (1992). Diaspora literacy and consciousness in the struggle against miseducation in the Black community. *The Journal of Negro Education, 61*, 317–340.

King, J. E. (2014). Black education for human freedom: On the African renaissance and history in the present. In I. Nuñez, C. T. Laura, & R. Ayers (Eds.), *Diving in: Bill Ayers and the art of teaching into the contradiction* (pp. 155–166). New York, NY: Teachers College Press.

King, J. E. (2017). 2015 AERA Presidential Address. Morally engaged research/ers dismantling epistemological nihilation in the age of impunity. *Educational Researcher, 46*(5), 211–222.

King, J. E., Goss, A., & McArthur, S. (2014). Recovering history and the "parent piece" for cultural well-being and belonging. In J. King, E. Swartz et al., *"Re-membering" history in student and teacher and learning: An Afrocentric culturally informed praxis* (pp. 155–188). New York, NY: Routledge.

King, J. E, & Swartz, E. E. (2014). *"Re-membering" history in student and teacher learning: An Afrocentric culturally informed praxis.* New York, NY: Routledge.

Lawrence, H. G. (Kofi Wangara) (1992). Mandinga voyages across the Atlantic. In I. Van Sertima (Ed.), *African presence in early America.* New Brunswick, NJ: Transaction.

Lester, J. (1969). *Black folktales.* New York, NY: Grove Press.

Levine, L. W. (1977). *Black culture and Black consciousness: Afro-American folk thought from slavery to freedom.* New York, NY: Oxford University Press.

Maïga, H. O. (1996/2003). *Conversational Soŋay language of Mali.* New Orleans, LA: Murehm Books.

Maïga, H. O. (2002/2005). *Notes on classical Songhoy education and socialization: The world of women and child rearing practices in West Africa* (3rd ed.). Atlanta, GA: Murehm Books.

Maïga H. O. (2005). When the language of education is not the language of culture: The epistemology of systems of knowledge and pedagogy. In J. E. King (Ed.), *Black education: A transformative research and action agenda for a new century* (pp. 159–182). Washington, DC: American Education Research Association/Mahwah, NJ: Lawrence Erlbaum.

Maïga, H. O. (2010). *Balancing written history with oral tradition: The legacy of the Songhoy people*. New York, NY: Routledge.

Maïga, H. O. (2016). Africana sociocultural heritage. In M. J. Shujaa & K. J. Shujaa (Eds.), *The SAGE encyclopedia of African cultural heritage in North America* (Vol. 1, pp. 158–166). Thousand Oaks, CA: SAGE.

Major, C. (Ed.). (1970). *From juba to jive: A dictionary of African-American slang*. New York, NY: Penguin.

Mann, K. (1996). *African Kingdoms of the past: Ghana, Mali, Songhay*. Parsippany, NJ: Dillon Press.

Moore, R. B. (1976). *Racism in the English language: A lesson plan and study essay*. New York, NY: Council on Interracial Books for Children/Racism and Sexism Resource Center.

Moumouni, F. (2008). *Aux sources de la connaissance directe: La parenté entre l'Égyptien ancient et le Songhay* [Source of direct knowledge: The kinship between ancient Egyptian and Songhay]. Paris, France: MNAIBU.

Nobles, V. L. (1995). *EMI: The concept of spirit in selected plays of August Wilson*. (Ph.D. Dissertation). Temple University, Philadelphia, PA.

Nobles, V. L. (2015). Ebonics: The retention of African tongues. In M. J. Shujaa & K. J. Shujaa (Eds.), *The SAGE encyclopedia of African cultural heritage in North America* (Vol. 1, pp. 388–391). Thousand Oaks, CA: SAGE.

Nobles, W. W. (1978). *The archaeology of the spirit: Toward a deeper discourse of Black studies*. Retrieved from https://docs.wixstatic.com/ugd/b5ad7a_fb7119cf8c6e431b8b53f503a05941bb.pdf

Nobles, W. W. (2005). To be African or not to be: The question of identity or authenticity: Some preliminary thoughts. In G. G. Jackson (Ed.), *We're not going to take it anymore: Educational and psychological practices from an Africentric paradigm of helping* (pp. 183–206). Silver Spring, MD: Beckham.

Nobles, W. W. (2015). *The island of memes: Haiti's unfinished revolution*. Baltimore, MD: Black Classic Press.

Nobles, W. W., Baloyi, L., & Sodi, T. (2016). Pan African humanness and Sakhu Djaer as praxis for African knowledge systems. *Alternation Special Education, 18*, 36–59.

Robinson, C., Battle, R., & Robinson, E. (1992). *The journey of the Songhai people*. Philadelphia, PA: Songhai.

Royster, M. D. (2017). A review: Balancing written history with oral tradition. *Journal of Negro Education, 86*(2), 191–192.

Seck, I. (2014). *Bouki fait gombo: A history of the slave community of Habitation Haydel (Whitney Plantation), Louisiana, 1750–1860*. New Orleans, LA: University of New Orleans Press.

Skiba, R., & Williams, N. (2014). Are Black kids worse? Myths and facts about racial differences and behavior: A summary of the literature. *The Equity Project at Indiana University*. Retrieved from www.district287.org/uploaded/A_Better_Way/MythsandFactsAboutRacialDifferencesinBehavior.pdf

Smitherman, G. (1977). *Talkin and testifyin: The language of Black America*. Boston, MA: Houghton Mifflin.

Smitherman, G. (1994). *Black talk: Words and phrases from the hood to the Amen corner*. Boston: Houghton Mifflin.

Smitherman, G. (2006). *Word from the mother: Language and African Americans*. New York, NY: Routledge.

Stewart, J. (1997). *African proverbs and wisdom: A collection for every day of the year, from more than forty African nations.* New York, NY: Kensington.

Stuckey, S. (1987). *Slave culture: Nationalist theory and the foundations of Black America.* New York, NY: Oxford University Press.

Van Sertima, I. (1976). *They came before Columbus: The African presence in ancient America.* New York, NY: Random House.

Wa Thiong'o, N. (1981). *Decolonizing the mind.* London: James Currey.

Winters, C.-A. (1979). Manding writing in the New World, part 1. *Journal of African Civilization, 1*(1), 81–97.

Yankah, K. (1989). *The proverb in context of Akan rhetoric: A theory of proverb praxis.* New York, NY: Peter Lang.

4

WORLDVIEW, SCHOLARSHIP, AND INSTRUCTIONAL AGENCY

Ellen E. Swartz

> To tap this mighty reservoir of experience, knowledge, beauty, love, and deed, we
> must appeal not to the few, not to some souls, but to all. The narrower the appeal, the
> poorer the culture; the wider the appeal the more magnificent are the possibilities.
>
> (Du Bois, 1920a, p. 140)

In this chapter we explore the work of scholars in the Black intellectual tradition
in the context of the progressive era. Specifically, how does their work exhibit
the African worldview and cultural concepts brought here by their ancestors
and retained in their heritage knowledge (a group's cultural memory) (Clarke,
1992; King, 2006a; King & Swartz, 2016)? Adding to the existing scholarship
on African retentions (Carney, 2001; Gomez, 1998; Hall, 2005; Holloway, 1990;
Phillips, 1990; Piersen, 1993; Rucker, 2006; Thompson, 1990; Turner, 2002;
Wahlman, 2001; Walker, 2001), we explore the retention of African democracy
in North America. This retention is evident in the ongoing African pursuit of
democracy in the Diaspora—a democracy that was/is understood as communal,
cooperative, and participatory. To further examine African retentions in Diasporan
scholarship, we turn to the work of William Edward Burghardt Du Bois and
ask ourselves, "What are the pre-enslavement African sources of significant Du
Boisian themes and how can knowledge of African worldview and cultural
concepts locate those sources?" To demonstrate the instructional agency needed
to replace eurocratic school knowledge with knowledge that draws upon the
history and cultural heritage of all students, we provide numerous examples of
the African episteme that is consistently present in several Du Boisian themes,
and suggest how to use these themes—and the episteme that informs them—to
shape classroom practices.

Black Scholarship in the Progressive Era

To explore the African episteme in Black scholarship, we go back to the late nineteenth and early decades of the twentieth centuries to what historians call the progressive era. While this era or movement is variously dated, historians generally agree that the ideas and practices in Frances W. Parker's Quincy System (Massachusetts) in the 1870s were early emanations that sought to democratize the regimented and rule-driven education practices that commonly existed (Kliebard, 1986). In fact, John Dewey called Parker the father of progressive education—a movement that gained momentum and peaked in the 1930s, but by the 1950s was pushed underground by reactionary forces in the Cold War era (Cremin, 1961; Dewey, 1899, 1952; Dewey & Dewey, 1915; King, 2016a; Kliebard, 1986).

While eras are shaped by the ideas and actions of people who live in them, historians who write about the ideas and actions of those people shape the history of an era. During the progressive era the presence and participation of both Black and White scholars and educators shaped educational thought and practice. Yet, it was historians of the dominant group—mostly White university men— who molded public memory of this era by producing an explanatory but distorted grand narrative of progressive education during this period. While describing the variations among progressive educators from compliance-seeking to democratic-oriented (see Chapter 5), this narrative assigned only White progressive philosophers and educators of the late nineteenth and early twentieth centuries as the "carriers" of reform that sought to change the narrow, dull, and lifeless curriculum predominant in U.S. schools. Invisible in this grand narrative are the thought and accomplishments of Black philosophers and educators, like W.E.B. Du Bois, Carter G. Woodson, and Anna Julia Cooper, as well as the leadership and practices of educators like Nannie Helen Burroughs and Mary McLeod Bethune, among others. Given the ubiquity of this narrative and the master scripts that maintain it, the task of the rest of us is to "re-member" or put back together a history of this and other eras that is closer to what actually occurred (King & Swartz, 2014; Swartz, 2007). We do this in service to scholarly accuracy, but also to learn how African worldview and heritage inform our understanding of this period of history and beyond.

During the progressive era, W.E.B. Du Bois (1932, 1935,1945), Anna Julia Cooper (1892/1969), Carter G. Woodson (1919a, 1925a, 1933), Nannie Helen Burroughs (1934), Horace Mann Bond (1934, 1935), Mary McLeod Bethune (1939), Charles H. Thompson (1935), Ida B. Wells (1892), Monroe N. Work (1916, 1919, 1931), Lawrence D. Reddick (1933), and Dorothy B. Porter (1936) were only a few of the men and women of African ancestry who were educators, published scholars, activists, and leaders. In varied ways and to varying degrees they identified and opposed race, class, and/or gender inequalities in a democracy, and in so doing, exhibited the worldview of their African ancestors.

(See Chapter 1 in this volume and Chapter 1 in King & Swartz, 2016 for content about African worldview.) For example, Nannie Helen Burroughs (1934) and Horace Mann Bond (1935) provided strident critiques of white racial domination while advocating and demonstrating self-determination that considered the needs of the Black masses as a collective—a decidedly ancestral communal concept retained in the Diaspora (Gyekye, 1987; Karenga, 1999, 2005). Yet, most accounts of the progressive era, even those by so-called revisionist historians (Bowers, 1969; Cremin, 1961; Tanner, 1991; Tyack, 2003), omit the ideas and scholarly work of Black intellectuals, leaders, and educators—omissions that mirror the same racial disconnections exhibited by the White progressives about whom they wrote (Swartz, 2007). While a small number of White historians and educators have taken one step outside the master script to acknowledge the presence of Black scholars during the progressive era, they do so to either point out the omissions and conservative leanings of White progressives or to acknowledge "that they [Black scholars] had firsthand and accurate knowledge of the underside of American society and a realistic understanding of how great a task it would be to bring about real social justice" (Tyack et al., 1984, pp. 179–180). Even in these accounts, Black scholars and other people of African ancestry have a defined place and purpose as only receivers of injustice in a racist society (Goodenow, 1975, 1977a, 1977b, 1978, 1981). Absent is any attempt to identify what Black scholarship and advocacy contributed to expanding democratic discourse and practice during the progressive era. Also absent is any consideration of African worldview and cultural concepts that informed the work of these Black scholars.

African Episteme and Black Scholarship

During the progressive era, Black scholarship that countered the limited knowledge base of the white dominant racial hierarchy with more accurate and comprehensive knowledge about African Diasporan history and culture was informed by an African episteme—that is, by ways of knowing and conceptions of knowledge based on an African worldview and the cultural concepts that express that worldview. Emancipatory Black scholars/activists—including educators, philosophers, historians, and social scientists—understood community well-being as dependent upon access to unfettered knowledge about the collective African family (Bond, 1934, 1935; Du Bois, 1924, 1939; Woodson, 1919b, 1933; Work, 1916). What is observable in their work is the retention of a worldview and related concepts that were passed on from Africa to the Diaspora and from one generation to the next as heritage knowledge (a group's cultural memory) (Akbar, 1984; Clarke, 1992; Dixon, 1971; Karenga & Carruthers, 1986; King, 2006a, 2015; King & Swartz, 2016; Nobles, 1976, 1986). As discussed in our previous volume (King & Swartz, 2016) and further developed in this volume, one way to "see" worldview is through cultural concepts (italicized throughout) that we gathered from scholarship on a wide range of African philosophies, cosmologies, and oral and written traditions and cultural productions (Abímbólá, 1976; Anyanwu, 1981a, 1981b; Asimeng-Boahene, 2014; Aptheker, 1951/1969; Bennett, 1975; Boakye-Boaten, 2010; Fu-Kiau, 2001; Gyekye, 1987, 1988; Ikuenobe, 2006; Karenga, 1999, 2006a, 2006b; Nkulu-N'Sengha, 2005; Senghor, 1964; Waghid, 2014; Wiredu, 2001). Ahead are some examples of these cultural concepts carried across time and geographic location and sustained in the heritage knowledge of people of African ancestry:

- *sharing responsibility for communal well-being and belonging;*
- *pursuing knowledge as inseparable from pursuing wisdom;*
- *knowing as a communal experience in which everyone has something to contribute;*
- *exhibiting self-determination that considers the needs of the collective;*
- *love, dignity, and decency as shared by all;*
- *knowing that cultural sovereignty is a common right of all Peoples;*
- *pursuing freedom and justice as communal responsibilities;* and
- *protecting childhood as a collective responsibility (each child is everyone's child).*

Throughout this chapter we discuss these and other cultural concepts and the worldview they convey, and show how the ideas and practices of emancipatory Black scholars are informed by the African episteme that produced these concepts. With access to these concepts, PK-12 teachers, administrators, and community educators can transform the typically omitted or distorted elements of African Diasporan history and culture, and in so doing, inform their curriculum and the pedagogies they use with students.

African Democracy: Continental and Diasporan

Democracy is one example of a concept retained in the Diaspora from the ancestral legacy of African people. As is common to all Diasporas, people bring their knowledge, historical consciousness, and life experiences—in this case of African governance and communal ways of living and being together—with them wherever they go and under whatever conditions. Thus, identifying the democratic features of governance across African cultures offers an explanation for Black people's commitment to democracy in the Americas. Not only were/ are traditional African leaders elected and chosen to serve by people in their town, village, state, and nation, but also they serve(d) at the will of the people, who can destool (depose) them if they abuse or disrespect members of their communities, misuse ancestral land or other communal wealth, fail to share the community's economic benefits, refuse to listen to people's concerns, or fail to seek the advice of their councilors who represent the people (Ajisafe, 1924; Danquah, 1928; Gyekye, 1988, 1997; Maïga, 2010; Nyerere, 1965; Rattray, 1929;

Sithole, 1959). Teffo (2004) describes this relationship between leaders and the people with a South African maxim—*Kgosi ke kgosi ka batho* (A chief is a chief through the people)—to explain that "You become a king by consent of the people and you remain one as long as the consent is not withdrawn" (p. 446).

Our point here is that traditional African leaders were/are not above or separate from their community (Busia, 1967; Maïga, 2010). Accountability, discussion, representation, and reconciliation of opposing views until consensus is reached are essential aspects of all decision making in traditional African societies. As anthropologist R. S. Rattray described in 1929, democracy among the Asante (West Africa) is "in the hands of the many . . . . [and] there was not any such thing as government apart from the people" (p. 406, 407). In discussing democracy among the Asante, Kwasi Wiredu (1995) calls it consensual democracy compared to Western forms of democracy that he refers to as majoritarian democracy:

> The Ashanti system was a consensual democracy. It was a democracy because government was by consent and subject to the control of the people as expressed through their representatives. It was consensual because, at least as a rule, that consent was negotiated on the principle of consensus. (By contrast, the majoritarian system might be said to be, in principle, based on "consent" without consensus) . . . For all concerned, the [Asante] system was set up for participation in power not its appropriation, and the underlying philosophy was one of cooperation, not confrontation.
>
> *(pp. 58–59)*

In this sense, African consensual democracy is not about opposition and an ongoing quest for power, but about participation in reciprocal group decision making, collaboration, and compromise (Wiredu, 2001).

Of course variations in governance exist(ed) across African cultures. Yet, African and Western historians, philosophers, economists, and social anthropologists have identified some fundamental commonalities. African cultures are communal, with a collective worldview that is philosophically expressed through representative governance, openness to the views of others, collective social responsibility, and high value placed on participation, unity, solidarity, reciprocity, and consensus (Anyanwu, 1981a; Busia, 1967; Dixon, 1971; Gyekye, 1987, 1997; Kuper, 1947; Mbiti, 1990; Rattray, 1929; Teffo, 2004; Wamala, 2004; Wiredu, 2001). Exceptions can be found, and some postcolonial African governments reveal the difficulties of maintaining indigenous democratic values and practices in nations whose boundaries were drawn by European colonial powers. Moreover, political realities in postcolonial Africa have also been distorted by the machinations of neocolonial domination, including externally imposed governance structures and the miseducation of African elites (Nkrumah, 1966; Prah, 2009; Wiredu, 2001; Zuberi, 2015). However, what is clear is that traditional African governance—which was more common than not among Africans who were forced into enslavement in the Americas—was structured to be participatory, limit the power of leaders, encourage free expression of ideas, and gather and express the popular will of the people.

African Democracy in the Diaspora

To see people of African ancestry, including scholars, educators, and activists, in the forefront of U.S. struggles to democratize the society in general and the school experience in particular is not surprising, and it cannot be limited to a reaction to oppression. Rather, the African worldview that supported democracy in Africa was carried into the Diaspora through cultural concepts that people brought with them as heritage knowledge—concepts such as *the inherent right of freedom, knowing as a communal experience in which everyone has something to contribute, knowing that cultural sovereignty is a common right of all Peoples*, and *love, dignity, and decency as shared by all*. In other words, African democracy is not only a political system but also a way of living and being together that considers the collective needs, common rights, and contributions of all people who belong to a community.

There is no lack of empirical evidence that African Peoples had experience with democracy (Ajisafe, 1924; Anyanwu, 1981a; Busia, 1967; Danquah, 1928; Gyekye, 1987, 1997; Kuper, 1947; Mbiti, 1990; Nyerere, 1965; Rattray, 1929; Sithole, 1959; Wamala, 2004; Wiredu, 1995), even though this evidence has been submerged due to the challenges it presents to the grand narratives of European and American history. And there is no lack of empirical evidence that people of African ancestry continued to pursue democracy in the Diaspora (Aptheker, 1951/1968, 1951/1969, 1956; Bennett, 1968, 1975; Du Bois, 1945; Franklin, 1992; Harding, 1990; Quarles, 1969). Yet, to identify a connection between democratic practices in Africa and the Diaspora, scholars must still scale a canonical wall—a great divide maintained in standard historiography between African and Diasporan knowledge and practices in every discipline and area of life (King & Swartz, 2014). Whereas connections to Europe are assumed, cultural connections between Africa and the Diaspora have been contested in academic scholarship, which is reinforced in school knowledge through ubiquitous Euro-American cultural referents, agreed-upon accounts of the past, a literary canon weighted with European and White American literature, and the teaching of European social, political, and economic values and practices as normative (Asante, 1991/1992, 2007a, 2014; Goodwin & Swartz, 1993, 2004; King & Swartz, 2016).

Scholarship in the Black intellectual tradition refutes this rupture—from the historiography that makes African Diasporan history visible and reclaims African humanity and identity in the formation of "slave culture" (Du Bois, 1920a, 1920b; Gomez, 1998; Stuckey, 1987) to Afrocentricity and the Afrocentric paradigm (Asante, 1987/1998, 2007a; Mazama, 2003) to evidence of the African roots of American culture (Holloway, 1990; Walker, 2001; Piersen, 1993) to the encyclopedic documentation of African cultural heritage in North America (Shujaa & Shujaa, 2015). For example, scholarship on the ongoing resistance to enslavement, including the well-known and lesser-known revolts throughout the Americas—with African-born and first-generation Africans often in leadership positions—has identified African cultural concepts and practices at their foundation (Rucker, 2006; Starobin, 1970; Stuckey, 1987). Knowing that freedom was an inherent right, cultural sovereignty was a common right, and communal well-being was a collective responsibility were African cultural concepts that served as a wellspring for resistance and revolt. While being well aligned with African democratic principles and practices, these concepts were in direct conflict with a supremacist system that restricted any vestige of democracy to those in power. This scholarship on continuity between Africa and the Diaspora is part of removing the imposed divide between Africa and the Diaspora by making visible African history and culture and the presence of an African worldview and cultural concepts in the ideas and actions of African Diasporan communities, leaders, educators, and scholars.

Montgomery Bus Boycott

Recall that in Chapter 1 Ms. Singleton discussed a culturally centered approach to teaching about the Montgomery Bus Boycott. She explained that by using African cultural concepts like *the inherent worth of all people, exhibiting self-determination that considers the needs of the collective,* and *sharing responsibility for community well-being and belonging,* she could teach what moved Montgomery's Black citizens to unite around ending bus segregation. The African cultural concepts in their heritage knowledge locate the boycott as an effort to democratize the Montgomery community. This is a departure from the typical instructional framing of Montgomery's Black community as reacting to discrimination by fighting *against* bus segregation. Ms. Singleton had no doubt that a goal of the boycott was to end segregation, but she explained that a culturally centered approach focuses on what people are *for,* not what they are *against.* In Montgomery, Black people acted *for* justice, self-determination, and human welfare—actions that were shaped by their African heritage knowledge of democracy.

How Do We Know?

The culturally centered approach suggested by Ms. Singleton to teach about the democratic values in African American heritage knowledge, which is evident in the Montgomery Bus Boycott, raises an important question . . . and you may already have thought of it. Can we claim that the ideas and actions of Black people who participated in the boycott (or any other movement or event in the Diaspora) were influenced by an African worldview and cultural concepts even if those who participated and wrote about it (King, 1958; Parks, 1992; Robinson, 1987) didn't reference an African worldview or name the cultural concepts that informed their actions? In other words, can cultural influences be observed in people's ideas and actions without their naming or even being consciously aware of those influences? We answer these questions with an unequivocal "Yes!" In fact, regardless of whether consciously known and named, all ideas and actions—including the scholarship that examines them—exist in cultural contexts.

Let's look at an example in education. As U.S. educators we know that Puritans brought their heritage—their worldview and cultural concepts and practices—from England to North America; and most of us learned that the colonial schools established by Puritans reflected the cultural values and experiences they brought with them. However, few educators are aware that the current school practices in which they now participate were shaped and continue to be influenced by the same European heritage knowledge that shaped Puritan education. Individuality, Competition, Difference (as deficit), Survival of the Fittest, Control over Nature, "might makes right," and a hierarchy of human worth are some European worldview elements, which are visible in European cultural concepts that represent the norm in our schools (Akbar, 1984; Dixon, 1971; King & Swartz, 2016; Nobles, 1976). Some of these cultural concepts (with examples in brackets) are:

- *understanding achievement as excelling above others through competition [standardized testing];*
- *valorizing individual over group identity [color/culture blindness];*
- *expecting and accepting a certain amount of failure [accepting the bell curve as natural and immutable];*
- *distributing resources by status/rank [tracking];*
- *viewing authority as achieved through the use of rewards and punishments [behavior modification/management];*
- *conceptualizing education as the transmission of agreed-upon information [reliance on packaged programs designed by "experts"];* and
- *perceiving mistakes as negative and leading to loss [not having "right answers" leads to lowered status]* (Akbar, 1984; Dixon, 1971; Fendler & Muzaffar, 2008; Kliewer & Fitzgerald, 2001; Kohn, 1996, 2000).

If many of these cultural concepts sound familiar, it's because most of us were educated in school systems that were shaped by them. With the foregoing European worldview elements and cultural concepts forming the epistemic foundation of most schools across the country, educators in those schools participate in standard practices such as transmission pedagogy, dull and acritical curriculum based on low expectations, standardized testing, tracking, and behavior modification, often *without being aware of* the European worldview elements and cultural concepts that shaped and sustain those practices (Au, 2009; King &

Swartz, 2016; Kumashiro, 2008). In similar fashion, educators are unaware of the African worldview elements and cultural concepts that shaped and sustain, for example, (1) African democratic practices that were carried into and pursued in the Diaspora; and (2) the actions of participants in the Montgomery Bus Boycott.

Heritage Knowledge and Resisting Racism in School Knowledge

In another example of heritage knowledge in action, Black educators and community leaders stood on an African epistemic foundation in their efforts to remove demeaning and crude representations of African Diasporan people from school textbooks before and after WWII (Bond, 1935; Dillard, 2007; King, 2016b; Moreau, 2003; Reddick, 1933; Zimmerman, 2004). These textbooks contained racial slurs (Morison & Commager, 1942, pp. 537–538; Rugg, 1931, p. 269); typically characterized and justified slavery "as a transitional status between barbarism and civilization" (Morison & Commager, 1942, p. 539); referred to slave-owners as "kindly, humane men" (Harlow, 1947, p. 195); ridiculed, maligned, and denigrated freedmen (Bailey, 1956, pp. 463–465); and rationalized the Black Codes and justified the origin of secret societies such as the Ku Klux Klan (Bailey, 1956, pp. 464–465, 477–478; Gavian & Hamm, 1945, p. 331; Muzzey, 1933, pp. 35–36).

When Black scholars and activists identified these textbooks and related curricula as forms of racism white supremacy embedded in school knowledge (Bond, 1935; Du Bois, 1935; Reddick, 1933; Woodson, 1919b), they sought to protect all children from being taught harmful distortions and misconceptions. In so doing they enacted an African cultural concept of *protecting childhood as a collective responsibility (each child is everyone's child)*(Boakye-Boaten, 2010; Ikuenobe, 2006). As part of the African epistemic foundation retained by these leaders in their heritage knowledge, they also displayed other African cultural concepts, such as:

- *sharing responsibility for communal well-being and belonging*;
- *exhibiting self-determination that considers the needs of the collective*;
- *demonstrating concern for human welfare through actions based on community-mindedness and service to others*; and
- *being responsible to bring good into the world through actions that are ethical, just, generous, compassionate, and peaceable* (Boakye-Boaten, 2010; Clarke, 1992; Gyekye, 1987, 1997; Karenga, 1999, 2006a, 2006b; King, 1992, 2006a; Waghid, 2014).

These concepts make visible a worldview that includes Collectivity, Interdependence, Self-Determination, and Reciprocity (capitalized because they have been identified by scholars cited herein as "the" elements of specific sets of ontological orientations, virtues, and principles), and right action, community-mindedness, and justice (not capitalized because they are selected by the authors among many possible examples of epistemologies and values). By resisting racism in school knowledge, Black educators and leaders displayed their heritage knowledge of democratically informed communal concepts, which suggests why they (and not their White contemporaries) took responsibility to protect all children from blatantly false representations in school knowledge that served to maintain racial divisions, limit democracy, and disrupt the welfare of whole communities.

It is important to note that before and during the progressive era Diasporan scholars in the Black intellectual tradition had developed conceptual frameworks, such as self-determination, self-reliance, service to others, cultural representation, and analysis of domination (Burroughs, 1934; Du Bois, 1897, 1903a, 1920a, 1920b; Bond, 1934; Cooper, 1892/1969; Fontaine, 1940; Garnet, 1843/1972, 1859; Walker, 1829/1965; Wells, 1892; Wesley, 1935; Woodson, 1919a, 1933). These frameworks could come only from men and women with a communal, reciprocal, and justice-oriented worldview—one they expressed through cultural concepts, such as *sharing responsibility for communal well-being and belonging, love, dignity, and decency as shared by all,* and *pursuing freedom and justice as communal responsibilities.* In other words, the thoughts and actions of these scholars were generated within an African episteme.

W.E.B. Du Bois: Recognition and Silence

To further pursue the presence of an African epistemic foundation in Diasporan scholarship and make it available to practitioners, we turn to the work of William Edward Burghardt Du Bois—a prolific Black scholar during and after the progressive era. In so doing, we trust that our selection of examples from his vast body of work will be adequate to open a discussion about how PK–12 curricula can make visible the cultural continuity that exists between Africa and the Diaspora. While a similar examination is needed of his contemporary Carter G. Woodson—also a prolific scholar during the progressive era whose work was shaped by an African episteme—we save that study for another venue (Dagbovie, 2007; Goggin, 1993; Greene, 1989; Wesley, 1951; Woodson, 1915, 1919a, 1919b, 1922, 1925b, 1928, 1935, 1944, 1945).

Du Bois is now recognized as a paramount scholar, educator, and activist of the late nineteenth and twentieth centuries, authoring sociological and historical studies, academic articles, biographical and autobiographical texts, editorials, essays, reviews, historically informed novels, stories, children's literature, and poetry (Franklin, 1992, 1995; Lewis, 2000; Marable, 1986, 2005; Rabaka, 2007; Rampersad, 1976; Wesley, 1970). His vision of democracy as "a method of realizing the broadest measure of justice to all human beings" (1920a, p. 142)—including women, workers, and all exploited groups—stood apart from the more limited democratic visions and practices of most scholars, educators, and activists during the progressive era (Aptheker, 1989; Zamir, 1995). His social scientific studies and analyses of the experiences of Black people served as internal correctives for racial uplift and as external correctives for racist histories and other inaccurate and distorted representations of Black people (Butchart, 1994; Du Bois, 1897, 1899, 1904, 1935/1962). His massive body of work reveals the changes and shifts that occurred over many decades in a scholar who continued to creatively respond to new information and changing contexts. This can be seen in the multiple genres and venues Du Bois used to present indigenous representations of Black life and advance freedom and justice, to explain how racism leads to the inevitability of war, to conduct scientific studies of the centuries-long impact of a racial hierarchy on U.S. life in general and on Black people in particular, and to analyze African Diasporan history and community needs in a global context (Du Bois, 1899; 1904; 1915a, 1919, 1920b, 1924, 1935/1962, 1939, 1940/1968, 1945, 1947, 1973, 1976).

What Has Been Suppressed

Reviews, critiques, literary analyses, and biographical accounts of Du Bois and his wide-ranging corpus are extensive (Aptheker, 1989; Broderick, 1959; Franklin, 1995; Gooding-Williams, 2009; Lewis, 1993, 2000; Logan, 1971; Marable, 2005; Meier, 1971; Morris, 2015; Rabaka, 2007, 2008, 2010; Rampersad, 1976; Rudwick, 1968; Stepto, 1979; Stuckey, 1987; Walters, 1993; Zamir, 1995). He is studied and acknowledged as a race theorist, Pan-Africanist, anticolonial theorist, Marxist theorist, male feminist, critical theorist, Black nationalist, peace advocate, and fore-thinker of Africana studies (see Rabaka, 2007, for extensive references related to most of these intellectual traditions). Du Bois is clearly a man of multidimensional complexity whose eight decades of scholarly work have been widely studied. Yet, in all this study—even when Du Bois is noted for acknowledging African influences in the Americas, identifying the importance of African Diasporan unity, and affirming the cultural and political connections between Africa and its Diaspora—there is virtual silence about the African epistemic influences on his scholarship. It appears that his biographers and other authors see his heritage as adequate enough to explain his interest in and commitment to African and Diasporan Peoples—including his Pan-African involvements—but not adequate enough to trace how retentions of that heritage informed his scholarship. In terms of African retentions, scholars do mention Du Bois (1903a) using a bar of the "Sorrow Songs" (Spirituals) to introduce each chapter in *The Souls of Black Folk* and an African song sung by his great-great-grandmother and passed down through the generations, but they seem to view these as among a few limited fragments that close rather than open a door to the pre-enslavement African heritage influence on his scholarship and advocacy (Broderick, 1959; Lewis, 1993; Sundquist, 1993; Zamir, 1994, 1995). With this loud academic silence, what *is* African (not what is *about* Africa) in Du Boisian scholarship has remained unimagined and unexplored—effectively walled off from the African episteme that informed it. Note that this is only one example of how a hegemonic academic knowledge base can and has systematically excluded African epistemology and how this exclusion has shaped knowledge in every discipline. According to Wynter (1992), the cultural model in which conceptual blackness functions in alter ego relation to whiteness is the foundation of this hegemonic episteme that suppresses, distorts, and omits African realities (Wynter, 1992). It is for this reason that we need to rewrite knowledge to make such suppressed African epistemological influences visible and available for our use in democratic educational practice.

Rewriting W.E.B. Du Bois: Making African Epistemic Continuity Visible

Toward the end of the nineteenth century, Du Bois completed an elite Western classical education that epistemologically privileged everything European, justified European domination and colonialism, taught scientific racism, and fostered the denigration of Africa and African (and Indigenous) Peoples (Gould, 1981; Mills, 1997, 1998; Stuckey, 1987; Wilder, 2013). Navigating his way through this academic quagmire of white supremacy, Du Bois emerged to define himself as African, a position he consistently held and built upon (1897, 1915b, 1940/1968; 1947). While some scholars have suggested that Du Bois's early commitment to moral suasion and uplift was assimilationist and informed by dominant race, class, and gender ideologies (Kendi, 2016; Lewis, 1993), his culturally grounded connections to Africa predominate his publications and advocacy. These publications (1) document the history and achievements of early African civilizations; (2) connect domination and structural racism in the United States to a global system of racial exploitation; (3) theorize Pan-Africanism and African independence and support the organizing of Pan-African Congresses; (4) insist on self-determination and cultural sovereignty for African Peoples; and (5) counter whiteness and its theories and practices of cultural supremacy in Africa and the world (Aptheker, 1989; Law, 2007; Meier, 1971; Morris, 2015; Rabaka, 2007, 2010; Rampersad, 1976; Rudwick, 1968; Shepperson, 1970; Stuckey, 1987; Sundquist, 1993). Well before anthropologists suggested the presence of Africanisms in the Diaspora (Herskovits, 1941; Bastide, 1971), Du Bois (1898, 1903a) acknowledged that (1) the Spirituals are of African origin; (2) the enslaved preacher who was concerned with community well-being was an African priest and institution builder (the Black Church); and (3) African folktales are sources of African philosophy and communal ideals—all of which were seminal in bringing enslaved people from diverse African nations together as one Diasporan people (Gomez, 1998; Stuckey, 1987). Du Bois drew upon his knowledge of African history and culture—that is to say, his African heritage knowledge—to make these cultural connections. To further explore these continuities we identify the pre-enslavement African episteme present in Du Boisean scholarship. For example, what is African about the concept of "double-consciousness" that Du Bois wrote about in 1897 and included six years later with minor changes in *Souls?*

Double-Consciousness Revisited

There has been extensive investigation of the Du Boisian concept of "double-consciousness." Numerous authors have identified and explored the influence of European and White American scholars such as Georg Wilhelm Friedrich Hegel, William James, Ralph Waldo Emerson, George Santayana, and Oswald Külpe on Du Bois's understanding of consciousness and his use of the term "double-consciousness." They agree that in the hands of Du Bois—who was familiar with these authors—double-consciousness either parallels or adapts these earlier European sources (Bruce, 1999; Gooding-Williams, 2009; Rampersad, 1976; Zamir, 1995). This analysis may ring true to scholars who are informed by only a European worldview and the understandings that come from its cultural outlook. Nevertheless, in the academic tradition of identifying and including early and relevant sources, we ask a to-date unasked question: What can an African world-view and cultural concepts add to our understanding of what Du Bois called double-consciousness? In his oft-quoted passage in *Souls* Du Bois wrote,

> After the Egyptian and Indian, the Greek and Roman, the Teuton and Mongolian the Negro is a sort of seventh son, born with a veil, and gifted with second sight in this American world,—a world which yields him no true self-consciousness, but only lets him see himself through the revelation of the other world. It is a peculiar sensation, this double-consciousness, this sense of always looking at one's self through the eyes of others, of measuring one's soul by the tape of a world that looks on in amused contempt and pity.
>
> *(1903a, pp. 16–17)*

Without knowledge of African worldview, one might view the double-consciousness of Du Bois as only a tragic outcome of a white racist world that has succeeded at controlling both the soul and psyche of people of African ancestry in the Diaspora—what Reiland Rabaka (2010) describes as "the ways in which blacks, however subtly, unceasingly accept and *internalize the diabolical dialectic of white superiority and black inferiority*" (p. 129, italics in the original) According to C. Eric Lincoln (1993), this seemingly immutable dialectic of double-consciousness became a standard reference that explains the uncertainty of Black identity. Yet, in the foregoing quote, Du Bois refers to "the Negro"—his People (not individuals, but his People)—as a seventh son, as born with a veil, and as gifted with second sight. These references invite us to move beyond the near-universal reading of double-consciousness as an imposed and group-accepted condition of negation. This dialectical trap of European dominance and African subjugation—while not experienced by Africans who have what Molefi Asante (1993) calls "a solid sense of identity" (p. 140)—requires the measuring of self (and one's People) only through the eyes of the oppressor, which many scholars have explained as a psychological condition of a divided self or what in psychopathology is referred to as a split personality (Bruce, 1999; Gooding-Williams, 2009; Rampersad, 1976; Wolfenstein, 2007).

We propose a different reading of "double-consciousness"—one that rejects the perception of a whole people as fragmented and dysfunctional. Sylvia Wynter has developed a concept of alterity (1992, 1997) as part of her analysis of the belief structure of race in which a hegemonically imposed black/white binary conceptualizes whiteness as all that is rational and good—what it means to be human—with blackness as its necessary opposite in alter ego fashion (King, 2006b; Morrison, 1992; Wynter, 1992, 2000, 2006). According to Wynter, alterity is a location that provides liminal groups with a perspective advantage from which to see the world. In our view, this vantage point of alterity uncovers the presence of agency when applied to double-consciousness. The perspective advantage of this standing place—what Du Bois calls "second sight"—includes the knowledge, experiences, ideals, and insights available to liminal groups. In addition, this interpretation suggests that being a "seventh son" and "born with a veil" (p. 16) or caul metaphorically refers to the insights, spiritual and predictive powers, and discernment of Africans in the Diaspora whose heritage knowledge of an African worldview and cultural concepts provides access to another way to be, to see, and to know the world. In this sense, double-consciousness is an epistemological location, not an ontological condition. This liminal location provides two ways to perceive the world: (1) from the autochthonous perceptions of African Diasporan people who know and define themselves; and (2) from exogenous, systemically sanctioned eurocratic perceptions. In the reading we propose, double-consciousness is the critical capacity to concurrently know/ experience your group's ideals *and* be discerning about the ideals of a system that in the past and present sanctions white supremacy. Du Bois describes this "twoness" or "double self" in this way:

> One ever feels his twoness,—an American, a Negro; two souls, two thoughts, two unrecognized strivings; two warring ideals in one dark body, whose dogged strength alone keeps it from being torn asunder.
>
> The history of the American Negro is the history of this strife,—this longing to attain self-conscious manhood, to merge his double self into a better and truer self. In this merging he wishes neither of the older selves to be lost. He would not Africanize America, for America has too much to teach the world and Africa. He would not bleach his Negro soul in a flood of white Americanism, for he knows that Negro blood has a message for the world. He simply wishes to make it possible for a man to be both a Negro and an American, without being cursed and spit upon by his fellows, without having the doors of Opportunity closed roughly in his face.
>
> *(p. 17)*

With double-consciousness as an epistemological location able to perceive two ideals/worlds, Du Bois suggests merging the best of what both have to offer so that neither imposes itself on the other and neither is lost. While many authors have seized on his idea of merging a "double self into a better and truer self" as an indication of Black negation and a nonexistent true self, Du Bois indicates that there *already is* a true cultural self when he states that Africa ("Negro blood") "has a message for the world." And it is this message that resides in African Diasporan heritage knowledge and can extricate us from the canonical reading of double-consciousness only as fragmentation, alienation, and dysfunction.

What is this "message" from the African side of "twoness"? What does it mean, from an African epistemic perspective, when Du Bois says that Black people represent "two souls, two thoughts, two unrecognized strivings; two warring ideals in one dark body"? What are these thoughts and ideals from the African side of "twoness" that conflict with "white Americanism"? With the ability to stand in two places through the gift of second sight, Black people clearly experience the denigrating and threatening messages and violent actions of "white Americanism," but they also experience messages from the African side of double-consciousness. And the "dogged strength" to remain whole *comes from that cultural location*—from the elements of an African worldview that include epistemological and ontological orientations, spiritual understandings, values, virtues, and principles. Ahead are some of these worldview elements and how enacting them recasts double-consciousness as a strategic asset in maintaining cultural identity and integrity (authenticity) in countering cultural supremacy:

- Collectivity and Interdependence are ontological orientations that maintain group solidarity and interconnectedness, both of which are necessary for maintaining cultural identity and resisting imposed standards that promote individualism and divisiveness;
- empathy and intuition-reasoning (learning from heart-mind knowledge, which produces wisdom) are epistemological orientations that facilitate seeing yourself as others might *and* knowing and defining yourself—a "twoness" that is possible (not pathological) when heart and mind knowledge remain connected;
- right action (ethical and wholesome action) and community-mindedness are African values that encourage ethical and wholesome actions, communal ethos, and group well-being as both normative and as a counter to external aggression;
- Justice and Truth are *Maatian* Virtues or standards of excellence that are cultural understandings of being human and bringing good into the world— even in the face of inhumanity; and
- Self-Determination and Unity are *Nguzo Saba* Principles of human conduct that identify how to make decisions in consideration of the collective needs and sovereign interests of African Diasporan people.

These are some of the worldview elements in support of an African epistemic reading of double-consciousness. These elements frame the "message" African Diasporan people have for the world—a message of ideals kept alive in heritage knowledge, and in the case of Du Bois, reflective of the following African cultural concepts we observe in his scholarship and activism:

- *pursuing freedom and justice as communal responsibilities:* Du Bois (1903a, 1915a, 1920a, 1985) repeatedly named racism, the "color line," and hierarchies of gender and class as injurious to the whole of humanity (Rabaka, 2010);
- *exhibiting self-determination that considers the needs of the collective:* Du Bois (1899, 1901, 1935/1962) conducted social scientific studies that made accessible indigenous and more accurate representations of Black life;
- *gaining knowledge for the purpose of bringing goodness, harmony, and balance into the world:* Du Bois (1915a, 1920a, 1947) countered the disparities and disharmony created by false historiography and European supremacist ideology and practices with knowledge of African history, the achievements of African civilizations, and the central, albeit subjugated, place of Africa in world affairs;
- *knowing that cultural sovereignty is a common right of all Peoples:* Du Bois (1915a, 1947) advocated self-determination and cultural sovereignty for African Peoples and an end to the exploitation of African Diasporan Peoples;
- *sharing responsibility for communal well-being and belonging:* Du Bois (1968) participated in organizing Pan-African Congresses that brought together African and Diasporan scholars and activists in a global pursuit of freedom and justice (Du Bois & Padmore, 1962; Walters, 1993); and
- *love, dignity, and decency as shared by all:* Du Bois (1903a, 1915a) advocated for justice, dignity, and an end to the exploitation and disenfranchisement of all historically oppressed groups in the pursuit of world democracy and full humanity (Rabaka, 2007, 2010).

The foregoing examples of what African worldview elements maintain and facilitate, and how Du Bois exhibited African cultural concepts, suggest that viewing double-consciousness within an African episteme makes it possible to know about and activate the "message" or ideals that Africa has for the world. Enacting this message—which is retained in heritage knowledge—facilitates measuring one's soul through African Diasporan ideals, whereas the canonical interpretation of double-consciousness leads to measuring one's soul using the tape of the dominant worldview. Furthermore, interpretations of double-consciousness that ignore pre-enslavement and enduring African epistemologies, values, and virtues endlessly bind the soul to the strife and struggle that the doctrine of white supremacy has produced.

In order to understand Du Bois and other emancipatory scholars who take positions outside of eurocratic frameworks and interpretations, we need to "Go back and fetch what we need" in order to then move forward (Willis, 1998,

p. 189). Guided by this Akan *Sankofan* philosophical concept (see Chapter 1), we propose retrieving and repossessing the African epistemic foundation that makes it possible to step outside of exogenous and often supremacist interpretations of the past (and present) and to learn from the message that Africa has for the world. One context for gaining access to this "message" is proverbial wisdom. Ahead are just a few examples of proverbial wisdom and the cultural concepts they embody—African ideals and dispositions that glimpse aspects of the message Africa has for the world (see Chapters 3 and 5 for more detail on African proverbs):

- "Wisdom is not in the head of one person" (Akan, Ghana) (*knowing as a communal experience in which everyone has something to contribute*);
- "Be a neighbor to a human being and not a fence" (Kenya) (*sharing responsibility for communal well-being and belonging*); and
- "A good wind is no use to a sailor who does not know his direction" (Zambia) (*inquiring as a source of true knowledge*) (Asimeng-Boahene, 2014).

African proverbial wisdom teaches us that true knowledge comes from openness to questions and from more than one source. We have attempted to follow that course by examining what is African in Du Boisean scholarship. Doing so opens the door to the suppressed influence of African heritage knowledge on his scholarship and on the scholarship of other emancipatory scholars, educators, and activists of African ancestry.

Connections to the Classroom

By making visible the African epistemic foundation of emancipatory Black scholarship, which is missing from the record of progressive era thinking, we aim to show how educators can (1) identify and use emancipatory content and instructional practices that center all students culturally and individually; (2) use African worldview elements and cultural concepts to frame the teaching of content and skills as a context for critical thinking, character development, right action, and community building; (3) develop relationships with students that build on who they are and what they know; and (4) communicate that student success is a communal responsibility by bringing family presence and ideas into curriculum development and assessment practices. It is such instructional agency and emancipatory practices that can liberate all students from an education that limits and distorts their knowledge, experiences, and consciousness.

To demonstrate these practical applications made possible through familiarity with the African epistemic foundation of emancipatory Black scholarship, we have identified five themes that are consistently (not exclusively) evident in the work of W.E.B. Du Bois during the progressive era and beyond: (1) African excellence versus externally imposed decline, (2) developing character,

(3) leadership, (4) democracy, and (5) education, freedom, and agency. Presentation of the African epistemic foundation (worldview elements and cultural concepts) upon which each theme rests is followed by a subsection entitled "Instructional Connection." For each theme we suggest how the epistemic foundation that informed it can be used to identify relevant content and conceptualize and shape PK-12 instruction.

African Excellence Versus Externally Imposed Decline

In an article titled "On Being Black" in the *New Republic*, Du Bois (1920b) described the purposely hidden and unmatched excellence of ancient cultures in Africa and Asia:

> Europe has never produced and never will in our day bring forth a single human soul who cannot be matched and over-matched in every line of human endeavor by Asia and Africa. Run the gamut, if you will, and let us have the Europeans who in sober truth over-match Nefertari, Mohammed, Rameses, and Askia, Confucius, Buddha, and Jesus Christ. If we could scan the calendar of thousands of lesser men in like comparison, the result would be the same; but we cannot do this because of the *deliberately educated ignorance of white schools* by which they remember Napoleon and forget Sonni Ali.
>
> *(p. 341, emphasis added)*

Du Bois went on to explain that this "deliberately educated ignorance" and denial of African excellence has been used to obfuscate the European imposition of decline on Africa—initially through enslavement and then through colonization. In numerous publications he provided data to correct eurocratic historiography that denied ancient African to modern Diasporan excellence (1920b, 1935/1962, 1939, 1945), and he called for African unity and "Africa for Africans," including both Continental and Diasporan Africans (1915b, 1920a, p. 61). These are the actions of a man whose worldview included Collectivity, Wholeness (all nature/life and knowledge are viewed as interconnected), community-mindedness, and right action. By viewing the long span of Continental and African Diasporan history and culture as a whole—not as disconnected parts—and by using scholarship to demonstrate that more accurate knowledge was available and needed, Du Bois exhibited this worldview by framing his scholarship within African cultural concepts, such as *gaining knowledge for the purpose of bringing goodness, harmony, and balance into the world*; *pursuing knowledge as inseparable from pursuing wisdom*; and *exhibiting self-determination that considers the needs of the collective*. In so doing, the African episteme that informed his work invited him to pursue knowledge/wisdom that could stimulate right action toward the whole human collective, not only part of it.

Instructional Connection

Teachers who know that African Diasporan history and culture are long and whole do not begin teaching about people of African ancestry with the *Maafa*—the European system of chattel slavery designed to dehumanize African people and enrich the enslavers (Ani, 1994). The first reason is that the *Maafa* occurred thousands of years after the beginning of African history and culture, so that introducing people of African ancestry in the curriculum through enslavement is incorrect and suggests that Africa gave nothing of value and importance to the world prior to the *Maafa*, which, as Du Bois (1915b, 1947) makes clear, is also incorrect. The second reason is that if you first present any people as conquered and enslaved, particularly to young children, it is more difficult to teach about the contributions of those people to humanity and the ways in which they have acted in the world as subjects with agency. While insurrection that includes multiple forms of resistance, self-liberation, and the secret maintenance of spiritual practices are examples of agency during enslavement, beginning with enslavement—which erases thousands of years of history and culture—makes it difficult for teachers to even identify let alone teach about these acts as representative of agency. The third reason is related to identity. How are young children supposed to understand—as one first-grade textbook put it in a vignette about Harriet Tubman—that "some African Americans were not free" (Boyd et al., 2011b, p. 68)? What did "some African Americans" (actually millions) do to be not free? When curriculum truncates your history, and your people incorrectly enter as victims of others, it suggests that something about your group—and you—is deficient and less worthy. While five- or six-year olds experience this through what they feel, the authority of school knowledge that omits and marginalizes the fullness of African history and culture over 12 or more years serves to reinforce and reify this early impression. The result is that children of African ancestry are systematically obstructed from identifying with their people.

Instead, begin with a developmentally appropriate unit on the history and culture of Africa as the birthplace of humanity. Continue with the knowledge, advanced technology, cultural productions, and resources of African Peoples that made Africa attractive to Arabs, West and East Asians, and Europeans centuries before the *Maafa* as a place for university study, spiritual enlightenment, travel, and trade (Asante, 1994, 2007b; Asante & Mazama, 2005; Diop, 1974). Over years, students can learn about the civilizational accomplishments of Nubia (Sudan and Egypt) and Kemet (Egypt) in Northeast Africa, educational centers and universities at Timbuktu, Jenné, and Gao (Mali) in West Africa, and the architectural feats and trading centers in the South African state of Great Zimbabwe (Zimbabwe) (Asante, 1994, 2007b; Diop, 1974; Maïga, 2010; C. Williams, 1974). They can learn about African democracy, spirituality, cultural unity, and trade among African Peoples on the continent and between Africa and other continents (Davidson, 1991; Danquah, 1928; Dike, 1956; Diop, 1959/1990, 1987, 2000; Gyekye, 1997;

Miller, 1988). With regard to the capture and enslavement of African Peoples that enriched competing nations of Europe, students can learn about how Europeans introduced and used their weaponry in conquest, trade, and domination strategies of divide and conquer that included inciting conflicts among African Peoples (Rodney, 1966, 1982). These purposely manipulated conflicts, which were strategically facilitated with European weaponry, weakened and depleted the African continent and made the capture, enslavement, and death of millions of Africans possible; not only did these actions result in a massive transfer of knowledge, skills, and wealth from Africa to Europe and its colonial outposts, but also this underdevelopment of the entire continent by European nations continues today (Carney, 2001; Clarke, 1992; Davidson, 1961, 1972; King & Swartz, 2016; Rodney, 1982; C. Williams, 1974; E. Williams, 1944/1966). All of this content is of course not presented at the primary level, but what can be presented at *all* levels is what makes people subjects with agency whose actions are connected to and informed by their ongoing cultural legacy. If, as Du Bois, you present the long-standing history and cultural excellence of African Peoples at home and in the Diaspora, when the time comes to teach about the European system of chattel slavery, you can teach it as an historical experience of horrific proportions, not as a definer of identity. This, however, requires accurate knowledge of Africa and Europe prior to the *Maafa* and the reality of Africa's legacy in the Diaspora.

Developing Character

In *Souls* (1903a), Du Bois exemplifies a scholar who as social scientist both studied and loved his people. In this and other texts (Du Bois, 1924, 1975), he explains how America would not be what it is without the gifts of Black people, yet squarely faces how three centuries of enslavement and "Jim Crow" have impacted both Black and White people. In his framing of education that can extricate Black people and Black achievements from centuries of denial and imposed limitations, Du Bois calls upon the virtues of Right and Truth, and proposes that racial uplift through education is essential to developing the character of men—a theme that repeats throughout much of his work. Unlike the accommodationist approach of Booker T. Washington, which limited Black education to industrial training and acquiesced on the white denial of civil and political rights, Du Bois and several contemporaries advocated that education develop multiple talents and strengths (Franklin, 1995). In so doing, he sidestepped the false dichotomy of whether Black men and women should be manual workers or intellectuals. As David Levering Lewis (1993) explained,

> Du Bois must have also clearly understood that to attack Washington was to mistake shadow for substance, to fall into a trap of internecine battling instead of laying the ground for all-out war on the real enemy—the white people who ordained that an entire race should remain indefinitely subordinate.
>
> (p. 275)

Instead, Du Bois laid out his democratic vision of education:

> We are training not isolated men but a living group of men . . . And the
> final product of our training must be neither a psychologist nor a brick-
> mason, but a man. And to make men, we must have ideals, broad, pure,
> and inspiring ends of living . . . The worker must work for the glory of
> his handiwork, not simply for pay; the thinker must think for truth, not
> for fame. And all this is gained only by human strife and longing; by
> ceaseless training and education; by founding Right on righteousness and
> Truth on the unhampered search for Truth.
>
> *(1903a, p. 72)*

This vision of education evolved within and in spite of what Du Bois called
the veil of white supremacy. Informed by an African episteme (ways of knowing
and conceptions of knowledge based on African worldview and cultural concepts), Du Bois did not allow this veil—with its assumptions of race and class
hierarchy—to cloud his vision. In other words, education is a means to develop
character, whether one is a professional, artisan, or laborer. Working to produce
quality (not only pay) and thinking to produce truth (not only fame) are values
and ideals that Du Bois proposed as elements of building character and community. With an African episteme as the source of this democratic vision and
collective (not individual) approach to racial uplift, Du Bois proposed building
character in all people, with their diverse talents, interests, and strengths.

Instructional Connection

When teaching about historical figures, ask students to identify their character
qualities. In Chapter 2 you read about Benjamin Banneker and read a classroom
scenario in which fifth-grade students learned about him from a "re-membered"
student biography. Building on the knowledge students gained about Banneker's
cultural background, accomplishments, the time period in which he lived, and
the letter he wrote to Thomas Jefferson advocating freedom for his enslaved
brothers and sisters, the teachers in the scenario asked students critical questions
about Banneker's character and their own:

- In order to do all of this, what kind of character traits or qualities do you think
  Banneker had?
- What character traits do you see in yourself that might be like Benjamin
  Banneker? Turn to a partner and talk about which of Banneker's character
  qualities you see in yourself. Explain to your partner why you think so, and
  then write your character qualities or traits on the Smart Board.

If as Du Bois suggests, education is first and foremost for the purpose of developing character, helping students to identify the character traits of historical

figures who brought just and right action into the world places importance on developing good character (Karenga, 1999, 2006b; Tedla, 1995). Importantly, the teachers in the scenario framed instruction about Banneker with two African cultural concepts that are visible in his actions (*being responsible to bring good into the world through actions that are ethical, just, generous, compassionate, and peaceable*; and *exhibiting self-determination that considers the needs of the collective*). This teaches students that his agency and character are linked to his African heritage. Thus, teaching about the character of historical figures—not only what they did—is a way to keep these men and women connected to their ancestry as well as a way for students to identify and further develop good character in themselves.

Leadership

Du Bois thought that under the circumstances of racial domination, higher education was a context for preparing "exceptional men" (1903b, p. 34) to advance the race through "right ideals" and knowledge of life and the world. He wrote, "Education and work are the levers to uplift a people. Work alone will not do it unless inspired by the right ideals and guided by intelligence. Education must not simply teach work—it must teach Life" (p. 75).

Early in his long career, Du Bois wrote and spoke about the relationship between education and racial uplift, suggesting that it be led by what he initially called the "Talented Tenth" (1903b). Numerous authors point out that the "Talented Tenth" was an assimilationist and elitist approach to leadership—albeit one that Du Bois changed over time (Kendi, 2016; Lewis, 1993; Meier, 1971; Rampersad, 1976; Zamir, 1995). Nonetheless, this notion of elitism has lingered in the literature—and while economic status is relevant to how one views and experiences the world—class has often been used to stoke internal division by scholars who ignore what is African about Du Bois's ideas of leadership. In his advocacy of education for life and community uplift that serves the needs of artisans and intellectuals alike, Du Bois did not limit leadership to educated professionals and saw Black workers as essential to group liberation (Rabaka, 2007, 2008; Wesley, 1970). He knew that everyone's participation was essential to the well-being of the whole community—an African worldview expressed in the cultural concept that *knowing is a communal experience in which everyone has something to contribute* (Fu-Kiau, 2001). In the heritage knowledge (a group's cultural memory) that informed his idea of leadership were African values (e.g., human welfare, right action, community-mindedness) and principles (e.g., Unity, Self-Determination, Collective Work and Responsibility)—elements of a worldview conveyed in other cultural concepts that shaped his thinking, such as *sharing responsibility for communal well-being and belonging* and *demonstrating concern for human welfare through actions based on community-mindedness and service to others* (Gyekye, 1997; Karenga, 1999, 2006a; Nkulu-N'Sengha, 2005; Nobles, 1976). Du Bois viewed all social groups as essential to community well-being—a position that contradicts the lingering hierarchal conception of leadership often attributed to him.

Instructional Connection

The communal idea that everyone has responsibility for community well-being is at the core of the African epistemic foundation upon which emancipatory pedagogies stand (see Table 2.2 in Chapter 2 for descriptions of six emancipatory pedagogies). In terms of leadership, the emancipatory pedagogies called Eldering and Question-Driven Pedagogy guide teachers to be leaders in developing right relationship with their students. Teachers who use these pedagogies exhibit authentic authority based on knowledge, wisdom, and expertise; develop authentic relationships with students and families; and foster learning through inquiry that builds on who students are and what they know. They understand that everyone is an essential participant and that knowledge is a communal experience in which everyone has something to contribute. As shown in Figure 4.1, Eldering and Question-Driven Pedagogy stand on an African epistemic foundation that African Peoples carried into the Diaspora and sustained in their heritage knowledge (Fu-Kiau, 2001; Gyekye, 1987; Karenga, 2006a; King & Swartz, 2016; Nkulu-N'Sengha, 2005).

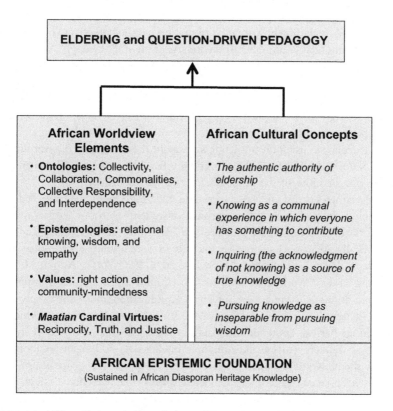

FIGURE 4.1 African Epistemic Foundation of Emancipatory Pedagogies: Eldering and Question-Driven Pedagogy

Eldering and Question-Driven pedagogies position students at the center of teaching and learning and therefore as essential to the well-being and effectiveness of their classrooms. For example, when learning about the Underground Railroad, a teacher can ask students, "If your home had been a station on the Underground Railroad, how would you have helped your family protect and care for the men, women, and children who came to your home on their journey to freedom"? This critical question (Question-Driven Pedagogy) asks students to place themselves in an historical period and engage in right action as they learn about the Underground Railroad; it invites each student to imagine specifically what he or she might do; and it tells students that everyone—including themselves—can demonstrate leadership, be of service to others, and contribute to community well-being.

In another example, after completing a unit of study on the history of voting in the United States—including information about voting restrictions that still exist—involve small groups of students in working collaboratively with each other and with parents/families and teachers to find out what kinds of obstacles to voting exist in their community and what they can do about it. Ask parents to share their knowledge of community standards for participation in the electoral process and to be part of developing a way to assess what they produce together with students, including how their collaboration has the potential to bring benefit to the community (Culturally Authentic Assessment Pedagogy). After student groups gather and organize input from their groups and from parents and family members, teach the class how to use consensus to decide which proposal for ending these obstacles to voting they want to present and how they plan to present it (e.g., speeches, poems, reports, murals/images/charts, dramatizations). Invite parents and family members to observe and assess student presentations and performances using the authentic assessment they were part of creating. And lead a follow-up discussion about how you, family members, and students can pursue one or more of the proposals for change (Eldering).

The examples in this subsection show how Eldering, Question-Driven Pedagogy, and Culturally Authentic Assessment involve students in continued learning and critical thought, bring family presence and ideas into the curriculum, and more authentically (than testing) involve students in demonstrating what they know, are able to do, and are like (King & Swartz, 2016; RTC, 2007). As quoted earlier, Du Bois wrote, "Work alone will not do it [uplift a people] unless inspired by the right ideals and guided by intelligence. Education must not simply teach work—it must teach Life" (1903a, p. 75). Emancipatory pedagogies, which are built on an African epistemic foundation, "teach life"; they prepare all students for life as thinkers—to use their multiple intelligences and create solutions that benefit themselves and others—not to be compliant laborers, artisans, or intellectuals in a raced, classed, and gendered society that benefits the few at the expense of everyone else. Using emancipatory pedagogies is a way to carry forward the African and Du Boisian idea of leadership—that community well-being depends on everyone contributing their diverse talents, knowledge, and skills.

Democracy

Through many of his well-known sociological, historical, and other writings (1899, 1903a, 1920a, 1935, 1945) Du Bois provided abundant evidence of the existence of inequalities and disproportionate applications of democracy across race. His oft-quoted statement that "[t]he problem of the twentieth century is the problem of the color-line" (1903a, p. 23) refers to these raced realities. Furthermore, Du Bois understood that the exclusionary character of U.S. democracy—with its limited opportunities and life chances for women, workers, and all other marginalized cultures and groups—was fundamentally flawed (Rabaka, 2007). Shaped by his African heritage knowledge and carried in his group memory, democracy for Du Bois was a community-wide and community-enhancing practice. Almost 100 years ago, he claimed that the denial of democracy was

> simply the old cry of privilege, the old assumption that there are those in the world who know better what is best for others than those others know themselves . . . In fact no one knows himself but that self's own soul . . . [and] to tap this mighty reservoir of experience, knowledge, beauty, love, and deed we must appeal not to the few, not to some souls, but to all. The narrower the appeal, the poorer the culture; the wider the appeal the more magnificent are the possibilities.
>
> *(1920a, p. 140)*

You see this concern for full participation when Du Bois explained that "no state can be strong which excludes from its expressed wisdom the knowledge possessed by mothers, wives, and daughters" (p. 143). Quite simply, to have democracy, full participation must be available to everyone.

Within an African worldview, democracy is both a form of governance *and* a way of being and interacting with others that sees people's Commonalities (not Differences) and depends on people being Interdependent (not Independent) (Dixon, 1971; Gyekye, 1997; Nobles, 1976). As discussed earlier in this chapter, democracy informed by an African worldview considers people's collective needs and common rights *because* they belong to a community, and values reciprocity and right action that depend on principles of justice and unity. Given this worldview, Du Bois logically advocated for full participation.

Instructional Connection

An accurate account of democracy in North America would describe the democracy practiced by Indigenous Americans prior to the arrival of European colonists and the democratic understandings and values that African people brought with them to the Americas. The "re-membered" student text entitled *Freedom and Democracy, A Story Remembered* (Swartz, 2013) explains the different ideas about freedom and democracy held by Native Americans, Europeans, and Africans when these three groups came into contact in North America. (To inquire about copies of this text, contact omnicentricpress@gmail.com.) Intermediate students learn about the knowledge and experience with democracy that each of these cultural groups had prior to meeting; that before and after the U.S. Constitution was written, freedom and democratic rights in colonial America were limited to White wealthy men, and that by law there was no freedom for millions of Indigenous and enslaved African Peoples and severely limited rights and opportunities for poor White men, all women, and free people of color (Franklin, 1992, 1995; Martin, 1973); and that even though the cultural sovereignty of Native American and African Peoples was not honored, African and Indigenous leaders tried to teach White colonists that freedom was an inherent right, and that good relations were possible if one group did not try to force its ways on another (Aptheker, 1951/1969; Bennett, 1968; Franklin, 1992; Grinde & Johansen, 1991; Lyons & Mohawk, 1992; Tehanetorens, 1970/1999).

Since then, constitutional amendments have been passed, other laws and institutional practices have been changed, and incremental improvements have been made. Yet, current data on the U.S. criminal justice system, health, environment, education, income, access to voting, and policing practices in Black, Native American, and other Communities of Color indicate that we are far from realizing democracy (Alexander, 2012; Brown, 2016; Bullard, 2005; Cheney-Rice, 2015; Davis, 2014; King, 2017; Regnier, 2015; Sanders, 2015; McVeigh, 2014; Young, 2016). The historical record and these current data suggest that *the inherent worth of all humanity, knowing that cultural sovereignty is a common right of all Peoples*, and *pursuing freedom and justice as communal responsibilities* are not organizing cultural concepts within the dominant Euro-American culture (Dunbar-Ortiz, 2014).

A curriculum that teaches the foregoing culturally informed content about democracy—using emancipatory pedagogies such as Eldering, Question-Driven Pedagogy, Multiple Ways of Knowing, and Culturally Authentic Assessment—locates people in the past and present, including your students, as subjects with agency whose heritage knowledge shaped(es) their actions. Think about how the following ideas (presented in *Freedom and Democracy, A Story Remembered*) might be part of your instruction about democracy:

- Before their contact with Europeans, both Native American (with the Haudenosaunee as an example) and African Peoples understood democracy as a way that people live and work together in communities where everyone's ideas are considered, leaders serve at the will of the people, and freedom is the natural right of everyone.
- Haudenosaunee and African Peoples knew that maintaining their cultures and their ancestral lands was a common right and they tried to teach White colonists this understanding of democracy.

While teaching these ideas—and depending on and adjusted to students' developmental level—you might ask critical questions, such as the following:

• The student text explains that in the early colonial period some White leaders were open to hearing what Indigenous and African leaders had to say. Why do you think so?
• Indigenous and African Peoples knew that freedom was an inherent right and that maintaining their cultures was a common right. What is the connection between having this knowledge and the actions taken by Indigenous and African Peoples when Europeans began to take their land, conquer, kill, and enslave them?

As students are learning about the history of democracy in the United States, engage them in a project that connects this history to the present—for example:

• You have learned that Native Americans viewed their freedom as an inherent right, and that African Peoples brought this same idea about freedom to the Americas. How do Native American and/or African American people show that they still view freedom as an inherent right today (e.g., indigenous movement to protect land, water, and sacred sites at Standing Rock; Black Lives Matter movement)? After explaining to a family member(s) what you have learned about Native American and African ideas about freedom and justice, ask your family member the same question and write down their ideas. Work with a partner, in a small group, or by yourself to show how Native American and/or African American people show that they still view freedom as an inherent right today. You can write an essay or poem, or do an oral performance that includes images and music. Be sure to include your family member's ideas in what you produce.

Like his African ancestors, Du Bois understood democracy as communal—as seeking to enhance the well-being of the whole community. Framing your instruction about democracy within this African worldview counters the agreed-upon approach to teaching about Western democracy. This "consensual national narrative" justifies the supposedly "civilizing" mission of Native American conquest and African enslavement with claims that even though it has been exclusionary, Western democracy is the most egalitarian form of governance whose full realization is inevitably gradual (Dunbar-Ortiz, 2014, p. 2). By having access to culturally informed content and knowing Du Bois's African-informed ideas about democracy, we can teach students that they have the capacity to contribute to democracy's egalitarian possibilities and to realizing those possibilities in the present.

Education, Freedom, and Agency

Du Bois (1935, 1973) did not support legally enforced segregation, but he also understood that separate schools could be of benefit, since white schools taught filiopietistic accounts of history that omitted or distorted Black history and heritage. Thus, he explained the weakness of white education as a model and suggested that educators avoid

> trying to parallel the history of white folk with similar boasting about black and brown folk, but rather an honest evaluation of human effort and accomplishment, without color blindness, and without transforming history into a record of dynasties and prodigies.
>
> *(Du Bois, 1935, p. 334)*

It would be unwise, he said, to mirror the approach used in White schools as a model for education about the history and culture of Black people. Instead, Du Bois proposed that Black education be based on ethical standards of truth, justice, and right action. Mutombo Nkulu-N'Sengha (2005) explains that in African societies all knowledge has an ethical dimension and that wisdom is necessary in the pursuit of true knowledge. Du Bois displayed this cultural concept (*pursuing knowledge as inseparable from pursuing wisdom*) when he asked for an honest record of human accomplishments in school knowledge. In the quote ahead, his vision for Black schools also displayed another African Diasporan cultural concept: *knowing that cultural sovereignty is a common right of all Peoples* (Akbar, 1984; Hart, 1985/2002; Hilliard, 1995; Karenga, 1999, 2006a, 2006b). Du Bois wrote,

> Thus, instead of our schools being simply separate schools, forced on us by grim necessity, they can become centers of a new and beautiful effort at human education, which may easily lead and guide the world in many important and valuable aspects. It is for this reason that when our schools are separate, the control of the teaching force, the expenditure of money, the choice of textbooks, the discipline and other administrative matters of this sort ought, also, to come into our hands [sovereignty], and be incessantly demanded and guarded.
>
> *(1935, pp. 334–335)*

Informed by African heritage knowledge—the cultural memory passed through the generations by his African ancestors—Du Bois understood that education for freedom was connected to ethics and agency. Thus, he advocated being in control of how children were educated; and using ethics and agency as a way to turn the negative and imposed disservice of segregation into an education for freedom that served the Black community.

Instructional Connection

Du Bois was masterful at conceptualizing how to transform systems of oppression into systems that encourage agency and freedom. How can we do the same in the classroom—that is, encourage agency in our students and well-being in their communities (King & Swartz, 2016)? At the heart of this effort is (1) transforming the way we present topics to be more reflective of the cultures that inform them; and (2) selecting content and pedagogies that can strengthen our relationships with students and families. For example, when teaching a unit on the oldest known human civilizations, which are located in Africa along the Nile River, use content that shows how these civilizations, such as Kemet (ancient Egypt) and Ta-Seti (Nubia), produced the earliest achievements in science, mathematics, philosophy, architecture, agriculture, medicine, literature, and the arts (Asante, 2014; Diop, 1967, 1974). To connect students to this ancient knowledge, especially African American students—for whom this knowledge is a foundational element of their heritage, yet disappeared in most school curriculum—explain that these Nile Valley civilizations (that preceded the Indus river valley civilization between the Tigris and Euphrates) lasted for thousands of years by being community-minded. This "common-unity" (communication with Odis Jones, 4/2004) was an outcome of a worldview and philosophy based on the spiritual and ethical practice of *Maat* with its Seven Virtues (Truth, Justice, Balance, Reciprocity, Harmony, Order, and Propriety). The Kemetic philosophers who developed *Maat* taught that living together in harmony means that all life is sacred and connected (Asante, 2000, 2007b; Diop, 1959/1990; Karenga, 1990, 2006a; Obenga, 1989).

One way to connect families to this study of education, freedom, and agency is to teach lessons on the role of elders who were the leaders and wisdom keepers in ancient Kemet. Elders were priests, peacemakers, healers, counselors, and educators who were appreciated and loved while they lived and even after they passed on to the next life (Goodwin & Swartz, 2009). This idea of highly regarding elders has been a central tenet in African societies and can be seen in all places where African people live throughout the world (Gyekye, 1987; Karenga, 1999, 2006a; Nkulu-N'Sengha, 2005; Ikuenobe, 2006; Tedla, 1995; Waghid, 2014). After sharing and discussing this content about the ancient Kemetic origins of eldership, ask family members to share their knowledge about how elders are viewed in their families and discuss the similarities they see with African ideas about eldership. Invite family members to participate in the development of assessments for a range of possible projects (e.g., student interviews of parents/elders; a book project, mural, or exhibition about family elders; student presentations of poetry, dramas, stories, research reports) in which students demonstrate (1) what they have learned about eldership in Nile Valley civilizations that was passed through the generations and throughout the world as part of the worldview and philosophies of African Peoples; and (2) how this historical knowledge relates to their families' knowledge about elders.

Conclusion

The world in which W.E.B. Du Bois lived—and in which we live—was shaped by centuries of enslavement, conquest, imperial exploitation, and systemically supported denial of opportunities to people of African ancestry, other Peoples of Color, workers, poor people, and women. Like Du Bois, we can teach how knowledge can enable people to transform an oppressive system—in this case an educational system that has excluded and distorted knowledge, maintained a hierarchy of human worth, and weakened our relationships with students and families. While Du Bois and other Black scholars/activists felt compelled to respond to these conditions during the progressive era and beyond, their work was not limited to a *reaction* to oppression. Rather, their work was an exercise of African agency—of the will and capacity to act in the interests of self, family, community, peoplehood, and humanity—an agency that Du Bois thought could be fostered through appropriate education grounded in history and culture (Du Bois, 1973). Thus, during the progressive era he reiterated his position in *Souls* (stated earlier) when he wrote, "The object of education was not to make men carpenters, but to make carpenters men" (1932, p. 61). He explained that it is necessary to learn the skills needed for all types of work, but equally or more important is the need to educate men and women to be self-determined and collectively responsible participants in the life of their communities.

As seen in DuBois's work, his social outlook is African—it asks for *sharing responsibility for communal well-being and belonging*; his advocacy for collective ways of improving the community, responding to social conditions, and serving others is African—it models *demonstrating concern for human welfare through actions based on community-mindedness and service to others*; and his pursuit of democracy is African—it is informed by and advances concepts such as *pursuing freedom and justice as communal responsibilities, knowing that cultural sovereignty is a common right of all Peoples*, and *love, dignity, and decency as shared by all* (Abímbólá, 1976; Anyanwu, 1981a; Fu-Kiau, 2001; Gyekye, 1997; Karenga, 2006b). By locating the scholarship of Du Bois and other emancipatory Black scholars, educators, and activists within an African epistemic foundation, and by using their ideas to conceptualize and shape instruction, we can extricate ourselves from the hegemonic straitjacket that has framed school knowledge before and during the progressive era and still today. Through our agency as educators we can replace eurocratic curricular content with content that acknowledges African Diasporan people as subjects with agency whose knowledge and actions remain connected to their heritage knowledge and cultural legacy. Likewise, we can replace authoritarian, competitive, punitive pedagogies with emancipatory pedagogies that center all students, are communal and relational, and invite students to use their voices by defining themselves and their ideas during instruction. In these ways, teachers can use knowledge of an African worldview and cultural concepts to transform the curriculum and develop instruction that draws upon the history and cultural heritage of all students.

References

Abímbólá, W. (1976). *Ifá will mend our broken world: Thoughts on Yoruba religion and culture in Africa and the Diaspora.* Roxbury, MA: Aim Books.

Ajisafe, A. K. (1924). *The laws and customs of the Yoruba people.* London: George Routledge & Sons.

Akbar, N. (1984). Africentric social sciences for human liberation. *Journal of Black Studies, 14*(4), 395–414.

Alexander, M. (2012). *The new Jim Crow: Mass incarceration in the age of color blindness.* New York: New Press.

Ani, M. (1994). *Yurugu, an African-centered critique of European cultural thought and behavior.* Trenton, NJ: Africa World Press.

Anyanwu, K. C. (1981a). The African world-view and theory knowledge. In E. A. Ruch & K. C. Anyanwu (authors), *African philosophy: An introduction to the main philosophical trends in contemporary Africa* (pp. 77–99). Rome: Catholic Book Agency.

Anyanwu, K. C. (1981b). Artistic and aesthetic experience. In E. A. Ruch & K. C. Anyanwu (authors), *African philosophy: An introduction to the main philosophical trends in contemporary Africa* (pp. 270–282). Rome: Catholic Book Agency.

Aptheker, H. (1951/1968). *A documentary history of the Negro people in the United States: From the Reconstruction era to 1910* (Vol. 2). New York: The Citadel Press.

Aptheker, H. (1951/1969). *A documentary history of the Negro people in the United States: From colonial times through the Civil War* (Vol. 1). New York: The Citadel Press.

Aptheker, H. (1956). *Toward Negro freedom.* New York: New Century.

Aptheker, H. (1989). *The literary legacy of W.E.B. Du Bois.* White Plains, NY: Kraus International.

Asante, M. K. (1987/1998). *The Afrocentric idea.* Philadelphia: Temple University Press.

Asante, M. K. (1991/1992). Afrocentric curriculum. *Educational Leadership, 49*(4), 28–31.

Asante, M. K. (1993). Racism, consciousness, and Afrocentricity. In Gerald Early (Ed.), *Lure and loathing: Essays on race, identity, and the ambivalence of assimilation* (pp. 127–143). New York, NY: Allen Lane, the Penguin Press.

Asante, M. K. (1994). *Classical Africa.* Maywood, NJ: Asante Imprint Books and Peoples.

Asante, M. K. (2000). *The Egyptian philosophers: Ancient African voices from Imhotep to Akhenaten.* Chicago: African American Images.

Asante, M. K. (2007a). *An Afrocentric manifesto.* Malden, MA: Polity Press.

Asante, M. K. (2007b). *The history of Africa: The quest for eternal harmony.* New York, NY: Routledge.

Asante, M. K. (2014). *Facing South to Africa.* Lanham, MD: Lexington Books.

Asante, M. K., & Mazama, A. (Eds.). (2005). *Encyclopedia of Black studies.* Thousand Oaks, CA: SAGE.

Asimeng-Boahene, L. (2014). Mirror of a people: The pedagogical value of African proverbs as cultural resource tools in content area social studies classrooms. In L. Asimeng-Boahene & M. Baffoe (Eds.), *African traditional and oral literature as pedagogical tools in content area classrooms K-12* (pp. 111–128). Charlotte, NC: Information Age.

Au, W. (2009). *Unequal by design: High-stakes testing and the standardization of inequality.* New York: Routledge.

Bailey, T. A. (1956). *The American pageant: A history of the republic.* Boston, MA: D. C. Heath.

Bastide, R. (1971). *African civilizations in the New World.* New York, NY: Harper & Row.

Bennett, L., Jr. (1968). *Pioneers in protest.* Chicago: Johnson.

Bennett, L., Jr. (1975). *The shaping of Black America.* Chicago: Johnson.

Bethune, M. M. (1939). The adaptation of the history of the Negro to the capacity of the child. *The Journal of Negro History, 24*(1), 9–13.

Boakye-Boaten, A. (2010). Changes in the concept of childhood: Implications on children in Ghana. *The Journal of International Social Research, 3*(10), 104–115.

Bond, H. M. (1934). *The education of the Negro in the American social order.* New York: Octagon Books.

Bond, H. M. (1935). The curriculum and the Negro child. *The Journal of Negro Education, 4*(2), 159–168.

Bowers, C. A. (1969). *The progressive educator and the Depression: The radical years.* New York, NY: Random House.

Boyd, C. D., Gay, G., Geiger, R., Kracht, J. B., Ooka Pang, V., Risinger, C. F., & Sanchez, S. M. (2011). *All together.* Boston, MA: Pearson.

Broderick, F. L. (1959). *W.E.B. Du Bois: Negro leader in a time of crisis.* Stanford, CT: Stanford University Press.

Brown, A. (2016). *Standing rock demonstrators file class-action lawsuit over police violence.* Retrieved from http://readersupportednews.org/news-section2/318-66/40565-standing-rock-demonstrators-file-class-action-lawsuit-over-police-violence

Bruce, D. D. (1999). W.E.B. Du Bois and the idea of double consciousness. In H. L. Gates, Jr. & T. H. Oliver (Eds.), *W.E.B. Du Bois: The souls of Black folk: Authoritative text, contexts, criticism* (pp. 236–244). New York, NY: W. W. Norton .

Bullard, R. D. (2005). *The quest for environmental justice: Human rights and the politics of pollution.* Berkeley, CA: Counterpoint Press.

Burroughs, N. H. (1934, February 17). Nannie Burroughs says that hound dogs are kicked but not bull dogs. *The Baltimore Afro-American,* p. 5.

Busia, K. A. (1967). *Africa in search of democracy.* New York: Praeger.

Butchart, R. E. (1994). Outthinking and outflanking the owners of the world: An historiography of the African American struggle for education. In M. J. Shujaa (Ed.), *Too much schooling, too little education: A paradox of Black life in white societies* (pp. 85–122). Trenton, NJ: Africa World Press.

Carney, J. A. (2001). *Black rice: The African origins of rice cultivation in the Americas.* Cambridge, MA: Harvard University Press.

Cheney-Rice, Z. (2015). *The police are killing one group at a staggering rate, and nobody is talking about it.* Retrieved from http://mic.com/articles/109894/the-police-are-killing-one-group-at-a-staggering-rate-and-nobody-is-talking-about-it#.DU9SB9SRw

Clarke, J. H. (1992). *Christopher Columbus and the Afrikan holocaust: Slavery and the rise of European capitalism.* Brooklyn, NY: A & B Books.

Cooper, A. J. (Haywood) (1892/1969). *A voice from the South, by a black woman of the South.* New York: Negro Universities Press.

Cremin, L. A. (1961). *The transformation of the school: Progressivism in American education 1876–1957.* New York: Alfred A. Knopf.

Dagbovie, P. G. (2007). *The early Black history movement: Carter G. Woodson and Lorenzo Johnston Greene.* Chicago, IL: University of Illinois Press.

Danquah, J. B. (1928). *Gold coast: Akan laws and customs and the Akim Abuakwa constitution.* London: G. Routledge & Sons.

Davidson, B. (1959). *The lost cities of Africa.* Boston: Little, Brown.

Davidson, B. (1961). *Black mother: The years of the African slave trade.* Boston, MA: Little, Brown.

Davidson, B. (1972). *In the eye of the storm: Angola's people.* Garden City, NY: Doubleday .

Davidson, B. (1991). *African civilization revisited: From antiquity to modern times.* Trenton, N.J.: Africa World Press.

Davis, B. (2014). *America's summer of white supremacy: A postmortem.* Retrieved from http://readersupportednews.org/opinion2/277-75/26127-americas-summer-of-white-supremacy-a-postmortem

Dewey, J. (1899). *The school and society.* Chicago: University of Chicago Press.

Dewey, J. (1952). Introduction to *The use of resources in education* (E. R. Clapp, author). New York, New York: Harper and Brothers.

Dewey, J., & Dewey, E. (1915). *School of to-morrow.* New York, NY: E. P. Dutton .

Dike, K. O. (1956). *Trade and politics in the Niger Delta, 1830–1885: An introduction to the economic and political history of Nigeria.* London: Oxford at the Clarendon Press.

Dillard, A. D. (2007). *Faith in the city: Preaching radical social change in Detroit.* Ann Arbor: University of Michigan Press.

Diop, C. A. (1959/1990). *The cultural unity of Black Africa.* Chicago: Third World Press.

Diop, C. A. (1967). *Anteriority of Negro civilizations.* Paris: Presence Africaine.

Diop, C. A. (1974). *The African origins of civilization: Myth or reality?* (M. Cook, Trans.). Westport, CT: Lawrence Hill.

Diop, C. A. (1987). *Pre-colonial Black Africa.* Westport, CT: Lawrence Hill.

Diop, C. A. (2000). *The cultural unity of Black Africa.* London: Karnak House.

Dixon, V. J. (1971). African-oriented and Euro-American-oriented world views: Research methodologies and economics. *The Review of Black Political Economy, 7*(2), 119–156.

Du Bois, W.E.B. (1897). The conservation of races. *Occasional Papers, American Negro Academy, 2,* 1–15.

Du Bois, W.E.B. (1898). Results of the investigation. In W.E.B. Du Bois (Ed.), *Some efforts of American Negros for their own social betterment: Report of an investigation under the direction of Atlanta University; together with the proceeding of the Third Conference for the study of the Negro problems, held at Atlanta University, May 25–26, 1898* (pp. 4–44). Atlanta, GA: Atlanta University Press.

Du Bois, W.E.B. (1899). *The Philadelphia Negro: A social study.* New York: Schocken Books.

Du Bois, W.E.B. (1901). *The Negro common school: Report of a social study made under the direction of Atlanta University, together with the proceedings of the sixth Conference for the Study of the Negro Problems, held at Atlanta University, on May 28th, 1901.* Atlanta, GA: University Press.

Du Bois, W.E.B. (1903a). *The souls of Black folks.* Greenwich, CT: Fawcett.

Du Bois, W.E.B. (1903b). The talented tenth. In B. T. Washington et al. (authors), *The Negro Problem: A series of articles by representative American Negroes of today* (pp. 31–75). New York, NY: James Pott.

Du Bois, W.E.B. (1904). *The suppression of the African Slave-Trade to the United States of America, 1638–1870.* New York: Longmans, Green. (Original work published in 1896)

Du Bois, W.E.B. (1915a, May). The African roots of war. *Atlantic Monthly, 65,* 707–714.

Du Bois, W.E.B. (1915b). *The Negro.* Mineola, NY: Dover.

Du Bois, W.E.B. (1919). The real cause of two race riots. *The Crisis, 19*(2), 56–62.

Du Bois, W.E.B. (1920a). *Darkwater.* New York: Harcourt, Brace.

Du Bois, W.E.B. (1920b, February 18). On being Black. *New Republic, 21,* 338–341.

Du Bois, W.E.B. (1924). *The gift of Black folk, the Negroes in the making of America.* Boston: Stratford. (Rundell, 326 D816g 1–1)

Du Bois, W.E.B. (1932). Education and work. *The Journal of Negro Education, 1*(1), 60–74.

Du Bois, W.E.B. (1935). Does the Negro need separate schools? *Journal of Negro Education, 4,* 329–335.

Du Bois, W.E.B. (1935/1962). *Black reconstruction in America: An essay toward a history of the part which Black folk played in the attempt to reconstruct democracy in America, 1860–1880.* Cleveland: World, Meridian Books.

Du Bois, W.E.B. (1939). *Black folk, then and now: An essay in the history and sociology of the Negro race.* New York, NY: Henry Holt.

Du Bois, W.E.B. (1940/1968). *Dusk of dawn: An essay toward an autobiography of a race concept.* New York, NY: Schocken Books.

Du Bois, W.E.B. (1945). *Color and democracy.* New York: Harcourt Brace.

Du Bois, W.E.B. (1947). *The world and Africa: An inquiry into the part which Africa has played in world history.* New York: Viking Press.

Du Bois, W.E.B. (1968). *The autobiography of W.E.B. Du Bois.* New York: International.

Du Bois, W.E.B. (1973). *The education of Black people, ten critiques 1906–1960.* Amherst: The University of Massachusetts Press.

Du Bois, W.E.B. (1975). *The gift of Black folk.* Millwood, NY: Kraus-Thomson Organization.

Du Bois, W.E.B. (1976). *The ordeal of Mansart* (book one of *The Black flame: A trilogy*). New York, NY: Mainstream. (Original work published 1957, Mainstream)

Du Bois, W.E.B. (1985). *Against racism: Unpublished essays, papers, addresses, 1887–1961.* Amherst: The University of Massachusetts Press.

Du Bois, W.E.B., & Padmore, G. (Ed.). (1962). *History of the Pan-African Congress.* London: Hammersmith Bookshop.

Dunbar-Ortiz, R. (2014). *An indigenous peoples' history of the United States.* Boston, MA: Beacon Press.

Fendler, L., & Muzaffar, I. (2008). The history of the bell curve: Sorting and the idea of normal. *Educational Theory, 58*(1), 63–82.

Fontaine, W. T. (1940). An interpretation of contemporary Negro thought from the standpoint of the sociology of knowledge. *Journal of Negro History, 25*(1), 6–13.

Franklin, V. P. (1992). *Black self-determination: A cultural history of African American resistance.* Chicago: Lawrence Hill Books.

Franklin, V. P. (1995). *Living our stories, telling our truths.* New York: Oxford University Press.

Fu-Kiau, K.K.B. (2001). *African cosmology of the Bântu-Kôngo, tying the spiritual knot: Principles of life and living.* New York: Athelia Henrietta Press.

Garnet, H. H. (1843/1972). Address to the slaves of the United States of America (Rejected by the National Convention held in Buffalo, NY, 1843). In S. Stuckey (Ed.), *The ideological origins of Black nationalism* (pp. 168–170). Boston: Beacon Press.

Garnet, H. H. (1859, September 17). Speech to the Colored citizens of Boston, 1859. *The Weekly Anglo African, 1*(9).

Gavian, R. W., & Hamm, W. A. (1945). *The American story: A history of the United States of America.* Boston: D. C. Heath.

Goggin, J. (1993). *Carter G. Woodson: A life in Black history.* Baton Rouge: Louisiana State University Press.

Gomez, M. A. (1998). *Exchanging our country marks: The transformation of African identities in the colonial and antebellum South.* Chapel Hill: University of North Carolina Press.

Goodenow, R. K. (1975). The progressive educator, race and ethnicity in the depression years: An overview. *History of Education Quarterly, 15*(4), 365–394.

Goodenow, R. K. (1977a). Racial and ethnic tolerance in John Dewey's educational and social thought: The Depression years. *Educational Theory, 26*(Winter), 48–64.

Goodenow, R. K. (1977b). The progressive educator on race, ethnicity, creativity, and planning: Harold Rugg in the 1930s. *Review Journal of Philosophy and Social Science, 1*(Winter), 105–128.

Goodenow, R. K. (1978). Paradox in progressive educational reform: The South and the education of Blacks in the depression years. *Phylon, 39*(1), 49–65.

Goodenow, R. K. (1981). The Southern progressive educator on race and pluralism: The case of William Heard Kilpatrick. *History of Education Quarterly, 21*(2), 147–170.

Gooding-Williams, R. (2009). *In the shadow of Du Bois: Afro-modern political thought in America.* Cambridge, MA: Harvard University Press.

Goodwin, S., & Swartz, E. E. (1993). Multiculturality: Liberating classroom pedagogy and practice. *Raising Standards: Journal of the Rochester Teachers Association, 1*(1), 19–33.

Goodwin, S., & Swartz, E. E. (Eds.). (2004). *Teaching children of color: Seven constructs of effective teaching in urban schools.* Rochester, NY: RTA Press.

Goodwin, S., & Swartz, E. E. (2009). *Document-based learning: Curriculum and assessment.* Rochester, NY: RTA Press.

Gould, S. J. (1981). *The mismeasure of man.* New York: Norton.

Greene, L. J. (1989). *Working with Carter G. Woodson, the Father of Black History: A diary, 1928–1930.* Edited with an introduction by A. E. Strickland. Baton Rouge: Louisiana State University Press.

Grinde, D. A., Jr., & Johansen, B. E. (1991). *Exemplar of liberty: Native America and the evolution of democracy.* Los Angeles: American Indian Studies Center, University of California.

Gyekye, K. (1987). *An essay on African philosophical thought: The Akan conceptual scheme.* Cambridge: Cambridge University Press.

Gyekye, K. (1988). *The unexamined life: Philosophy and the African experience.* Accra: Ghana Universities Press.

Gyekye, K. (1997). *Tradition and modernity: Philosophical reflections on the African experience.* New York: Oxford University Press.

Hall, G. M. (2005). *Slavery and African ethnicities in the Americas: Restoring the links.* Chapel Hill: University of North Carolina Press.

Harding, V. (1990). *Hope and history.* New York: Orbis Books.

Harlow, R. V. (1947). *Story of America.* New York: Henry Holt.

Hart, R. (1985/2002). *Slaves who abolished slavery: Blacks in rebellion.* Kingston, Jamaica: University of the West Indies Press.

Herskovits, M. J. (1941). *The myth of the Negro past.* New York, NY: Harper & Brothers.

Hilliard, A. G. III (1995). *The Maroon within us: Selected essays on African American community socialization.* Baltimore, MD: Black Classic Press.

Holloway, J. E. (Ed.). (1990). *Africanisms in American culture.* Bloomington: Indiana University Press.

Ikuenobe, P. (2006). *Philosophical perspectives on communalism and morality in African traditions.* Lanham, MD: Lexington Books.

Karenga, M. (Translator and Commentator). (1990). *The book of coming forth by day: The ethics of the Declarations of Innocence.* Los Angeles, CA: University of Sankore Press.

Karenga, M. (1999). *Odù Ifá: The ethical teachings.* Los Angeles: University of Sankore Press.

Karenga, M. (2005). Kwanzaa. In M. K. Asante & A. Mazama (Eds.), *Encyclopedia of Black studies* (pp. 303–305). Thousand Oaks, CA: SAGE.

Karenga, M. (2006a). *Maat, the moral ideal of ancient Egypt: A study in classical African ethics.* New York: Routledge.

Karenga, M. (2006b). Philosophy in the African tradition of resistance: Issues of human freedom and human flourishing. In L. R. Gordon & J. A. Gordon (Eds.), *Not only the master's tools: African American studies in theory and practice* (pp. 243–271). Boulder, CO: Paradigm.

Karenga, M., & Carruthers, J. H. (Eds.). (1986). *Kemet and the African worldview*. Los Angeles: University of Sankore Press.

Kendi, I. X. (2016). *Stamped from the beginning: The definitive history of racist ideas in America*. New York, NY: Nation Books.

King, J. E. (1992). Diaspora literacy and consciousness in the struggle against miseducation in the Black community. *Journal of Negro Education, 61*(3), 317–340.

King, J. E. (2006a). "If justice is our objective": Diaspora literacy, heritage knowledge and the praxis of critical studyin' for human freedom. *Yearbook of the National Society for the Study of Education, 105*(2), 337–360.

King, J. E. (2006b). Perceiving reality in a new way: Rethinking the Black/White duality of our times. In A. Bogues (Ed.), *Caribbean reasonings: After man toward the human: Critical essays on Sylvia Wynter* (pp. 25–56). Kingston, Jamaica: Ian Randle.

King, J. E. (2015). *Dysconscious racism, Afrocentric praxis, and education for human freedom: Through the years I keep on toiling, the selected works of Joyce E. King*. New York, NY: Routledge.

King, J. E. (2016a). *Liberatory research practice and ethics beyond epistemological nihilation*. Santa Cruz: UC Center for Collaborative Research for an Equitable California.

King, J. E. (2016b). We may well become accomplices: "To rear a generation of spectators is not to educate at all." *Educational Researcher, 45*(2), 159–172.

King, J. E., & Swartz, E. E. (2016). *The Afrocentric praxis of teaching for freedom: Connecting culture to learning*. New York, NY: Routledge.

King, J. E., & Swartz, E. E., Campbell, L., Lemons-Smith, S., & López, E. (2014). *"Remembering" history in student and teacher learning: An Afrocentric culturally informed praxis*. New York, NY: Routledge.

King, M. L., Jr. (1958). *Stride toward freedom: The Montgomery story*. New York: Harper.

King, S. (2017). *Soul snatchers: How New York City's criminal justice system conspires to destroy Black and Brown lives*. Retrieved from http://readersupportednews.org/opinion2/277-75/45414-soul-snatchers-how-new-york-citys-criminal-justice-system-conspires-to-destroy-black-and-brown-lives

Kliebard, H. M. (1986). *The struggle for the American curriculum 1893–1958*. New York: Routledge.

Kliewer, C., & Fitzgerald, L. M. (2001). Disability, schooling, and the artifacts of colonialism. *Teachers College Record, 103*(3), 450–470.

Kohn, A. (1996). *Beyond discipline: From compliance to community*. Alexandria, VA: Association for Supervision and Curriculum Development.

Kohn, A. (2000). *The case against standardized testing: Raising the scores, ruining the schools*. Portsmouth, NH: Heinemann.

Kumashiro, K. K. (2008). *The seduction of common sense: How the right has framed the debate on America's schools*. New York: Teachers College Press.

Kuper, H. (1947). *An African aristocracy: Rank among the Swazi*. London: Oxford University Press for the International African Institute.

Law, R. (2007). Du Bois as pioneer of African history: A reassessment of *The Negro*. In M. Keller & C. J. Fontenot, Jr. (Eds.), *Re-cognizing W.E.B. Du Bois in the twenty-first century* (pp. 14–33). Macon, GA: Mercer University Press.

Lewis, D. L. (1993). *W.E.B. Du Bois: Biography of a race, 1868–1919*. New York: Henry Holt.

Lewis, D. L. (2000). *W.E.B. Du Bois: The fight for equality and the American century, 1919–1963*. New York: A John Macrae Book/Henry Holt.

Lincoln, C. E. (1993). The Du Boisian dubiety and the American dilemma: Two levels of lure and loathing. In G. Early (Ed.), *Lure and loathing: Essays on race, identity, and the ambivalence of assimilation* (pp. 194–206). New York, NY: Allan Lane, The Penguin Press.

Logan, R. W. (Ed.). (1971). Introduction. In R. W. Logan (Ed.), *W.E.B. Du Bois: A profile* (pp. vii–xxii). New York, NY: Hill and Wang.

Lyons, O., & Mohawk, J. (Eds.). (1992). *Exiled in the land of the free: Democracy, Indian nations, and the U.S. Constitution*. Santa Fe, NM: Clear Light.

Maïga, H. O. (2010). *Balancing written history with oral tradition: The legacy of the Songhoy people*. New York: Routledge.

Marable, M. (1986). *W.E.B. DuBois, Black radical democrat*. Boston, MA: Twayne.

Marable, M. (2005). *W.E.B. Du Bois: Black radical democrat*. Boulder, CO: Paradigm.

Martin, J. K. (1973). *Men in rebellion: Higher government leaders and the coming of the American Revolution*. New Brunswick, NJ: Rutgers University Press.

Mazama, A. (2003). *The Afrocentric paradigm*. Trenton, NJ: Africa World Press.

Mbiti, J. S. (1990). *African religions and philosophy* (2nd ed.). Portsmouth, NH: Heinemann Educational Books.

McVeigh, K. (2014). *Equal pay for US women taken up by Senate as study highlights gender gap*. Retrieved from http://readersupportednews.org/news-section2/314-18/23016-equal-pay-for-us-women-taken-up-by-senate-as-study-highlights-gender-gap

Meier, A. (1971). The paradox of W.E.B. Du Bois. In R. W. Logan (Ed.), *W.E.B. Du Bois: A profile* (pp. 64–85). New York: Hill and Wang.

Miller, J. C. (1988). *Way of death: Merchant capitalism and the Angolan slave trade, 1730–1830*. Madison: University of Wisconsin Press.

Mills, C. W. (1997). *The racial contract*. Ithaca, NY: Cornell University Press.

Mills, C. W. (1998). *Blackness visible: Essays on philosophy and race*. Ithaca, NY: Cornell University Press.

Moreau, J. (2003). *Schoolbook nation: Conflicts over American history textbooks from the Civil War to the present*. Ann Arbor: University of Michigan Press.

Morison, S. E., & Commager, H. S. (1942). *The growth of the American republic* (Vol. 1, 3rd ed.). New York: Oxford University Press.

Morris, A. D. (2015). *The scholar denied: W.E.B. Du Bois and the birth of modern sociology*. Oakland: University of California Press.

Morrison, T. (1992). *Playing in the dark, whiteness and the literary imagination*. Cambridge, MA: Harvard University Press.

Muzzey, D. S. (1933). *The United States of America, Volume II: From the Civil War*. New York, NY: Ginn.

Nkrumah, K. (1966). *Neo-colonialism: The last stage of imperialism*. London: Nelson.

Nkulu-N'Sengha, M. (2005). African epistemology. In M. K. Asante & A. Mazama (Eds.), *Encyclopedia of Black studies* (pp. 39–44). Thousand Oaks, CA: SAGE.

Nobles, W. W. (1976). Extended self: Rethinking the so-called Negro self-concept. *The Journal of Black Psychology, 2*(2), 15–24.

Nobles, W. W. (1986). Ancient Egyptian thought and the development of African (Black) psychology. In M. Karenga & J. H. Carruthers (Eds.), *Kemet and the African worldview* (pp. 100–118). Los Angeles: University of Sankore Press.

Nyerere, J. (1965). Democracy and the party system. In R. Emerson & M. Kilson (Eds.), *The political awakening of Africa* (pp. 122–128). Englewood Cliffs, NJ: Prentice-Hall.

Obenga, T. (1989). African philosophy of the Pharaonic period (2780–330 B.C.) (Excerpt from a work in translation). In I. Van Sertima (Ed.), *Egypt revisited* (2nd ed.) (pp. 286–324). New Brunswick, NJ: Transaction.

Parks, R., & Haskins, J. (1992). *My story.* New York: Dial Books.

Phillips, J. E. (1990). The African heritage of White Americans. In J. E. Holloway (Ed.), *Africanisms in American culture* (pp. 225–239). Bloomington: Indiana University Press.

Piersen, W. D. (1993). *Black legacy: America's hidden heritage.* Amherst: University of Massachusetts Press.

Porter, D. B. (1936). The organized educational activities of Negro literary societies, 1828–1846. *The Journal of Negro Education, 5*(4), 555–576.

Prah, K. K. (2009). Mother-tongue education in Africa for emancipation and development: Towards the intellectualization of African languages. In B. Brock-Utne & I. Skattum (Eds.), *Languages and education in Africa: A comparative and transdisciplinary analysis* (pp. 83–104). Oxford: Symposium Books.

Quarles, B. (1969). *Black abolitionists.* New York: Oxford University Press.

Rabaka, R. (2007). *W.E.B. Du Bois and the problems of the twenty-first century: An essay on African critical theory.* New York: Rowman & Littlefield.

Rabaka, R. (2008). *Du Bois's dialectics: Black radical politics and the reconstruction of critical social theory.* Lanham, MD: Lexington Books.

Rabaka, R. (2010). *Against epistemic apartheid: W.E.B. Du Bois and the disciplinary decadence of sociology.* Lanham, MD: Lexington Books, an imprint of Rowman & Littlefield.

Rampersad, A. (1976). *The art and imagination of W.E.B. Du Bois.* Cambridge, MA: Harvard University Press.

Rattray, R. S. (1929). *Ashanti law and constitution.* London: Oxford University Press.

Reddick, L. D. (1933). *Racial attitudes in the South's American history textbooks.* Nashville, TN: Fisk University.

Regnier, C. (2015). *America is locking its poor in debtor's prisons to fund police.* Retrieved from http://readersupportednews.org/opinion2/277-75/30433-america-is-locking-its-poor-in-debtors-prisons-to-fund-police

Robinson, J.A.G. (1987). *The Montgomery bus boycott and the women who started it: The memoir of Jo Ann Gibson Robinson.* Knoxville: The University of Tennessee Press.

Rodney, W. (1966). African slavery and other forms of social oppression on the upper Guinea coast in the context of the Atlantic slave trade. *The Journal of African History, 7*(3), 431–443.

Rodney, W. (1982). *How Europe underdeveloped Africa.* Washington, DC: Howard University Press.

RTC (Rochester Teacher Center). (2007). *Cultural learning standards: What students are expected to know, be able to do, and be like.* Rochester, NY: Author.

Rucker, W. C. (2006). *The river flows on: Black resistance, culture, and identity formation in early America.* Baton Rouge: Louisiana State University Press.

Rudwick, E. M. (1968). *W.E.B. Du Bois: Propagandist of the Negro protest.* New York, NY: Atheneum.

Rugg, H. O. (1931). *A history of American government and culture: America's march toward democracy* (Vol. IV). Boston, MA: Ginn.

Sanders, B. (2015). *Racial justice.* Retrieved from http://readersupportednews.org/opinion2/277-75/31883-focus-racial-justice

Senghor, L. S. (1964). *On African socialism.* (M. Cook, Trans.). New York: Frederick A. Praeger. (Original work published 1961)

Shepperson, G. (1970). Introduction to *The Negro* by W.E.B. DuBois. Oxford: Oxford University Press. (original work published 1915, Henry Holt)

Shujaa, M. J., & Shujaa, K. J. (2015). *The SAGE encyclopedia of African cultural heritage in North America* (2 vols.). Thousand Oaks, CA: SAGE.

Sithole, N. (1959). *African nationalism.* London: Oxford University Press.

Starobin, R. S. (Ed.). (1970). *Denmark Vesey: The slave conspiracy of 1822.* Englewood Cliffs, NJ: Prentice-Hall.

Stepto, R. B. (1979). *From behind the veil: A study of Afro-American narrative.* Chicago: University of Illinois Press.

Stuckey, S. (1987). *Slave culture: Nationalist theory and the foundations of Black America.* New York, NY: Oxford University Press.

Sundquist, E. J. (1993). *To wake the nations: Race in the making of American literature.* Cambridge, MA: The Belknap Press of Harvard University Press.

Swartz, E. E. (2007). Stepping outside the master script: Re-connecting the history of American education. *The Journal of Negro Education, 76*(2), 173–186.

Swartz, E. E. (2013). *Freedom and democracy: A Story Remembered.* Rochester, NY: RTA Press.

Tanner, D. (1991). *Crusade for democracy: Progressive education at the crossroads.* Albany: State University of New York Press.

Tedla, E. (1995). *Sankofa: African thought and education.* New York: Peter Lang.

Teffo, J. (2004). Democracy, kingship, and consensus: A South African perspective. In K. Wiredu (Ed.), *A companion to African philosophy* (pp. 443–449). Malden, MA: Blackwell.

Tehanetorens (Fadden, R.). (1970/1999). *Kaianerekowa Hotinonsionne: The great law of peace of the longhouse people.* Rooseveltown, NY: Akwesasne Notes/Mohawk Nation.

Thompson, C. H. (1935, July). Court action the only reasonable alternative to remedy immediate abuses of the Negro separate school. *The Journal of Negro Education, 4*(3), 419–434.

Thompson, R. F. (1990). Kongo influences on African American artistic culture. In J. E. Holloway (Ed.), *Africanisms in American culture* (pp. 148–184). Bloomington: Indiana University Press.

Turner, L. D. (2002). *Africanisms in the Gullah dialect.* Columbia: University of South Carolina Press. (originally published by University of Chicago Press, 1949)

Tyack, D. (2003). *Seeking common ground: Public schools in a diverse society.* Cambridge, MA: Harvard University Press.

Tyack, D., Lowe, R., & Hansot, E. (1984). *Public schools in hard times: The great depression and recent years.* Cambridge, MA: Harvard University Press.

Waghid, Y. (2014). *African philosophy of education reconsidered: On being human.* New York: Routledge.

Wahlman, M. S. (2001). *Signs and symbols: African images in African American quilts.* Atlanta, GA: Tinwood Books.

Walker, D. (1829/1965). *David Walker's appeal.* C. M. Wiltse (Ed.). New York: Hill and Wang.

Walker, S. S. (Ed.). (2001). *African roots/American cultures: Africa in the creation of the Americas.* Lanham, MD: Rowman & Littlefield.

Walters, R. W. (1993). *Pan Africanism in the African diaspora: An analysis of modern Afrocentric political movements.* Detroit, MI: Wayne State University Press.

Wamala, E. (2004). Government by consensus: An analysis of a traditional form of democracy. In K. Wiredu (Ed.), *A companion to African philosophy* (pp. 435–442). Malden, MA: Blackwell.

Wells, I. B. (1892). *Southern horrors: Lynch law in all its phases*. New York: The New York Age Print.

Wesley, C. H. (1935). The reconstruction of history. *Journal of Negro History, 20*(4), 411–427.

Wesley, C. H. (1951). Carter G. Woodson—as a scholar. *The Journal of Negro History, 36*(1), 12–24.

Wesley, C. H. (1970). W.E.B. Du Bois: The historian. In J. H. Clarke, E. Jackson, E. Kaiser, & J. H. O'Dell (Eds.), *Black Titan W.E.B. Du Bois: An anthology by the editors of Freedomways* (pp. 82–97). Boston, MA: Beacon Press.

Wilder, C. S. (2013). *Ebony and ivy: Race, slavery and the troubled history of America's universities*. New York, NY: Bloomsbury Press.

Williams, C. (1974). *Destruction of Black civilization: Great issues of a race from 4500 B.C. to 2000 A.D.* Chicago, IL: Third World Press.

Williams, E. (1944/1966). *Capitalism and slavery*. New York: Capricorn Books.

Willis, B. (1998). *Adinkra dictionary: A visual primer on the language of Adinkra*. Washington, DC: Pyramid Complex.

Wiredu, K. (1995). Democracy and consensus in African traditional politics: A plea for a non-party polity. *The Centennial Review, 39*(1), 53–64.

Wiredu, K. (2001). Democracy by consensus: Some conceptual considerations. *Philosophical Papers, 30*(3), 227–244.

Wolfenstein, E. V. (2007). *A gift of the spirit: Reading the souls of Black folk*. Ithaca, NY: Cornell University Press.

Woodson, C. G. (1915). *The education of the Negro prior to 1861: A history of the education of the Colored people of the United States from the beginning of slavery to the Civil War*. New York, NY: Putnam's.

Woodson, C. G. (1919a). Negro life and history as presented in the schools. *The Journal of Negro History, 4*, 273–280.

Woodson, C. G. (1919b). *The education of the Negro prior to 1861: A history of the education of the Colored people of the United States from the beginning of slavery to the Civil War* (2nd ed.). Washington, DC: Associated.

Woodson, C. G. (1922). *The Negro in our history*. Washington, DC: Associated.

Woodson, C. G. (1925a). Ten years of collecting and publishing the records of the Negro. *The Journal of Negro History, 10*(4), 598–606.

Woodson, C. G. (1925b). *Negro Orators and their orations*. Washington, DC: Associated.

Woodson, C. G. (1928). *Negro makers of history: The story of the Negro retold*. Washington, DC: Associated.

Woodson, C. G. (1933). *The mis-education of the Negro*. Washington, DC: Associated.

Woodson, C. G. (1935). Annual report of the director. *The Journal of Negro History, 20*(4), 363–372.

Woodson, C. G. (1944). *African heroes and heroines* (2nd ed.). Washington, DC: Associated. (Original work published 1939)

Woodson, C. G. (1945). *The story of the Negro retold* (3rd ed.). Washington, DC: Associated. (Original work published 1935)

Work, M. N. (1916). The passing tradition and the African civilization. *Journal of Negro History, 1*(1). Retrieved from www.gutenberg.org/files/13642/13642-h/13642-h.htm#a1-3

Work, M. N. (Ed.). (1919). *Negro year book: An annual encyclopedia of the Negro, 1918–1919*. Tuskegee, AL: The Negro Year Book, Tuskegee Institute Press.

Work, M. N. (Ed.). (1931). *Negro year book: An annual encyclopedia of the Negro, 1931–1932.* Tuskegee, AL: The Negro Year Book, Tuskegee Institute Press.

Wynter, S. (1992). *Do not call us "Negroes": How multicultural textbooks perpetuate racism.* San Francisco: Aspire Books.

Wynter, S. (1997). Alterity. In C. Grant & G. Ladson-Billings (Eds.), *Dictionary of multicultural education* (pp. 13–14). New York: Oryx.

Wynter, S. (2000). The re-enchantment of humanism: An interview with Sylvia Wynter by David Scott. *Small Axe, 8,* 119–207.

Wynter, S. (2006). On how we mistook the map for the territory, and re-imprisoned ourselves in our unbearable wrongness of being, of Désêtre: Black studies toward the human project. In L. R. Gordon & J. A. Gordon (Eds.), *Not only the master's tools: African American studies in theory and practice* (pp. 107–169). Boulder: Paradigm.

Young, N. (2016). *President Obama, you must end the violence against peaceful water protectors at Standing Rock.* Retrieved from http://readersupportednews.org/opinion2/277-75/40574-president-obama-you-must-end-the-violence-against-the-peaceful-water-protectors-at-standing-rock

Zamir, S. (1994). "The Sorrow Songs"/"Song of Myself": Du Bois, the crisis of leadership, and prophetic imagination. In W. Sollors & M. Diedrich (Eds.), *The Black Columbiad: Defining moments in African American literature and culture* (pp. 145–166). Cambridge, MA: Harvard University Press.

Zamir, S. (1995). *Dark voices: W.E.B. Du Bois and American thought, 1888–1903.* Chicago: University of Chicago Press.

Zimmerman, J. (2004). Brown-ing the American textbook: History, psychology, and the origins of modern multiculturalism. *History of Education Quarterly, 44*(1), 46–69.

Zuberi, T. (2015). *African independence: How Africa shapes the world.* Lanham, MD: Rowman & Littlefield.

5

WHITE PROGRESSIVE EDUCATION, AFRICAN WORLDVIEW, AND DEMOCRATIC PRACTICE

Ellen E. Swartz

Be a neighbor to a human being and not a fence.

(Kenyan proverb)

Good fences make good neighbors.

(Robert Frost, "Mending Wall")

This chapter examines the ideas of White progressive philosophers and educators in the early decades of the twentieth century, the provenance of their ideas, and the connection of these ideas to the present. It offers an explanation for the limited traction of progressive democratic theories and practices in PK-12 schools and explores African worldview and cultural concepts as a viable foundation for a democratic curriculum. Scholars have referred to the term "progressive" as vague and imprecise, since both social efficiency and child-centered educators wore the progressive label in the early decades of the twentieth century (Cohen & Mohl, 1979; Graham, 1967). While our interest is to examine and offer an alternative to the latter, taking a brief look at the ideas and actions of their social efficiency peers provides insight into the dominant societal context and continuum in which both groups lived and worked.

In the early twentieth century and in step with the growing influence of modern science and industrialization, social efficiency progressives advocated the scientific management and training of students to supply the labor needs of industry; they viewed student and teacher compliance and obedience as essential to the efficiency of the factory model of schooling they sought to implement (Cremin, 1961; Kliebard, 1986). Importantly, prominent social efficiency theorists, such as G. Stanley Hall (1911), Franklin Bobbitt (1909), Leta S. Hollingworth

(1924), and Edward L. Thorndike (1914), were strongly influenced by social Darwinism and eugenics ideology. These educators published work in support of eugenics—a now discredited "science" that advocated selective breeding, segregation, anti-miscegenation laws, immigration restrictions and bans, and institutionalization and sterilization of the poor and "unfit" (Gould, 1981; Kevles, 1985; Ordover, 2003; Pickens, 1968). Along with other social efficiency educators they pursued school policies and practices that assumed a biologically determined hierarchy of human worth and ability that placed White upper-class Anglo-Saxons at the top (Selden, 1999; Winfield, 2007). To confirm this assumption, they claimed that newly developed norm-referenced assessments could measure and sort people by intelligence (Fendler & Muzaffar, 2008; Kevles, 1985; Oakes et al., 1997). Social efficiency progressives pushed this form of mental measurement in the early 1900s, which produced a groundswell of testing, sorting, ranking, and tracking of students, who then received different school experiences designed to "fit" them to their biologically determined and test-affirmed station in life (Stoskopf, 2009; Wallace & Graves, 1995; Winfield, 2007).

Bolstered by the pseudoscience of eugenics, this group of progressives planted their supremacist ideology of inborn human worth and ability into the bureaucratic structure of schooling by force-fitting the "measurement" of intelligence and ability to a bell curve. Based on their assumption that intelligence and learning capacity were determined by heredity, there was no point in having high expectations of millions of students who scored below what they determined to be average intelligence. Although few educators would admit to viewing students this way today, their participation in the current testing regime and their wide acceptance of bell-curve thinking as an accurate description of "the way it is" (most students have average intelligence, a smaller number of students are either above or below this average, and a few students have either a lot of intelligence or very little) suggest otherwise. If we want students to learn what we teach and have the possibility of success, we would *never* want the distribution of their achievement to follow a bell curve that expects—actually requires—some students to fail (Bloom, 1971). Notwithstanding pockets of resistance to high-stakes testing (Bale, 2015; Hagopian, 2014a; Karp, 2013–2014), the eugenic-informed legacy of social efficiency progressives remains firmly in place 100 years later as seen in the centrality of norm-referenced test comparisons in current education policy that continue to determine who is "gifted" and who is "at risk."

Historians tell us that at the same time, the second group of White progressives viewed teaching and learning as intellectual inquiry and wrote about engaging students in problem-solving and purposeful activities that could stimulate social imagination and cooperation (Dewey, 1899, 1915, 1938a; Cremin, 1961; Kilpatrick, 1918; Kliebard, 1986). These child-centered progressive theorists also valued science, but they wrote about science as a useful tool in solving social problems—that is, finding ways for schools to prepare students as citizens in and builders of a free and more democratic society (Bode, 1938; Coe, 1932; Counts, 1930, 1946; Dewey, 1916, 1937; Kilpatrick, 1918, 1935a; Newlon, 1939; Rugg, 1932, 1941; Tomlinson, 1997). Among these educators were a smaller group of social reconstructionists who envisioned public schools as sites for social action leading to a major restructuring of society that more equitably distributed social and economic goods (Bowers, 1964; Counts, 1932a, 1932b; Coe, 1935; Curti, 1936; Rugg, 1932).

The child-centered White progressive educators were part of organizations like the Progressive Education Association, the John Dewey Society for the Study of Education, and the Society for Curriculum Study; they operated and contributed to journals such as *Progressive Education* and *Social Frontier, A Journal of Educational Criticism and Reconstruction*, later called *Frontiers of Democracy* (Tanner, 1991; Tyack et al., 1984). Their efforts to identify schools as locations for deepening democratic practice and rethinking curriculum and pedagogy were buttressed by the advocacy of local reform-minded community groups, the economic upheaval of the Great Depression, and the work of economists and historians whose critical assessments of business practices and government's protection of property interests and private ownership lent credence to the idea that public schools should be places for the thoughtful examination of all institutions in society (Beard, 1914, 1922; Bowers, 1969; Reese, 1986, 2011). So, it appears that child-centered and social efficiency progressive educators were quite different. While historians generally support this view, how accurate is it?

Changing the Social Order

When social reconstructionist George S. Counts spoke to the Progressive Education Association (PEA) and the National Education Association (NEA) in 1932, he posed his now famous question, "Dare the school build a new social order?" He believed that educators were well positioned to advance a program of social reconstruction that would lead the way to equal opportunities and justice (Tyack et al., 1984). To do this, Counts advocated a "new" doctrine of collectivism—one that would "develop in the individual devotion to the common good" and in so doing replace the doctrine of capitalism (Counts, 1946, p. 94). He seemed unaware that collective practices had been central to the worldview, philosophies, and practices of African and other indigenous cultures for millennia. So, Counts and others explained, with the enthusiasm of adherents to a bold "new" idea, that the influence of business on school policies and practices—especially on the curriculum—generated and sustained economic inequalities that privileged the upper class at the expense of equality of opportunity, social justice, and the common good (Coe, 1935; Counts, 1932a, 1932b, 1939, 1946; Dewey, 1936). The seemingly heady ideas of social reconstructionists can be viewed—as most historian do—as a positive if idealistic response to the typically rigid school practices that trained future generations to be compliant workers, not problem-solvers and thinking leaders able to revamp inequitable social systems (Spring, 2011; Tanner, 1991).

At the same time, there was another way to view what schools do. Regardless of whether intended as a response to George S. Count's suggestion that schools build a new social order, Black educator Horace Mann Bond (1935) included this statement in his discussion of curriculum: "Let us confess that the schools have never built a new social order, but have always in all times and in all lands been the instruments through which social forces were perpetuated" (p. 168). If, as Bond proposed, schools take their cues from society, not the other way around, then racism and other forms of supremacy that were so embedded in U.S. society were at home in the curriculum. Bond cautioned that the curriculum revisions undertaken in the name of progressive reform had little possibility of changing what Black students experienced in schools unless curriculum managers and builders removed from their work "the social orthodoxies" (p. 168) based on racial inequalities that determined what they produced. As we explain and exemplify in this chapter, notwithstanding the egalitarian rhetoric of Counts and other White progressive educators—which was never matched by their actual practices—their ideas about what schools could accomplish were informed by their location at the top of an unacknowledged (by them) racial hierarchy.

A Continuum of Whiteness

Historians have correctly cast progressive educators such as John Dewey and George Counts and their organizations as liberal in philosophy and action when compared to organizations such as the America Legion, the National Association of Manufacturers (NAM), the Advertising Federation of America, and Guardians of American Education. These organizations campaigned to control the content of curriculum so that free enterprise was taught as inseparable from patriotism, good citizenship, and democracy (Rudd, 1957; Spring, 2011; Tyack et al., 1984). They used media and public forums to attack as un-American, socialist, and communist any efforts to engage students in critical inquiry related to social conditions. When compared to these groups, White progressives were different.

However, in terms of race, the differences among White educators virtually disappear in a "continuum of whiteness." This phrase refers to a range of practices that are outcomes of white supremacist ideology—all assuming dominance that ranges from literal violence to the hegemony that supports it. The term "whiteness" is used here (and throughout) to describe an ideological mind-set or way of thinking that varies from tacit support to participation in violent actions toward people of color. Not all White people have this mind-set, although a society shaped by racism white supremacy "invites" members of this group to take on this way of thinking and doing. Our point here is that a "continuum of whiteness" represents a range of actions produced by racism white supremacy.

At one end of this continuum in the early to mid-twentieth century were overt assaults and genocidal actions, such as mob attacks on Black people and communities, lynching, police/state violence, forced enrollment and deculturalization of Indigenous children in government-run boarding schools, eugenic-driven anti-immigration, sterilization, and anti-miscegenation laws, debt peonage, incarceration and forced labor, medical abuse and experimentation, terror-driven economic exploitation, and other forms of life-threatening Jim Crow that denied civil and human rights to people of African, indigenous, and Asian ancestry and all other people of color (Bennett, 1975; Du Bois, 1919; Franklin, 1995; Gould, 1981; Liliuokalani, 1898; Loewen, 2005; Lomawaima & McCarty, 2006; Mills, 2004; Spring, 1997; Coates, 2017; Washington, 2006; Wells-Barnett, 1970; Winfield, 2007).

Identifying the source of support for this well-documented violence and terror takes us to the other end of the continuum of whiteness. There we find various forms of hegemony—a term that refers to the dominant distribution of power through social, economic, political, and other cultural forces (Giroux & McLaren, 1992). These forces produce covert or less visible forms of oppression through systems of meaning that seep into the fabric of a society through interconnected sets of ideologies, everyday institutional practices, media representations, values, and assumptions (Williams, 1989). These systems of meaning are a reservoir of enough social support to feed the overt violence at the other end of the continuum. In the early to mid-twentieth century, these hegemonies included inaccurate and stereotypic media portrayals of people of color and immigrants and overtly racist and xenophobic scholarship; state-sanctioned educational curricula and instructional materials that omitted or denigrated African, Indigenous, and other people of color with misinformation and racial slurs; eugenic-driven educational practices that lowered expectations and opportunities for students of color and immigrants; limitations on Black scholarship due to white-only libraries and severely restricted publication opportunities for Black scholars; and agreed-upon historiography that supported colonial domination, Western imperialism, and the exploitation of the resources and labor of people of color throughout the world (Bond, 1934, 1935; Du Bois, 1903, 1932; Goggin, 1983, 1993; Grande, 2004; Mills, 1997; Morison & Commager, 1942; NAACP, 1939; Reddick, 1933, 1937; Semmes, 1992; Williams, 2007/1980; Winfield, 2007; Woodson, 1919). The ideas, assumptions, and work of early twentieth-century progressive philosophers and educators were informed by both ends of the "continuum of whiteness," since its "opposite ends" of violence and hegemony actually require each other, with each being unable to exist without the other. While the space between one end of the continuum and the other appears to offer choices, they all fall within a range of supremacist stances. Even though child-centered progressive educators espoused more egalitarian ideas and democratic rhetoric compared to their social efficiency peers, we demonstrate ahead how they failed to step outside the "continuum of whiteness" that encapsulated them.

A Hierarchy of Human Worth

While child-centered White progressives mentioned segregation, intolerance, educational inequalities, and the denial of rights to people of color as incompatible with democracy (Counts, 1932a, 1946, 1952; Dewey, 1934, 1938b; Kilpatrick, 1935a, 1939), they preferred gradual change. They denounced segregation as a concept, yet supported it in practice; they failed to support anti-lynching legislation or denounce violence against people of African ancestry and land theft and genocide against Indigenous people; and they advanced their child-centered practices as universal and race-neutral in a white supremacist society that they refused to acknowledge, much less challenge (Margonis, 2007, 2009; Taylor, 2004; West, 1989). In his discussion of John Dewey and race, Shannon Sullivan (2003) explains that Dewey's failure to acknowledge and confront racism amounted to supporting it. Sullivan wrote, "The disregard of race in a racist world is not a neutral position because its effects are not neutral" (p. 124). In other words, White child-centered educators like Dewey made pronouncements describing their democratic visions without acknowledging that educational and other inequalities were undemocratic outcomes of white supremacy (Du Bois, 1932, 1935; Bond, 1934, 1935; Thompson, 1935a, 1935b; Woodson, 1919, 1925). They espoused democracy and denounced inequalities in their progressive journal, entitled *Social Frontier, A Journal of Educational Criticism and Reconstruction*, between 1934 and 1939 (Swartz, 2007). Yet during those six years there was only one article that called for full equality—including anti-lynching legislation and an end to all forms of racial segregation and discrimination (Lovestone, 1938)—and only one essay by a Black author about the severe obstacles experienced by Black research scholars in the South (Reddick, 1937). This almost total exclusion of Black voice—along with other contradictory and gradualist actions—shows that White progressive educators held fast to their (unacknowledged by them) socially assigned position in the racial hierarchy of human worth. Their claim to a democratic agenda was contradicted by their practices.

Hegemonic Use of the Academic Canon

The Afrocentric theoretical concepts and culturally informed principles described in Chapter 2 were formalized after the early to mid-twentieth-century progressive movement, yet most of these concepts and principles were familiar to scholars in the early decades of the twentieth century. For example, academic canons have long required scholars to be attentive to evidence and accurate scholarship, and to provide substantive portrayals of topics and avoid distortions. The concepts of maintaining history and heritage and the principle of critical thinking were also valued by scholars during the progressive era. However, what seemed outside the understanding of White scholars, even democratically oriented progressive ones, was that these familiar practices of scholarship were applicable to *all* cultures and groups. For example, John Dewey wrote and spoke about racial inequalities as unjust. Yet, in the scholarly work of his Chicago years for which he is most noted, he still adhered to genetic inheritance as explaining variations in societies; he held a linear view of historical development as occurring in stages that positioned modern civilization (read European/white) as the most advanced and far beyond all others, which he viewed as socially undeveloped and deficient (Fallace, 2010, 2015; Margonis, 2009; Sullivan, 2003). While Dewey (1916) did not support biological determinism—or for that matter mental measurement that categorized students and denied their individuality (Selden, 1999; Tomlinson, 1997), he definitely viewed "others" as being at lower stages of human development (Fallace, 2010, 2015; Sullivan, 2003). In so doing, he located himself at the top of a racial hierarchy, which reveals his ignorance (or ignoring) of Black scholarship on African Diasporan history and culture published during the same period (Cooper, 1892/1969; Du Bois, 1903, 1915; Lynch, 1913; Woodson, 1915; Work, 1916). Dewey and his progressive peers made both selective and hegemonic use of the academic canon. In so doing, they demonstrated lack of familiarity with the principle of a Collective Humanity recognized by Black scholars of that era. This principle serves as an epistemic foundation for understanding that there is no hierarchy of human worth that places some groups above others.

White progressives also did not apply the principle of Indigenous Voice to all groups, so they spoke *about* and *for* "others." While Black philosophers and educators called for ending the institutionally supported racial hierarchy in education and all other social, political, and economic arenas (Bond, 1935; Du Bois, 1903, 1935; Locke, 1935; Woodson, 1933), their White progressive counterparts called only for changing attitudes through education in order to foster tolerance and cultural pluralism (Dewey, 1936; Goodenow, 1975, 1977a, 1978, 1981; Kilpatrick, 1935b, 1939).

Both Northern and Southern White progressive educators failed to see Black people as normative subjects of their own experiences, with those in the South being blatant about their adherence to a racial hierarchy. They even managed to use the progressive rhetoric of tolerance, equal opportunity, and learning by doing to revise curriculum built around the assumption of white superiority and the maintenance of racial segregation (Goodenow, 1975, 1978). In efforts to modernize education in the South following Reconstruction, their racist agenda was clear, with representations of Black people in curriculum that contained racial slurs, stereotypes, distortions, and justifications of economic exploitation (Cooking and Sewing, 1899; Division of Instruction, 1937; Georgia Department of Education, 1937; Washburne, 1942). The findings of a 1933 study by Lawrence D. Reddick of American history textbooks used in the South revealed a similar pattern of representing Black people through stereotypes, distortions, and justifications of economic exploitation during and after the *Maafa* (the European enslavement of African people).

George S. Counts

While more outspoken than most social reconstructionists about the need for equality among the races, George S. Counts (1922, 1938, 1946) exemplified the ways in which White progressives adhered to a hierarchy of human worth. In fact, his epistemological rendition of progressivism belied his stated commitment to a democratic society. For example, he decried mob violence, exploitation, and the denial of opportunities to the original inhabitants and people of African ancestry, yet in the same text extolled, with eurocratic flair, the European conquest of the Americas (1946). He acknowledged the right of European settlers to decide their fate and control their lives, yet he didn't apply the same principle of self-determination to Indigenous and African Peoples whose sovereignty was trampled by those settlers. In *School and Society in Chicago* (1928) Counts failed to include Black people at a time when Chicago's Black population had significantly increased due to Southern migration, and restrictive housing covenants had produced segregated communities and schools. Counts did include Black people in *The Prospects of American Democracy* (1938), but only as victims of discrimination, not as men and women whose ideas and practices advanced American democracy (Bond, 1934, 1935; Cooper, 1892/1969; Du Bois, 1903, 1924; Thompson, 1935a, 1935b; Woodson, 1928, 1933/1990).

In a 1922 study of high school students, Counts compromised accurate scholarship when he proffered inaccurate assumptions of Black family life *even though they were unsupported by his study's findings.* He claimed that Black families were "notoriously unstable" and that "the home is not the center of stimulation and inspiration that it is among other groups in the population" (p. 122). Yet, his study found that Black students showed less indecision about their expectations following graduation and higher expectations of going to college than White students. In an apparent attempt to explain the gap between his assumptions and the study's findings, Counts referred to the "struggle for secondary education" of Black students in St. Louis as an exception—as *"really unique* in the annals of American education" (p. 122, emphasis added).

Counts also failed to acknowledge that he worked in the same organizations, on the same boards, and on the same social issues with Black people. For example, during Counts's tenure as president of the American Federation of Teachers (AFT) between 1939 and 1943, New York City social studies teacher Layle Lane was one of the union's vice presidents. In 1940 she was a Counts supporter in a hotly contested AFT convention, and was the only representative from the New York local who was elected to the Executive Council because she was a Counts supporter (Iversen, 1959). As chair of the Human Relations Committee, Lane wrote articles for *The American Teacher*, the AFT organ, during and after Counts's tenure as president (e.g., 1941a, 1941b, 1944, 1945–1953). The two educators also appear together in a newspaper photograph and article about a 1953 AFT convention at which Counts was a speaker in support of the union amending their constitution to end segregated locals (Schierenbeck, 2000–2001, p. 16). Yet, Counts fails to reference Lane and her work as well as the work of other Black educators and leaders, such as Doxey Wilkerson (1934, 1939), Robert C. Weaver (1946, 1948), and Ralph Bunche (1936), who also served on the AFT Executive Council, on commissions, and/or at conventions that Counts attended (Eaton, 1975; Berleman, 1944; Schierenbeck, 2000–2001). Related to people of color, Counts's exclusion of Black scholarship and leadership in advancing democracy; his inclusion of Black people only as victims; his unquestioned acceptance of European/White conquest, domination, and manifest destiny; and his exogenous and false assumptions about Black family life exhibit unacknowledged agreement with a racial hierarchy that positions Euro-Americans at the top.

John Dewey and William Heard Kilpatrick

John Dewey (1927, 1938a) and William Heard Kilpatrick (1935b, 1939) both followed a cautious and gradualist approach to ending racial inequalities (Tyack et al. 1984; Margonis, 2009). In fact, neither took issue with segregated elementary and secondary schools (Goodenow, 1977b, 1981; Kluger, 2004). In *Schools of To-morrow* (Dewey & Dewey, 1915), John Dewey and his daughter Evelyn Dewey extolled the policies, structural efficiencies, pedagogy, and ways in which the public school system in Gary, Indiana, served the community—including European immigrants. Based on Evelyn Dewey's observations, Gary schools were run democratically based on the needs of students and community, and represented an example of progressive educational theories successfully put into practice. The Deweys failed to mention or express any concern, however, that schools in Gary were segregated, with schools for Black students being significantly underfunded and understaffed compared to White schools (Cohen & Mohl, 1979). In the same text the Deweys described another segregated public school—No. 26 in a poor Black community in Indianapolis—as having "a bad reputation for lawlessness and disorder" (p. 209). Here students learned by doing, they said, with the school supplying "opportunities for useful work" (p. 216) to meet the needs of students and their community. All academic courses were tied to the school's focus on the vocational skills needed by students to earn a living. In neither case do the authors take issue with legal segregation, education for Black children as only training for vocations, or the racist policies and practices in Indianapolis that facilitated and maintained the conditions in the Black community which they viewed and called the school's "immoral surroundings" (p. 210). Thus, in the book's presentation of segregated public schools that they considered successful applications of John Dewey's theories about democratic school practices, there was no critique of the undemocratic policy and practice of segregation, which the authors seemed to accept as practical and expedient. It appears that the racial hierarchy of human worth that segregation represented—with its objectives of economic exploitation, political disenfranchisement, and the maintenance of raced roles and status—was too assumed (yet unacknowledged) to produce any critique in the white world of their experience.

In 1951 William Heard Kilpatrick was asked by the NAACP to testify in *Briggs v. Elliott*, a school desegregation case in South Carolina that was the first of five cases to become part of *Brown v. Board* (1954). He declined, saying that he looked forward to an end to segregation, but added,

> I must confess that I seriously doubt the wisdom of seeking to have the Courts attempt to abolish at this stage the existing segregation in the elementary and secondary schools. I fear the results in the South would put back the long-run cause. I think some time is necessary first to digest the change at the highest level.
>
> *(Quoted in Kluger, 2004, p. 336)*

Kilpatrick's concern that Southern White people needed to "digest the change" is an example of the gradualism required to maintain a hierarchy of human worth. To claim that people in power, and those who support them, aren't "ready"—in this case to end segregation—is a strategy for putting off any change that might challenge the relations of power and the privilege of those at the top of the hierarchy.

Thus, both Dewey and Kilpatrick wrote in favor of equality of opportunity, yet advocated that the racially privileged be tolerant and of good will and that the racially oppressed accept current racial conditions in a process of orderly and gradual change. Dewey and Kilpatrick were not alone. White child-centered progressives typically failed to consider the knowledge, experiences, insights, and actions of Black people, let alone the scholarship and agency of Black philosophers and educators (Margonis, 2009; Swartz, 2007). In their published work, it was as if Black people existed only to exemplify an egalitarian nadir, and Black scholars and educators didn't exist at all.

For Their Time

There is a well-worn caveat that asks us to consider scholarship on its own terms and in its own time—to avoid what Bernard Bailyn (1960) has called viewing the past as "simply the present writ small" (p. 9). With this in mind, shouldn't we measure White child-centered educators by the norms of their era? Weren't they progressive "for their time"? To these questions we respond, "Whose norms and whose time?" It is risky at best to excuse earlier work by suggesting that there is a common way to read and understand the past or the present. While there are dominant or agreed-upon readings, there are not common readings of either one. Race, class, and gender supremacies provide a good example. As seen by people who experience them—not by those who consciously or dysconsciously perpetuate them—(King, 1991, 2015) supremacies of the past *are* the present writ small. While specifics differ due to the sensibilities and politics of each era, the *experience* of racist, sexist, and other supremacist ideologies and related practices remains the same (Davis, 2014; Chomsky & Yancy, 2015; McVeigh, 2014; Quigley, 2015; Shabazz, 2013). Critiquing earlier authors who exhibited racial privilege from the vantage point of the present acknowledges the dominance they exhibited in the past, and is an effort to avoid replicating it in the forms it takes in the present. Importantly, as we have seen in the work of Black scholars and educators during the same period (see Chapter 4), they did not accept racially privileged positions as normative. While their educational ideas, interests, and practices—as well as their approaches to bringing about change—varied, their work has consistently reflected the idea of a common humanity—that there is no hierarchy of human worth. As for individual White progressive philosophers and educators, we note that this chapter's assessment of their work exemplifies a systemic indictment of whiteness as a location of white supremacy more than a critique of individuals (Mills, 2004). That said, we are all responsible for how we locate ourselves when studying and writing about any topic, and it *is* possible for White educators and scholars to avoid collapsing into a mind-set of whiteness, with Herbert Aptheker (1951/1968, 1951/1969, 1974, 1976/1990, 1993) and Robert Farris Thompson (1983, 1990, 1993, 1999) coming at once to mind.

Worldview and Cultural Continuity

As discussed in Chapter 1, standard historical accounts provide cultural continuity for Americans of European descent, which explains the regular references made by White progressive educators, and the historians who write about them, to the work of earlier European scholars, philosophers, and movements in education. For instance, who can imagine a discussion of the child-centered approaches of early to mid-twentieth-century progressive educators without references to European Enlightenment philosophers and educators, such as Jean-Jacques Rousseau or Johann Heinrich Pestalozzi (Fallace, 2015)? As stated in the language of today, Rousseau's *Émile* (1762) and other writings espoused ideas about learning as developmental, teachers as facilitators of knowledge, and the value of children exploring their own interests and drawing their own conclusions (Darling, 1993; Rousseau, 1933). Pestalozzi built on Rousseau's philosophy and advanced ideas such as learning through observation and self-activity/action, the inner dignity of each child, love as a foundation for learning, and encouraging children to arrive at their own answers through exploration, self-discipline, and inquiry (Brühlmeier, 2010; Kilpatrick, 1951; Silber, 1960). The philosophies and practices of these men, like the White progressive educators who later built on their work, were clearly on the fringe of the societies in which they lived. Rousseau's *Émile* was banned and burned in eighteenth-century France and he was forced to live in exile for several years; and Pestalozzi's late eighteenth-century efforts to use his method for educating poor children either failed or attracted minimal support until much later in his life.

Our point here is that the work of both Rousseau and Pestalozzi was in many ways a departure from the central tendencies of a European worldview exhibited by other European philosophers and educators of their day. They did not conform their thinking to commonly held dogmas about the nature of man and how to educate children (Stewart & McCann, 1967). For example, Rousseau wrote about man as born free (in contrast to the doctrine of original sin) and that man and nature were connected and in harmony—ideas that contradicted European cosmology and a worldview of nature as alien, hostile, and existing to be conquered and controlled (Akbar, 1984; Dixon, 1971). He proposed that children came into the world good, and that the role of educators was to facilitate the development of that nature. Unlike his contemporaries, Pestalozzi thought that both poor and rich children should be educated, that excessive use of authority was unjust and obstructed a child's autonomy to learn, and that observation and reason led to children arriving at their own solutions; and he proposed that love was required for children to develop the inherent good within them (Brühlmeier, 2010; Kilpatrick, 1951; Silber, 1960). Both men denounced social injustice—at least in their own societies—and seemed less bound by the assumption of genetically endowed human worth than their peers. It should be noted, however, that their dependency on aristocratic regimes and patrons who themselves depended on eighteenth- and nineteenth-century colonial domination and chattel slavery for their wealth and power was the social, economic, and political context in which they worked and lived their lives. Thus, while their theories stepped aside from some of the central tendencies of a European worldview, they nonetheless reaped the benefits of Europe's "right to rule" and the worldview that supported it.

As discussed earlier, the same was true for White progressive educators like John Dewey (1915, 1916), George Counts (1932b, 1939), and William Heard Kilpatrick. By contesting authoritarian, obedience-seeking, and student-ranking practices, these progressive philosophers and educators did depart from some of the central tendencies of a European worldview. Yet, their positions on race and unacknowledged compliance with the racial hierarchy are seen in their approval of and participation in the segregated schools that put their progressive theories into practice—private schools located in suburban and rural areas (e.g., Marietta Johnson School for Organic Education in Fairhope, Alabama; Arthurdale in Arthurdale, West Virginia); elite lab schools at urban universities (Dewey's Laboratory School at the University of Chicago and the Lincoln School at Teachers College Columbia in New York) whose student profiles were White middle- and upper-class; and segregated public school systems (e.g., Winnetka in Illinois, Pasadena in California, Gary in Indiana, Denver in Colorado) (Cohen & Mohl, 1979; Condliffe Lagemann, 1989; Heffron, 1999; Margonis, 2009; Newman, 1999;

Zilversmit, 1993). In other words, a number of private and public schools incorporated progressive theories and practices designed to foster a more democratic society at the same time as adhering to the undemocratic practices of racial segregation and class privilege. Yes, segregation was typical in the South and North during the progressive era, but claiming interest in a more democratic society at the same time as supporting legal practices that deny democracy to millions of citizens raises an important question: Who were White child-centered progressive educators trying to benefit with a "more democratic society"? Who were they seeking to center? Rhetoric notwithstanding, the cultural continuity of their Euro-American experience paved the way for participation in a racial hierarchy of human worth. In a white supremacist society White progressives remained within a "continuum of whiteness," along with their social efficiency peers and other more conservative White educators.

Today

Child-centered ideas that date to the eighteenth century still have currency in the twenty-first century. Yet, this approach to education does not currently have a strong presence in U.S. education. There are only about 50 private schools defining themselves as based on progressive principles, and public schools, with few exceptions, exhibit practices that favor state-sanctioned curricula, high-stakes testing, tracking, and behavior modification practices that seek obedience and compliance (About education, 2015; Au, 2009; Johnson, 2015; Kohn, 2000, 2008; Little, 2013; Pianta et al., 2007). Even so, educators continue to theorize, practice, and advocate ways to expand democratic and inquiry-based approaches, and to limit practices that position students as passive receivers of information. Much of their work follows in the tradition of Dewey, Counts, Kilpatrick, and others, with more recent monikers (from the 1960s to the present) like open classrooms, constructivist teaching, experiential education, relational pedagogy, and connected learning (Apple, 1999; Bowers, 1969; Brooks & Brooks, 1999; Brownlee & Berthelsen, 2008; Fishman & McLaren, 2000; Higgins, 2009; Ito et al., 2013; Kim, 2005; Kilpatrick, 1951; Kohn, 1999; Meier, 1994, 1995). What is striking about these student-centered approaches in PK-12 schools, since the progressive days of the early twentieth century, is that they have appeared and disappeared as if through a revolving door that turns on shifting political, social, and economic winds. Educator Larry Cuban (2004) has described these shifts as educational trends that mirror social and political changes in the general society from one decade to another.

Today, progressive approaches are found in some classrooms and taught in some education courses, yet most schools and teacher preparation programs have bent under government pressure to foster teaching that purportedly aims to leave no child behind while racing to the top of some test-determined hierarchy designed to do the opposite (Au, 2009; Bale, 2015; Hagopian, 2014b; Karp,

2013–2014; Kumashiro, 2015; Ravitch, 2010, 2013; Winfield, 2007). As of this writing, early reviews of NCLB's 2015 replacement—Every Student Succeeds Act (ESSA), which won't be fully implemented until the 2017–2018 school year—describe the new act as more flexible than NCLB, but also suggest that ESSA is not fundamentally different in terms of policy initiatives that can significantly improve teaching and learning experiences for the most vulnerable students (Battenfield & Crawford, 2015; Severns, 2015). Also, after several years of protest, Common Core State Standards are being reexamined, with recommendations for replacement in a number of states (Bidwell, 2015; Taylor, 2015). Yet, even with these changes—which appear more cosmetic than substantive—scripted curriculum, tracking, and excessive student testing tied to teacher evaluations remain ensconced in most education systems, with predictable outcomes. These authoritarian and antidemocratic policies and practices, which reflect the eugenic practices of the early twentieth century, are now cloaked in the equal opportunity language of "reform" and bear down hardest in urban schools. When students, teachers, and schools don't meet these one-size-fits-all measures, current educational systems punish such "failures" with job loss, labels of deficiency, harsh discipline policies and practices, state takeovers, and school closures that threaten to replace public schools with charter schools at public expense (Au et al., 2013; Farrell, 2010; Karp, 2013–2014; Hagopian, 2014b; Kumashiro, 2008; Ravitch, 2013; Winfield, 2007). While we agree with Larry Cuban (2004) that educational trends mirror social and political changes in the general society from one decade to another, we ask, "What explains the persistence of compliance-driven practices and the revolving door of progressive practices in schools?"

Cultural Continuity

Molefi Kete Asante (1993) explains that "we inherit a unified field of culture," meaning that culture is "one whole fabric of the past" that is passed on from one generation to the next (p. 140). Thus, even with internal regional variations (e.g., in Africa, in Europe, in Asia) and cross-cultural influences, broad cultural groups represent unified contexts that result in continuity across time and location. Europeans and their descendants view cultural continuity as given; it is understood as the way in which the heritage and legacy of Western civilization are transmitted to them. In Chapter 4 we discussed this continuity to explain the shaping and maintaining of school norms informed by European worldview elements and cultural concepts that Europeans brought with them to the Americas. The more democratic and egalitarian ideas of Euro-American educators have been and remain marginalized, but their ideas are still contained within that cultural field. These progressive educators seek to change the form of an ineffective system—to make an authoritarian, agreed-upon, compliance-driven system less so. Their challenge to the hierarchy of human worth is limited to nonexistent, which places them within the continuum of whiteness discussed earlier. White progressive educators understand that children need to inquire, think critically, discover, problem solve, and use their imaginations; and they know that there is a connection between the absence of these school experiences and a citizenry largely compliant with societal practices that are not in the best interest of individuals, let alone the common good. Yet, stepping outside the continuum of whiteness rarely occurs since it would require knowledge of another worldview(s) and a willingness to seek guidance from thinkers and practitioners whose work embodies diverse cultural bases that view *knowing as a communal experience in which everyone has something to contribute* and *self as defined in relation to others* (Berrigan & Hanh, 1975; King & Swartz, 2016; Nguyễn Vũ Hoàng, 2009; Nkulu-N'Sengha, 2005). With the support of worldviews and cultural concepts more compatible with the collective achievement of academic and cultural excellence and the development of good character, school knowledge and the pedagogies used to teach it can locate *all* students and their families and communities at the center of the learning experience (Hilliard, 2003; Karenga, 1999, 2006a, 2006b; King, 2006).

What drives the educational system we have inherited, however, is a worldview that obstructs achieving academic and cultural excellence and the development of good character for all students. Think about how Competition, Individualism (the "I" is more important than the "We"), and Survival of the Fittest (ontological orientations) affect achievement. Think about how excessive use of authority (an epistemology), a hierarchy of human worth and individual mindedness (values), and the assumption that there is a scarcity of resources (principle) affect how educators view the possibility of developing self-knowledge and good character as a communal practice. These worldview elements become apparent in cultural concepts that sound all too familiar: *achievement understood as excelling above others, competition as essential to making progress, expecting and accepting a certain amount of student failure, distributing resources by status/rank (based on the assumption that there isn't enough to go around), teaching as the transmission of agreed-upon information,* and *perceiving mistakes as negative and leading to loss* (Fendler & Muzaffar, 2008; King & Swartz, 2016). These are the cultural concepts that shape what we do in school—and the policies that support them—such as scripted curriculum (state-sanctioned knowledge), transmission pedagogy, norm-referenced high-stakes assessments, behavior modification control strategies, and tracking (Au, 2009, Au et al., 2013; Bale, 2015; King & Swartz, 2016; Kohn, 2000; Oakes, 1985; Ravitch, 2010). In the absence of other worldview influences and concepts—and even when White progressive educators try to do otherwise—their best-laid theories and practices are marginalized by a European worldview, concepts, and practices that have been carried forward from one generation to the next. It is this cultural continuity that keeps both standard and progressive ideas encased in the cultural field that produced them.

There are, however, other worldviews and cultural concepts to consider. The African worldview and the cultural concepts that express it—which are ancient and accessible—have been/are typically unknown by Europeans and their descendants—even those who go against the grain of commonly held educational ideas and practices in Europe and the United States. There is a similar lack of knowledge about Indigenous American, East and South Asian, and other world-views and cultural concepts that could be part of transforming school policies and practices that fail to meet the needs of all children (Berrigan & Hanh, 1975; Cajete, 1994, 2001; Grande, 2004; Nguyễn Vũ Hoàng, 2009; Nhat Hanh, 2001, 2008; Mohawk, 1993, 2002). We have selected the African worldview and cultural concepts as the cultural foundation of a model that demonstrates the support needed to produce more scholarly, inclusive, and democratic curricula that center all children, not only some.

African Cultural Foundation

If school curriculum—which includes content and pedagogy as well as the ways of knowing, being, and doing that schools promulgate—is to be responsive to *all* students, we need to learn from a worldview that can support this outcome. We propose that an African worldview—and the cultural concepts and produc-tions that express it—has the capacity to produce such democratized curriculum and learning environments due to its communal, relational, and interdependent characteristics. One way to explore this is to consider Steven Covey's Habit 2: Begin With the End in Mind (2005)—that is, to envision what most of us cur-rently don't know about or can't see. Covey explains that phenomena are created twice, once through the mind and then in practice. We interpret this to mean that our role here is to offer knowledge in the form of mental pictures based on African Diasporan scholarship. Then, with support and collaboration, PK-12 practitioners can turn these pictures—this knowledge—into practice. The mental pictures we provide ahead are drawn from the cultural productions and practices of specific African cultures and can guide the creation of learning environments that foster academic and cultural excellence and the development of good character.

Maat

Maat is an ancient Kemetic (Egyptian) philosophy with seven Cardinal Virtues (Truth, Justice, Harmony, Balance, Order, Reciprocity, and Propriety) that define excellence as an ethical ideal (Asante, 2011; Hilliard, 1997; Karenga, 2006a). As the foundation of Kemetic spirituality and ethics, *Maat* defines African axiological commitments to community-mindedness, service to others, human welfare, right action, equanimity, and the sacredness of both the spiritual and the material (Anyanwu, 1981; Gyekye, 1987; Karenga, 1980, 2006b; Obenga, 1989). Scholar-ship on *Maat* is extensive, varied, and complex; and it provides insight into the process of developing order, rightness, justice, and harmony in the universe and in oneself. As such, *Maat* offers a context for discussing, identifying, and attaining standards of excellence.

For example, if we want to teach children to know, respect and protect all forms of life—to sustain themselves, their communities, and the planet—we would teach that life is whole and interconnected. This involves valuing the general welfare and engaging in reciprocal and sustainable ways of thinking and acting that benefit the common good. Teaching in social studies guided by *Maat* can produce accurate, inclusive, and indigenously voiced scholarship that includes the effects of past practices on the natural world and encourages students to envision sustainable practices in the present. Students can read and discuss oral and written text (ELA) to learn about how all life is connected and how people are responsible to maintain, not disrupt, the balance and harmony that exist in the natural world. The arts and music can foster experiences of connection and reciprocal interactions so that students can feel/experience interconnectedness. And science and mathematics can be contexts for discovering the harmony, balance, and order in the natural world.

Maat teaches that an "an *interrelated order of rightness*" exists in the universe (Karenga, 1999, p. 7, italicized in the original). With such an understanding, achieving academic and cultural excellence is not a competition. It is not *achievement understood as excelling above others, competition as essential to making progress*, and *expecting and accepting a certain amount of student failure*. These eurocratic cultural concepts result in standards that fail to produce excellence since failure is expected and some students gain at the expense of others. In practices informed by *Maat*, academic excellence and cultural excellence are outcomes of reciprocal, relational, and interdependent experiences. Individual excellence is linked to the excellence of the group because there is *sharing responsibility for communal well-being and belonging, knowing as a communal experience in which everyone has something to contribute*, and *gaining knowledge for the purpose of bringing goodness, harmony, and balance into the world* (Gyekye, 1987, 1997; Nkulu-N'Sengha, 2005; King & Swartz, 2016, p. 120). These African cultural concepts and the worldview elements they express can be part of structuring learning environments that intend to draw out from our children their individual and collective excellence.

Odù Ifá

The *Odù Ifá* is the sacred wisdom text of the Yoruba People (Nigeria). Its ethical teachings are found in a text of 256 *Odù* (chapters) and many *ese* (verses) of poems, proverbs, stories, chants, and ethical narratives that reflect Yoruba cosmology, epistemology, and communal values (Abímbólá, 1976a, 1976b; Karenga, 1999). As quoted from our previous text (King & Swartz, 2016, p. 6),

> the *Odù Ifá is* based on the principles of a well-ordered universe able to provide insights into every human action (Abímbólá, 1976a; Karenga, 2005).

The African worldview elements evident in the *Odù Ifá* are representative of the ways of being and knowing, values, principles, and virtues that African people brought with them to the Americas (Hazzard-Donald, 2012). For example, *Odù* 202:1 refers to "the principle of grouping together" that defines how all forms of life are gathered in groups "[s]o that the goodness of togetherness could come forth at once. Indeed all goodness took the form of a gathering together in harmony."

(Karenga, 1999, pp. 361, 364)

Maulana Karenga (2006b) explains that this "goodness of togetherness" refers to sharing what is good:

the great goods of freedom, justice, love, family, friendship, sisterhood, brotherhood, a life of peace, a life of dignity and decency, and the world itself are all shared goods. And they are not real if only some people are deemed worthy of them or worthier than others.

(pp. 269–270)

Notice that the *Odù Ifá* is a Yoruba cultural production that was created due to the presence and support of African worldview elements (e.g., Collectivity, Interdependence, empathy, right action, community-mindedness) expressed in cultural concepts such as *gaining knowledge for the purpose of bringing goodness, harmony, and balance into the world*; *demonstrating concern for human welfare through actions based on community-mindedness and service to others*; *pursuing freedom and justice as communal responsibilities*; and *love, dignity and decency as shared by all* (Fu-Kiau, 2001; Gyekye, 1987; Karenga, 1999, 2006b; King & Swartz, 2016, p. 120; Nkulu-N'Sengha, 2005; Waghid, 2014). If we want to teach children to develop good character and bring good into the world, we would give them opportunities to experience harmony, justice, community-mindedness, love, and dignity as shared goods in the classroom. In other words, the *Odù Ifá* teaches that good character (which includes good behavior) is a collective endeavor. In a classroom this means that we begin by acknowledging the goodness in all students and developing content and emancipatory pedagogies that draw out that collective good.

In contrast, eurocratic cultural concepts do not produce good character as a shared good. Concepts such as *valorizing individual identity over group identity*; *understanding good behavior as controlled behavior due to rules, rewards, and punishments*; *teaching as transmission of agreed-upon information*; and *perceiving mistakes as negative and leading to loss* fail to produce good behavior since "bad" behavior is assumed and agreed-upon information typically omits examples of historical figures who exemplify good character *as a shared good*. In a classroom framed by concepts in the *Odù Ifá*, good character would be taught through examples of men and women (e.g., Benjamin Banneker, Audrey Shenandoah, Austin Steward, Harriet Tubman, Canassateego, Septima Clark, Oren Lyons, Rosa Parks) who exhibited good character by showing that freedom, justice, love, brotherhood, sisterhood, a life of peace, and a life of dignity and decency can exist only when everyone experiences them. In other words, there is no justice, no sisterhood, no freedom, and so forth if only some people experience them.

You can have students identify the character qualities of historical figures who lived by this inclusive principle of a shared good, and think about how such qualities led these men and women to develop life commitments to right action. You can also ask students to identify which character qualities of an historical figure(s) they also see in themselves and to give examples (oral and/or written). This is a way for students to gain self-knowledge and to experience connections between themselves and their ancestors. The knowledge gained from African texts like the *Odù Ifá* is a foundation on which to build classroom learning environments that intend to produce good character as a collective and shared experience.

Adinkra

Adinkra is an indigenous Akan (West African) script whose many symbols express Akan philosophical concepts. These symbols are epistemic expressions or visual markers of Akan cosmology, values, cultural concepts, and practices (Arthur, 2001). Akan symbols are stamped on fabric used to make clothing for funereal services and ceremonies (Willis, 1998). The Akan understand death as a stage in life or a transition, and Adinkra symbols give family and community members opportunities to communicate to and about the person who has passed. For example, if the person exhibited wisdom and insight, the *Matemasie* symbol could be on the fabric of a garment worn during funereal ceremonies. Akan symbols are used today in general attire, sculpture, pottery, logos, and architecture. While their use has broadened over time and place, Adinkra are enduring representations of Akan epistemology. They teach that gaining knowledge is for a purpose of developing good character, being resourceful and interdependent, and bringing excellence and harmony into the world (Gyekye, 1987; Nkulu-N'Sengha, 2005; Willis, 1998).

There are many Adinkra symbols that can be used to teach the positive qualities needed to develop good character. After learning about these symbols, students can select one that represents qualities they see in themselves. They can write an essay, speech, or poem/rap, and/or use/create images to show how the selected symbol represents them. They can select a symbol that represents a family member or ancestor and tell a story about that person to explain how s/he exhibits the quality(ies) of that symbol. Students might pair Adinkra symbols with historical figures. For example, what Adinkra symbols represent the character traits of Harriet Tubman and why do you think so? Ahead are some Adinkra symbols presented in *The Adinkra Dictionary* by W. Bruce Willis (1998) that can be used to teach about good character and to facilitate its development among all students in your classroom (Figures 5.1–5.6).

FIGURE 5.1 *Ananse Ntontan*

Ananse Ntontan (ah-nan-see n-to-n-tan): **The Spider's Web**—This Adinkra symbol stands for wisdom and creativity. The spider Ananse of African folklore fame is a small yet resourceful insect that weaves an intricate web to feed and protect itself. This symbol represents how individuals can creatively use the resources they have to bring good to themselves and their community.

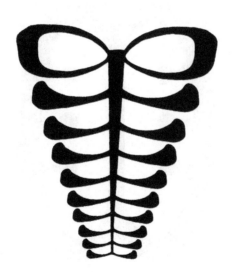

FIGURE 5.2 *Aya*

Aya (ah-yah): **The Fern**—This Adinkra symbol stands for endurance, independence, hardiness, perseverance, and resourcefulness. *Aya* is a hardy fern plant that grows in rough terrain yet survives. Its toughness represents the resourcefulness and endurance that individuals and communities need to survive and prosper.

FIGURE 5.3 *Dwennimmɛn*

Dwennimmɛn (djwin-knee-mann): **Ram's Horns**—This Adinkra symbol stands for strength of mind, body, and soul and for wisdom, humility, and learning. The ram uses its powerful horns to not only protect itself but also avoid conflict and seek peace. For people to excel, strength is understood as having integrity—heart wisdom—that comes from learning and humility, not forcefulness.

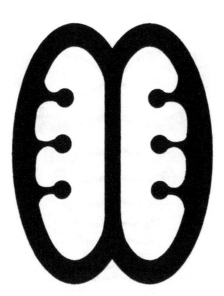

FIGURE 5.4 *Ɛse Ne Tɛkrɛma*

Ɛse Ne Tɛkrɛma (s-e knee teh-kra-mah): **The Teeth and the Tongue**—This Adinkra symbol stands for improvement, growth, and the need for friendliness and interdependence. The appearance of a child's teeth signals the growth of the child. Growth and improvement are needed to prosper and occur in the interdependent context of families and communities.

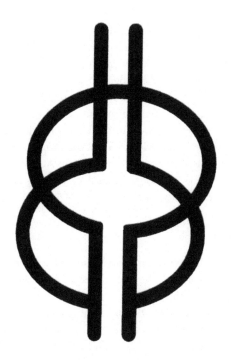

FIGURE 5.5 *Nyansapɔ*

Nyansapɔ (n-yahn-sah-poh): **Wisdom Knot**—This Adinkra symbol stands for intelligence, patience, and ingenuity. An Akan proverb says, "It is the wise who unties the wisdom knot." This means that it takes intelligence, patience, and being intuitive and imaginative to understand the meaning of an idea and apply that to achieving a practical goal.

FIGURE 5.6 *Ɔsram*

Ɔsram (o-srahm): **The Moon**—This Adinkra symbol is about leadership. It stands for understanding, patience, and determination, and having faith in oneself and growing through experiences. Just as the full moon, tides, and sunrise occur when they are ready, leadership abilities, understanding, and influence require the "patience" of time and seeing beyond the present.

You have probably noticed that most of the foregoing Adinkra symbols are visual markers based on observations of the natural world. This Akan epistemology (observation over time as a way of knowing) produced understandings, insights, and values about how to live and be together in families and community—how to learn, grow, and persevere, and how to be strong, patient, and resourceful. In addition to guiding students to see the qualities of good character in themselves and others, we can use these symbols to teach students that nature has been and continues to be a source of knowledge from which to learn. By now you have probably thought of several other ways to use these Adinkra symbols in addition to those suggested earlier. We look forward to hearing about them! You can write us at omnicentricpress@gmail.com.

Proverbial Wisdom

Proverbs are a way of knowing or epistemology that Vernon J. Dixon (1971, 1976) calls symbolic imagery. They are collected wisdom over time—distilled into short expressions of the philosophy, cosmology, and values of a People. For example, the Akan proverb "One head does not hold a discussion" (Kwame, 1995, p. xxxi) is the metaphoric essence of a concept about the collaboration that it takes to consider, examine, and analyze a topic. One head cannot do this. Congolese scholar Kimbwandende Kia Bunseki Fu-Kiau (2001) refers to African proverbs as a philosophical language having a law-like quality that communicates social theories, norms, principles, and values. Proverbs teach about all facets of life—about eldership, ways to know and learn, the interconnectedness of all life, unity, justice, complementarity, communal responsibility, right action, and right relationships. While proverbs are a form of oral literature, many have been collected and written down. We have selected and discussed two proverbs from Central African cultures to exemplify how proverbs can guide teaching for academic and cultural excellence and the development of good character.

• **Bântu-Kôngo** (Central Africa)
  Within the community everybody has the right to teach and to be taught. Education is a matter of reciprocity. True knowledge is acquired through sharing (Fu-Kiau, 2001, pp. 99–100).
     This proverb teaches that engagement and collaboration are ways to gain knowledge, and that everyone is a participant in that process. Knowledge is not a transmission of information but an understanding gained through reciprocal interactions. This proverb reflects African worldview elements of Collaboration, Interdependence, relational knowing (learning from reciprocal interactions), and community-mindedness that are expressed in the cultural concept of *knowing as a communal experience in which everyone has something to contribute* (Fu-Kiau, 2001; Nkulu-N'Sengha, 2005). Classrooms that foster

academic and cultural excellence are communities where instruction involves partnered and group work that engages students with each other; parents and families are part of the instructional program; and educators foster right relationships among and between themselves, students, and families (Heavy-Runner & DeCellus, 2002; King & Swartz, 2016; Moll & González, 2004; Simpson, 2014). Achieving excellence is understood as an inclusive and communal experience.

• **Baluba** (Central Africa)
 The child who raises questions is the one who will gain knowledge (Mutombo Nkulu-N'Sengha, 2005, p. 42).

 This proverb teaches that inquiry is the way to gain true knowledge. The Baluba teach that there is an art to not knowing and that coming to know involves critical inquiry and a dialogue between the head and the heart. This dialogue occurs in classrooms where question-driven pedagogy (Goodwin, 2004) draws out and builds on the knowledge that students have within them. By leading with thought-provoking questions, teachers model and encourage the use of questions. This emancipatory pedagogy is grounded in African epistemology, including intuition-reasoning (learning from heart-mind knowledge, which are linked, not separate), relational knowing, and the authentic authority of eldership, which are expressed in the cultural concept *inquiring (the acknowledgment of not knowing) as a source of true knowledge.* Question-driven pedagogy positions teaching and learning as a reciprocal experience that gives students the opportunity to demonstrate agency by defining themselves and their ideas during instruction.

 This way of teaching is the antithesis of scripted curriculum, since it involves an improvisational flow between teacher and students, who basically create the curriculum together. If you ask a critical question, the ensuing interaction depends on how students respond—on what they offer and what you can do with it to extend learning (King & Swartz, 2016, pp. 45–46).

As we know from being around young children, they are naturally curious. They seem to know without being taught that questions are a way to learn what they want to know. They constantly use the Five W's, which cannot be answered by a "yes" or "no"—often to the frustration of adults. This means that young students, unlike many of us who are grown, are adept at asking critical questions. However, something happens as children progress through eurocratic systems of education that seek compliance through transmission pedagogy, scripted curricula, standardized testing, and behavior modification strategies. These school practices stifle inquisitiveness, and now it is our job to recuperate it. Remember that critical thinking is there; it just went underground. Creating an environment that values questions as a way to learn and know will bring it back to the surface.

Conclusion

In the hierarchal grand narrative of the progressive era, historians have assigned White progressive philosophers and educators of the early to mid-twentieth century as the "carriers" of educational thought that challenged standard school practices. Invisible in this grand narrative are Black philosophers and educators who stood within an African episteme to develop theories, conduct research, and publish materials that sought to improve standard school practices. Their work not only challenged (and continues to challenge) these standard practices, but also—as exemplified in the work of W.E.B. DuBois (see Chapter 4)—is an example of what African Diasporan cultural continuity produces. While an African cultural framework could have informed the theories and practices proposed by White progressive educators, using this framework would have required these educators to step outside the "continuum of whiteness"—something we have shown they were unable to do. By staying within this continuum, their access to the worldview and concepts of "others" was blocked. The lesson learned here is that transforming social institutions such as schools may require familiarity with diverse cultural sources in order to replace commonly held approaches shaped by this society's predominant worldview. Becoming familiar with African worldview and cultural concepts through the cultural productions of diverse African Peoples brings African Diasporan cultural continuity to the foreground. We propose this as a step in the direction of identifying a viable epistemic foundation that can support schools as sites of democratic practice.

References

Abímbólá, W. (1976a). *Ifá will mend our broken world: Thoughts on Yoruba religion and culture in Africa and the Diaspora.* Roxbury, MA: Aim Books.

Abímbólá, W. (1976b). *Ifá: An exposition of the Ifá literary corpus.* Ibadan, Nigeria: Oxford University Press Nigeria.

About education. (2015). *Progressive schools.* Retrieved from http://privateschool.about.com/od/progressiveschools/

Akbar, N. (1984). Africentric social sciences for human liberation. *Journal of Black Studies, 14*(4), 395–414.

Anyanwu, K. C. (1981). The African world-view and theory knowledge. In E. A. Ruch & K. C. Anyanwu (authors), *African philosophy: An introduction to the main philosophical trends in contemporary Africa* (pp. 77–99). Rome: Catholic Book Agency.

Apple, M. W. (1999). *Official knowledge: Democratic education in a conservative age* (2nd ed.). New York, NY: Routledge.

Aptheker, H. (1951/1968). *A documentary history of the Negro people in the United States: From the Reconstruction era to 1910* (Vol. 2). New York: The Citadel Press.

Aptheker, H. (1951/1969). *A documentary history of the Negro people in the United States: From colonial times through the Civil War* (Vol. 1). New York, NY: The Citadel Press.

Aptheker, H. (1974). *American Negro slave revolts.* New York, NY: International.

Aptheker, H. (1976/1990). *Early years of the republic: From the end of the revolution to the first administration of Washington (1783–1793).* New York, NY: International.

Aptheker, H. (1993). *Anti-racism in U.S. history: The first two hundred years.* Westport, CT: Praeger.

Arthur, G.F.K. (2001). *Cloth As metaphor: (Re)reading the Adinkra cloth symbols of the Akan of Ghana.* Accra, Ghana: Cefiks.

Asante, M. K. (1993). Racism, consciousness, and Afrocentricity. In G. Early (Ed.), *Lure and loathing: Essays on race, identity, and the ambivalence of assimilation* (pp. 127–143). New York, NY: Allen Lane, the Penguin Press.

Asante, M. K. (2011). *Maat and human communication: Supporting identity, culture, and history without global domination.* Retrieved from www.asante.net/articles/47/maat-and-human-communication-supporting-identity-culture-and-history-without-global-domination/

Au, W. (2009). *Unequal by design: High-stakes testing and the standardization of inequality.* New York: Routledge.

Au, W., Bigelow, B., Christensen, L., Gym, H., Levine, D., Karp, S., Miller, L., Peterson, B., Salas, K. D., Sokolower, J., Tempel, M. B., & Walters, S. (2013). The trouble with the *Common Core. Rethinking Schools, 27*(4), 4–6.

Bailyn, B. (1960). *Education in the forming of American society: Needs and opportunities for study.* Chapel Hill: University of North Carolina Press.

Bale, J. (2015). English-only to the core: What the common core means for emergent bilingual youth. *Rethinking Schools, 30*(1), 20–27.

Battenfield, M., & Crawford, F. (2015). *Why every student succeeds act still leaves most vulnerable kids behind.* Retrieved from http://theconversation.com/why-every-student-succeeds-act-still-leaves-most-vulnerable-kids-behind-46247

Beard, C. (1914). *An economic interpretation of the constitution of the United States.* New York, NY: Macmillan.

Beard, C. (1922). *The economic basis of politics.* New York, NY: Alfred A. Knopf.

Bennett, L., Jr. (1975). *The shaping of Black America.* Chicago: Johnson.

Berleman, M. (Ed.). (1944). Experts in various educational fields serve on new AFT Commission. *The American Teacher, 29*(2), 2.

Berrigan, D., & Hanh, T. N. (1975). *The raft is not the shore: Conversations toward a Buddhist/Christian awareness.* Boston, MA: Beacon Press.

Bidwell, A. (2015). *Tennessee governor signs bill stripping common core.* Retrieved from www.usnews.com/news/articles/2015/05/12/tennessee-gov-bill-haslam-signs-bill-removing-common-core-standards

Bloom, B. S. (1971). Mastery learning. In J. H. Block (Ed.), *Mastery learning: Theory and practice* (pp. 47–63). New York, NY: Holt, Rinehart and Winston.

Bobbitt, F. (1909). Practical eugenics. *The Pedagogical Seminary, 13*(3), 385–394.

Bode, B. H. (1938). *Progressive education at the crossroads.* New York, NY: Newson .

Bond, H. M. (1934). *The education of the Negro in the American social order.* New York, NY: Octagon Books.

Bond, H. M. (1935). The curriculum and the Negro child. *The Journal of Negro Education, 4*(2), 159–168.

Bowers, C. A. (1964). The *Social Frontier* journal: A historical sketch. *History of Education Quarterly, 4*(3), 167–180.

Bowers, C. A. (1969). *The progressive educator and the Depression: The radical years.* New York, NY: Random House.

Brooks, J. G., & Brooks, M. G. (1999). *In search of understanding, the case for constructivist classrooms.* Alexandria, VA: Association for Supervision and Curriculum Development.

Brownlee, J., & Berthelsen, D. (2008). Developing relational epistemology through relational pedagogy: New ways of thinking about personal epistemology in teacher education. In M. S. Khine (Ed.), *Knowing, knowledge and beliefs: Epistemological studies across diverse culture* (pp. 405–422). New York, NY: Springer.

Brühlmeier, A. (2010). *Head, heart and hand: Education in the spirit of Pestalozzi.* Cambridge, UK: Open Book.

Bunche, R. J. (1936). *A world view of race.* Washington, DC: The Associates in Negro folk education.

Cajete, G. (1994). *Look to the mountain: An ecology of Indigenous education.* Durango, CO: Kivaki Press.

Cajete, G. (2001). Indigenous education and ecology: Perspectives of an American Indian educator. In J. A. Grim (Ed.), *Indigenous traditions and ecology: The interbeing of cosmology and community* (pp. 619–638). Cambridge, MA: Harvard University Press/Center for the Study of World Religions, Harvard Divinity School.

Chomsky, N., & Yancy, G. (2015). *Noam Chomsky on the roots of American racism.* Retrieved from http://opinionator.blogs.nytimes.com/?module=BlogMain&action=Click&regio n=Header&pgtype=Blogs&version=Blog%20Post&contentCollection=Opinion

Coates, T. (2017, September). *The first White president.* Retrieved from http://readersup-portednews.org/opinion2/277-75/45770-focus-the-first-white-president

Coe, G. A. (1932). *Educating for citizenship: The sovereign state as ruler and as teacher.* New York, NY: C. Scribner's Sons.

Coe, G. A. (1935). Education as social engineering. *The Social Frontier: A Journal of Educational Criticism and Reconstruction, 1*(4), 25–27.

Cohen, R. D., & Mohl, R. A. (1979). *The paradox of progressive education: The Gary Plan and urban schooling.* Port Washington, NY: Kennikat Press, National University.

Condliffe Lagemann, E. (1989). The plural worlds of educational research. *History of Education Quarterly, 29*(2), 185–214.

Cooking and Sewing in Colored Grade School of Durham, N.C. (1899, November). *North Carolina Journal of Education, 3*, 10–11.

Cooper, A. J. (Haywood) (1892/1969). *A voice from the South, by a black woman of the South.* New York, NY: Negro Universities Press.

Counts, G. S. (1922). *The selective character of American secondary education.* Chicago, IL: The University of Chicago.

Counts, G. S. (1928). *School and society in Chicago.* New York, NY: Harcourt, Brace.

Counts, G. S. (1930). *The American road to culture: A social interpretation of education in the United States.* New York: John Day.

Counts, G. S. (1932a). *Dare the school build a new social order?* New York: John Day.

Counts, G. S. (1932b). Dare progressive education be progressive? *Progressive Education, 9,* 257–263.

Counts, G. S. (1938). *The prospects of American democracy.* New York: NY: John Day.

Counts, G. S. (1939). *The schools can teach democracy.* New York, NY: John Day.

Counts, G. S. (1946). *Education and the promise of America.* New York: Macmillan. (Originally the 17th volume of the Kappa Delta Pi Lecture Series, 1945)

Counts, G. S. (1952). *Education and American civilization.* New York, NY: Teachers College, Columbia University.

Covey, S. R. (2005). *The 7 habits of highly effective people.* Kottayam, India: DC Books.

Cremin, L. A. (1961). *The transformation of the school: Progressivism in American education 1876–1957.* New York, NY: Alfred A. Knopf.

Cuban, L. (2004). The open classroom. *Education Next, 4*(2). Retrieved from http://educationnext.org/theopenclassroom/

Curti, M. (1936). Changing issues in the school's freedom. *The Social Frontier: A Journal of Educational Criticism and Reconstruction, 2*(6), 166–169.

Darling, J.E.M. (1993). *Child-centered education and its critics.* Thousand Oaks, CA: SAGE.

Davis, B. (2014). *America's summer of white supremacy: A postmortem.* Retrieved from http:// readersupportednews.org/opinion2/277-75/26127-americas-summer-of-white-supremacy-a-postmortem

Dewey, J. (1899). *The school and society.* Chicago, IL: University of Chicago Press.

Dewey, J. (1915). *The school and society and the child and the curriculum.* Mineola, NY: Dover.

Dewey, J. (1916). *Democracy and education: An introduction to the philosophy of education.* New York, NY: Macmillan.

Dewey, J. (1927). *The public and its problems.* New York, NY: H. Holt.

Dewey, J. (1934). Can education share in social reconstruction? *Social Frontier, a Journal of Educational Criticism and Reconstruction, 1,* 11–12.

Dewey, J. (1936). Liberalism and equality. *The Social Frontier: A Journal of Educational Criticism and Reconstruction, 2*(4), 105–106.

Dewey, J. (1937). Education and social change. *The Social Frontier: A Journal of Educational Criticism and Reconstruction, 3,* 235–238.

Dewey, J. (1938a). *Experience and education.* New York: Collier Macmillan.

Dewey, J. (1938b, October 25). Democracy ailing: Dr. Dewey asserts. *New York Times,* p. 7.

Dewey, J., & Dewey, E. (1915). *School of to-morrow.* New York, NY: E. P. Dutton.

Division of Instruction, State Department of Education, Montgomery. (1937). *Report of the committee on social and economic conditions in Alabama and their implications for education.* Montgomery, AL: Alabama Education Association.

Dixon, V. J. (1971). African-oriented and Euro-American-oriented world views: Research methodologies and economics. *The Review of Black Political Economy, 7*(2), 119–156.

Dixon, V. J. (1976). World views and research methodology. In L. M. King, V. J. Dixon, & W. W. Nobles (Eds.), *African philosophy: Assumptions and paradigms for research on Black persons* (pp. 51–102). Los Angeles, CA: Fanon Research and Development Center.

Du Bois, W.E.B. (1903). *The souls of Black folks.* Greenwich, CT: Fawcett.

Du Bois, W.E.B. (1915). *The Negro.* Mineola, NY: Dover.

Du Bois, W.E.B. (1919). The real cause of two race riots. *The Crisis, 19*(2), 56–62.

Du Bois, W.E.B. (1924). *The gift of Black folk, the Negroes in the making of America.* Boston, MA: Stratford.

Du Bois, W.E.B. (1932). Education and work. *The Journal of Negro Education, 1*(1), 60–74.

Du Bois, W.E.B. (1935). Does the Negro need separate schools? *Journal of Negro Education, 4,* 329–335.

Eaton, W. E. (1975). *The American Federation of Teachers, 1916–1961: A history of the movement.* Carbondale: Southern Illinois University Press.

Fallace, T. D. (2010). Was John Dewey ethnocentric? Reevaluating the philosopher's early views on culture and race. *Educational Researcher, 39*(6), 471–477.

Fallace, T. D. (2015). *Race and the origins of progressive education, 1880–1929.* New York, NY: Teachers College Press.

Farrell, W. C., Jr. (2010). *Dismantling public education from Reagan to Obama public school privatization Race to the Top (RTTT) and Common Core.* Retrieved from Issue # 621 http://blackcommentator.com/621/621_cover_dismantling_public_education_from_reagan_to_obama_farrell_guest.html

Fendler, L., & Muzaffar, I. (2008). The history of the bell curve: Sorting and the idea of normal. *Educational Theory, 58*(1), 63–82.

Fishman, G., & McLaren, P. (2000). Schooling for democracy: Toward a critical utopianism. *Contemporary Sociology, 29*(1), 168–179.

Franklin, V. P. (1995). *Living our stories, telling our truths*. New York: Oxford University Press.

Fu-Kiau, K.K.B. (2001). *African cosmology of the Bântu-Kôngo, tying the spiritual knot: Principles of life and living*. New York, NY: Athelia Henrietta Press.

Georgia Department of Education. (1937, May). Georgia program for the improvement of instruction: Guide to curriculum improvement. *Bulletin, 2*, 25–26.

Giroux, H. A., & McLaren, P. L. (1992). Media hegemony: Towards a critical pedagogy of representation. In J. Schwoch, M. White, & S. Reilly (Eds.), *Media knowledge* (pp. XV–XXXIV). Albany: Albany State University of New York Press.

Goggin, J. (1983). Countering White racist scholarship: Carter G. Woodson and *The Journal of Negro History. The Journal of Negro History, 68*(4), 355–375.

Goggin, J. (1993). *Carter G. Woodson: A life in Black history*. Baton Rouge: Louisiana State University Press.

Goodenow, R. K. (1975). The progressive educator, race and ethnicity in the depression years: An overview. *History of Education Quarterly, 15*(4), 365–394.

Goodenow, R. K. (1977a). The progressive educator on race, ethnicity, creativity, and planning: Harold Rugg in the 1930s. *Review Journal of Philosophy and Social Science, 1*(Winter), 105–128.

Goodenow, R. K. (1977b). Racial and ethnic tolerance in John Dewey's educational and social thought: The Depression years. *Educational Theory, 26*(Winter), 48–64.

Goodenow, R. K. (1978). Paradox in progressive educational reform: The South and the education of Blacks in the depression years. *Phylon, 39*(1), 49–65.

Goodenow, R. K. (1981). The Southern progressive educator on race and pluralism: The case of William Heard Kilpatrick. *History of Education Quarterly, 21*(2), 147–170.

Goodwin, S. (2004). Emancipatory pedagogy. In S. Goodwin & E. E. Swartz (Eds.), *Teaching children of color: Seven constructs of effective teaching in urban schools* (pp. 37–48). Rochester, NY: RTA Press.

Gould, S. J. (1981). *The mismeasure of man*. New York, NY: Norton.

Graham, P. A. (1967). *Progressive education: From Arcady to academe, a history of the Progressive Education Association, 1919–1955*. New York, NY: Teachers College Press.

Grande, S. (2004). *Red pedagogy: Native American social and political thought*. Lanham, MD: Rowman & Littlefield.

Gyekye, K. (1987). *An essay on African philosophical thought: The Akan conceptual scheme*. Cambridge, UK: Cambridge University Press.

Gyekye, K. (1997). *Tradition and modernity: Philosophical reflections on the African experience*. New York, NY: Oxford University Press.

Hagopian, J. (2014a). *More than a score: The new uprising against high-stakes testing*. Chicago, IL: Haymarket Books.

Hagopian, J. (2014b). The testocracy versus the education spring. In J. Hagopian (Ed.), *More than a score: The new uprising against high-stakes testing* (pp. 7–27). Chicago, IL: Haymarket Books.

Hall, G. S. (1911). *Educational problems*. New York: D. Appleton.

Hazzard-Donald, K. (2012). *Mojo Workin': The old African American Hoodoo system*. Urbana, Chicago: University of Illinois Press.

HeavyRunner, I., & DeCellus, R. (2002). Family education model: Meeting the student retention challenge. *Journal of American Indian Education, 41*(2), 29–37.

Heffron, J. M. (1999). The Lincoln School of Teachers College: Elitism and educational democracy. In S. F. Semel & A. R. Sadovnik (Eds.), *"Schools of Tomorrow," schools of today: What happened to progressive education* (pp. 141–170). New York, NY: Peter Lang.

Higgins, P. (2009). Into the big wide world: Sustainable experiential education for the 21st century. *Journal of Experiential Education, 32*(1), 44–60.

Hilliard, A. G. III (1997). *SBA: The reawakening of the African mind.* Gainesville, FL: Makare.

Hilliard, A. G. III (2003). No mystery: Closing the achievement gap between Africans and excellence. In T. Perry, C. Steele, & A. Hilliard, III (Eds.), *Young, gifted, and Black: Promoting high achievement among African American students* (pp. 131–165). Boston: Beacon Press.

Hollingworth, L. S. (1924). Provisions for intellectually superior children. In M. V. O'Shea (Ed.), *The child: His nature and his needs* (pp. 277–299). New York, NY: The Children's Foundation.

Ito, M., Gutiérrez, K., Livingstone, S., Penuel, B., Rhodes, J., Salen, K., Schor, J., Sefton-Green, J., & Watkins, S. C. (2013). *Connected learning: An agenda for research and design.* Retrieved from http://eprints.lse.ac.uk/48114/1/__lse.ac.uk_storage_LIBRARY_Secondary_libfile_shared_repository_Content_Livingstone,%20S_Livingstone_Connected_learning_agenda_2010_Livingstone_Connected_learning_agenda_2013.pdf

Iversen, R. W. (1959). *The communists and the schools.* New York, NY: Harcourt, Brace.

Johnson, H. (2015). *Welcome from the Head of School [Waverly School].* Retrieved from http://thewaverlyschool.org/about-us/welcome-from-the-head-of-school/

Karenga, M. (1980). *Kawaida theory.* Los Angeles, CA: Kawaida.

Karenga, M. (1999). *Odù Ifá: The ethical teachings.* Los Angeles: University of Sankore Press.

Karenga, M. (2005). Odù Ifá. In M. K. Asante & A. Mazama (Eds.), *Encyclopedia of Black studies* (pp. 388–390). Thousand Oaks, CA: SAGE.

Karenga, M. (2006a). *Maat, the moral ideal of ancient Egypt: A study in classical African ethics.* New York, NY: Routledge.

Karenga, M. (2006b). Philosophy in the African tradition of resistance: Issues of human freedom and human flourishing. In L. R. Gordon & J. A. Gordon (Eds.), *Not only the master's tools: African American studies in theory and practice* (pp. 243–271). Boulder, CO: Paradigm.

Karp, S. (2013–2014). The problems with the common core. *Rethinking Schools, 28*(2), 10–17.

Kevles, D. J. (1985). *In the name of eugenics: Genetics and the uses of human heredity.* Berkeley: University of California Press.

Kilpatrick, W. H. (1918). The project method. *Teachers College Record, 19*, 319–335.

Kilpatrick, W. H. (1935a). Loyalty oaths—a threat to intelligent teaching. *The Social Frontier: A Journal of Educational Criticism and Reconstruction, 1*(9), 10–15.

Kilpatrick, W. H. (1935b). Resort to courts by Negroes to improve their schools a conditional alternative. *The Journal of Negro Education, 4*(3), 412–418.

Kilpatrick, W. H. (1939). Education and intolerance. *The Social Frontier: A Journal of Educational Criticism and Reconstruction, 5*(45), 230–231.

Kilpatrick, W. H. (1951). Introduction to *The education of man, aphorisms* (J. H. Pestalozzi, author). New York, NY: Greenwood Press.

Kim, J. S. (2005). The effects of a constructivist teaching approach on student academic achievement, self-concept, and learning strategies. *Asia Pacific Education Review, 6*(1), 7–19.

King, J. E. (1991). Dysconscious racism: Ideology, identity, and the miseducation of teachers. *Journal of Negro Education, 60*(2), 133–146.

King, J. E. (2006). "If justice is our objective": Diaspora literacy, heritage knowledge and the praxis of critical studyin' for human freedom. *Yearbook of the National Society for the Study of Education, 105*(2), 337–360.

King, J. E. (2015). *Dysconscious racism, Afrocentric praxis, and education for human freedom: Through the years I keep on toiling, the selected works of Joyce E. King.* New York, NY: Routledge.

King, J. E., & Swartz, E. E. (2016). *The Afrocentric praxis of teaching for freedom: Connecting culture to learning.* New York, NY: Routledge.

Kliebard, H. M. (1986). *The struggle for the American curriculum 1893–1958.* New York, NY: Routledge.

Kluger, R. (2004). *Simple justice: The history of Brown v. Board of Education and Black America's struggle for equality.* New York, NY: Knopf. (Original work published 1976 by Alfred A. Knopf)

Kohn, A. (1999). *The schools our children deserve.* Boston, MA: Houghton Mifflin.

Kohn, A. (2000). *The case against standardized testing: Raising the scores, ruining the schools.* Portsmouth, NH: Heinemann.

Kohn, A. (2008). *Progressive education.* Retrieved from www.alfiekohn.org/article/progressive-education/

Kumashiro, K. (2008). *The seduction of common sense: How the right has framed the debate on America's schools.* New York, NY: Teachers College Press.

Kumashiro, K. (2015). *Against common sense* (3rd ed.). New York, NY: Routledge.

Kwame, S. (1995). *Readings in African philosophy: An Akan collection.* New York, NY: University Press of America.

Lane, L. (1941a). The Negro and national defense. *The American Teacher, 25*(7), 39–41.

Lane, L. (1941b). Negro teachers win fight for equal pay. *The American Teacher, 25*(6), 5–6.

Lane, L. (1944). Why not introduce high school students to some Negro publications? *The American Teacher, 29*(3), 15.

Lane, L. (1945–1953). The human relations front (48 monthly columns). *The American Teacher, 30*(2)–*37*(8).

Liliuokalani. (1898). *Hawaii's story by Hawaii's Queen Liliuokalani.* Boston, MA: Lee and Shepard.

Little, T. (2013). *Hubbard Woods, Winnetka, Illinois.* Retrieved from http://parkdaytom.blogspot.com/2013/05/hubbard-woods-winnetka-ill.html

Locke, A. (1935). The dilemma of segregation. *The Journal of Negro Education, 4*(3), 406–411.

Loewen, J. W. (2005). *Sundown towns: A hidden dimension of American racism.* New York, NY: New Press.

Lomawaima, K. T., & McCarty, T. L. (2006). *To remain an Indian: Lessons in democracy from a century of native American education.* New York, NY: Teachers College Press.

Lovestone, J. (1938). Toward the American commonwealth: IX. new frontiers for labor. *The Social Frontier: A Journal of Educational Criticism and Reconstruction, 5*(39), 54–59.

Lynch, J. R. (1913). *The facts of reconstruction.* New York, NY: Neale.

Margonis, F. (2007). John Dewey, W.E.B. Du Bois, and Alain Locke: A case study in white ignorance and intellectual segregation. In S. Sullivan & N. Tuana (Eds.), *Race epistemologies and ignorance* (pp. 173–195). New York: State University of New York Press.

Margonis, F. (2009). John Dewey's racialized visions of the student and classroom community. *Educational Theory, 59*(1), 17–39.

McVeigh, K. (2014). *Equal pay for US women taken up by Senate as study highlights gender gap.* Retrieved from http://readersupportednews.org/news-section2/314-18/23016-equal-pay-for-us-women-taken-up-by-senate-as-study-highlights-gender-gap

Meier, D. (1994). A talk to teachers. *Dissent,* (Winter), 80–87.

Meier, D. (1995). *The power of their ideas.* Boston, MA: Beacon Press.

Mills, C. W. (1997). *The racial contract.* Ithaca, NY: Cornell University Press.

Mills, C. W. (2004). Racial exploitation and the wages of whiteness. In G. Yancy (Ed.), *What White looks like: African American philosophers on the whiteness question* (pp. 25–54). New York, NY: Routledge.

Mohawk, J. (1993). Coming to wholeness: Native culture as safe place. *Akwe: kon, A Journal of Indigenous Issues, 10*(4), 31–36.

Mohawk, J. (2002). Nurturance is the responsibility of the nation and the people. *Native Americas, 14*(3 & 4), 58–62.

Moll, L. C., & González, N. (2004). Engaging life: A funds-of-knowledge approach to multicultural education. In J. A. Banks & C. A. McGee Banks (Eds.), *Handbook of research on multicultural education* (2nd ed., pp. 699–715). San Francisco, CA: Jossey-Bass.

Morison, S. E., & Commager, H. S. (1942). *The growth of the American republic* (Vol. 1, 3rd ed.). New York: Oxford University Press.

NAACP (National Association for the Advancement of Colored People). (1939). *Anti-Negro propaganda in school textbooks.* New York, NY: The National Association for the Advancement of Colored People.

Newlon, J. H. (1939). *Education for democracy in our time.* New York, NY: McGraw-Hill Book.

Newman, J. W. (1999). Experimental school, experimental community: The Marietta Johnson School of Organic Education in Fairhope, Alabama. In S. F. Semel & A. R. Sadovnik (Eds.), *"Schools of Tomorrow," schools of today: What happened to progressive education* (pp. 67–101). New York, NY: Peter Lang.

Nguyễn Vũ Hoàng, V. (2009). *Contrasting of English and Vietnamese addressing forms.* Retrieved from www.google.com/url?sa=t&rct=j&q=&esrc=s&source=web&cd=4&ved=0CDg QFjAD&url=http%3A%2F%2Fkhoaanh.net%2F_upload%2FCA2009%2FCqBT05_ Nguyen_Vu_Hoang_Van_Contrasting_of_English_and_Vietnamese_addressing_forms. docx&ei=6ptKVN79HvWCsQTIpoHoDQ&usg=AFQjCNFWRViB0g0ZgkGIfhdWgl I5UOtZLw&sig2=Iqkx2V7RvU3VAzdEOjSlzg

Nhat Hanh, T. (2001). *Thich Nhat Hanh essential writings.* Maryknoll, NY: Orbis Books.

Nhat Hanh, T. (2008). The environment is you: A talk by Thich Nhat Hanh—Denver, Colorado, August 29, 2007. *Human Architecture: Journal of the Sociology of Self-Knowledge, 6*(3), 15–20.

Nkulu-N'Sengha, M. (2005). African philosophy. In M. K. Asante & A. Mazama (Eds.), *Encyclopedia of Black studies* (pp. 45–52). Thousand Oaks, CA: SAGE.

Oakes, J. (1985). *Keeping track: How schools structure inequality.* New Haven, CT: Yale Press.

Oakes, J., Wells, A. S., Jones, M., & Datnow, A. (1997). Detracking: The social construction of ability, cultural politics, and resistance to reform. *Teachers College Record, 98*(3), 482–510.

Obenga, T. (1989). African philosophy of the Pharaonic period (2780–330 B.C.) (Excerpt from a work in translation). In I. Van Sertima (Ed.), *Egypt revisited* (2nd ed., pp. 286–324). New Brunswick, NJ: Transaction.

Ordover, N. (2003). *American eugenics: Race, queer anatomy, and the science of nationalism.* Minneapolis: University of Minnesota Press.

Pianta, R. C., Belsky, J., Houts, R., & Morrison, F. (2007, March 30). Opportunities to learn in America's elementary classrooms. *Science, 315*(5820), 1795–1796.

Pickens, D. K. (1968). *Eugenics and the progressives.* Nashville, TN: Vanderbilt University Press.

Quigley, B. (2015). *40 reasons our jails and prisons are full of Black, brown, and poor people.* Retrieved from http://readersupportednews.org/opinion2/277-75/30547-focus-40-reasons-our-jails-and-prisons-are-full-of-black-brown-and-poor-people

Ravitch, D. (2010). *The death and life of the great American school system: How testing and choice are undermining education.* New York, NY: Basic Books.

Ravitch, D. (2013). *Reign of error: The hoax of the privatization movement and the danger to America's public schools.* New York, NY: Alfred A. Knopf.

Reddick, L. D. (1933). *Racial attitudes in the South's American history textbooks.* Nashville, TN: Fisk University.

Reddick, L. D. (1937). Research barriers in the South. *The Social Frontier: A Journal of Educational Criticism and Reconstruction, 4*(30), 85–86.

Reese, W. J. (1986). *Power and the promise of school reform: Grassroots movements during the progressive era.* Boston, MA: Routledge & Kegan Paul.

Reese, W. J. (2011). *America's public schools: From the common school to "no child left behind."* Baltimore, MD: The John Hopkins University Press.

Rousseau, J.-J. (1933). *Émile* (Barbara Foxley, Trans.). London: J. M. Dent & Sons. (Original work published 1762)

Rudd, A. G. (1957). *Bending the twig: The revolution in education and its effect on our children.* New York, NY: New York Chapter Sons of the American Revolution.

Rugg, H. O. (1932). Social reconstruction through education. *Progressive Education, 9*(8), 11–18.

Rugg, H. O. (1941). *That men may understand: An American in the long armistice.* New York, NY: Doubleday, Doran.

Schierenbeck, J. (2000–2001, Winter). Lost and found: The incredible life and times of (Miss) Layle Lane. *American Educator, 24*(4), 4–19.

Selden, S. (1999). *Inheriting shame: The story of eugenics and racism in America.* New York, NY: Teachers College Press.

Semmes, C. E. (1992). *Cultural hegemony and African American development.* Westport, CT: Praeger.

Severns, M. (2015). *Congress set to dump no child left behind.* Retrieved from www.politico.com/story/2015/11/no-child-left-behind-education-bush-congress-216291

Shabazz, S. (2013). *Black Louisiana town latest victim of "environmental racism."* Retrieved from www.finalcall.com/artman/publish/health_amp_fitness_11/article_100643.shtml

Silber, K. (1960). *Pestalozzi: The man and his work.* London: Routledge and Kegan Paul.

Simpson, L. B. (2014). Land as pedagogy: Nishnaabeg intelligence and rebellious transformation. *Decolonization: Indigeneity, Education & Society, 3*(3), 1–25.

Spring, J. (1997). *Deculturalization and the struggle for equality: A brief history of the education of dominated cultures in the United States.* New York, NY: McGraw-Hill.

Spring, J. (2011). *The American school: A global context from the Puritans to the Obama era* (8th ed.). Boston, MA: McGraw-Hill.

Stewart, W. A. C., & McCann, W. P. (1967). *The educational innovators, 1750–1880.* New York, NY: Macmillan.

Stoskopf, A. (2009). The forgotten history of eugenics. In W. Au (Ed.), *Rethinking multicultural education: Teaching for racial and cultural justice* (pp. 45–51). Milwaukee, WI: Rethinking Schools.

Sullivan, S. (2003). (Re)construction zone. In W. Gavin (Ed.), *In Dewey's wake: The unfinished work of pragmatic reconstruction* (pp. 109–127). Albany: State University of New York Press.

Swartz, E. E. (2007). Stepping outside the master script: Re-connecting the history of American education. *The Journal of Negro Education, 76*(2), 173–186.

Tanner, D. (1991). *Crusade for democracy: Progressive education at the crossroads.* Albany: State University of New York Press.

Taylor, K. (2015). *Cuomo panel calls for further retreat from common core standards.* Retrieved from www.nytimes.com/2015/12/11/nyregion/cuomo-task-force-signals-further-retreat-from-common-core-school-standards.html?_r=0

Taylor, P. C. (2004). Silence and sympathy: Dewey's whiteness. In G. Yancy (Ed.), *What White looks like* (pp. 227–241). New York, NY: Routledge.

Thompson, C. H. (1935a). Court action the only reasonable alternative to remedy immediate abuses of the Negro separate school. *The Journal of Negro Education, 4*(3), 419–434.

Thompson, C. H. (1935b). The Association for the Study of Negro Life and History. *The Journal of Negro Education, 4*(4), 465–467.

Thompson, R. F. (1983). *Flash of the spirit: African and Afro-American art and philosophy.* New York, NY: Random House.

Thompson, R. F. (1990). Kongo influences on African American artistic culture. In J. E. Holloway (Ed.), *Africanisms in American culture* (pp. 148–184). Bloomington: Indiana University Press.

Thompson, R. F. (1993). *Face of the Gods: Art and altars of Africa and the African Americas.* New York, NY: Museum of African Art.

Thompson, R. F. (1999). An aesthetic of the cool: West African dance. In G. Dagel Caponi (Ed.), *Signifyin(g), sanctifyin', & slam dunking: A reader in African American expressive culture* (pp. 72–86). Amherst: University of Massachusetts Press. (originally printed in *African Forum*, 1966)

Thorndike, E. L. (1914). Eugenics: With special reference to intellect and character. In L. James Wilson (Ed.), *Eugenics: Twelve university lectures* (pp. 319–342). New York, NY: Dodd, Mead.

Tomlinson, S. (1997). Edward Lee Thorndike and John Dewey on the science of education. *Oxford Review of Education, 23*(3), 365–383.

Tyack, D., Lowe, R., & Hansot, E. (1984). *Public schools in hard times: The great depression and recent years.* Cambridge, MA: Harvard University Press.

Waghid, Y. (2014). *African philosophy of education reconsidered: On being human.* New York, NY: Routledge.

Wallace, B., & Graves, W. (1995). *Poisoned apple: The bell curve crisis and how our schools create mediocrity and failure.* New York, NY: St. Martin's Press.

Washburne, C. W. (1942). Preamble to Chapter IX, "summary of recommendations in regard to Negro education." In C. S. Johnson (researcher), *The Negro public schools: A social and educational survey* (pp. 239–241). Baton Rouge, LA: Louisiana Educational Survey Commission.

Washington, H. A. (2006). *Medical apartheid: The dark history of medical experimentation on Black Americans from colonial times to the present.* New York, NY: Doubleday.

Weaver, R. C. (1946). *Negro labor, a national problem.* New York, NY: Harcourt, Brace.

Weaver, R. C. (1948). *The Negro ghetto.* New York, NY: Harcourt, Brace.

Wells-Barnett, I. B. (1970). *Crusade for justice: The autobiography of Ida B. Wells.* A. M. Duster (Ed.). Chicago, IL: University of Chicago Press.

West, C. (1989). Black culture and post modernism. In B. Kruger & P. Mariani (Eds.), *Remaking history* (pp. 87–96). Dia Art Foundation Discussions in Contemporary Culture, No. 4. Seattle, WA: Bay Press.

Wilkerson, D. (1934). Racial differences and scholastic achievement. *Journal of Negro Education, 3*, 453–477.

Wilkerson, D. (1939). *Special problems of Negro education (staff study number 12 prepared for The Advisory Committee on Education).* Washington, DC: U.S. Government Printing Office.

Williams, R. (1989). Hegemony and the selective tradition. In S. DeCastell, A. Luke, & C. Luke (Eds.), *Language, authority, and criticism, readings on the school textbook* (pp. 56–60). New York, NY: Falmer Press.

Williams, W. A. (2007/1980). *Empire as a way of life.* Brooklyn, NY: Ig.

Willis, W. B. (1998). *Adinkra dictionary: A visual primer on the language of Adinkra.* Washington, DC: Pyramid Complex.

Winfield, A. G. (2007). *Eugenics and education in America: Institutionalized racism and the implications of history, ideology, and memory.* New York, NY: Peter Lang.

Woodson, C. G. (1915). *The education of the Negro prior to 1861: A history of the education of the Colored people of the United States from the beginning of slavery to the Civil War.* New York, NY: Putnam's.

Woodson, C. G. (1919). Negro life and history as presented in the schools. *The Journal of Negro History, 4*, 273–280.

Woodson, C. G. (1925). Ten years of collecting and publishing the records of the Negro. *The Journal of Negro History, 10*(4), 598–606.

Woodson, C. G. (1928). *Negro makers of history: The story of the Negro retold.* Washington, DC: Associated.

Woodson, C. G. (1933). *The mis-education of the Negro.* Washington, DC: Associated.

Work, M. N. (1916). The passing tradition and the African civilization. *Journal of Negro History, 1*(1). Retrieved from www.gutenberg.org/files/13642/13642-h/13642-h.htm#a1-3

Zilversmit, A. (1993). *Changing schools: Progressive education theory and practice, 1930–1960.* Chicago, IL: University of Chicago Press.

6

A CALL FOR A REPARATORY JUSTICE CURRICULUM FOR HUMAN FREEDOM

Rewriting the Story of Our Dispossession and the Debt Owed

Joyce E. King

The axe forgets; the tree remembers.

(African proverb)

You can't have a healthy democracy without an enlightened citizenry.

(Randall Robinson, 2013)

A Dedication. This chapter is dedicated to the memory of Celia, an enslaved 19-year-old, who was hanged in 1855 for killing the White man who had repeatedly raped her since he purchased her at the age of 14 (McLaurin, 1991), and Randall Robinson, author of *The Debt: What America Owes to Blacks.*

This chapter begins in Part 1 with three vignettes that illustrate our cultural dispossession or "Heritage Knowledge Denied." Such cultural dispossession results from miseducation and underscores that African American and global movements for reparations need to emphasize the importance of heritage knowledge in education for human freedom. Next, Part 2, "Rewriting the Story of Our Dispossession," presents five premises of a reparatory justice curriculum approach. These premises illustrate the importance of accurate scholarship informed by African epistemology and wisdom. Part 3, "The Debt Owed," situates this task of rewriting knowledge within the global movement for reparations and the work of the National African American Reparations Commission in particular. Part 4, "(Mis)Representing Slavery in a Global Online Game and Other Teaching Materials," presents four examples that illustrate the need for a reparatory justice curriculum approach: (mis)representations and distortions regarding African American enslavement in a controversial U.S. high school textbook, an online instructional video game created in Europe, a children's picture book, and demeaning classroom pedagogy. These examples illustrate that a debt is owed not only for centuries of enslavement, dehumanization, and stolen labor but also for ongoing wounds inflicted by miseducation that continue to obstruct human freedom.

Part 1: Heritage Knowledge Denied

Heritage knowledge, as I explained in a previous publication, "is a cultural birthright of every human being" (King, 2006, p. 345). It refers to group memory, and like what John Henrik Clarke referred to as "heritage teaching," permits "a people to develop an awareness and pride in themselves so that they can achieve good relationships with other people" (Clarke, 1994, p. 86). Three vignettes provide examples of heritage knowledge that is being denied to African Americans.

Vignette #1

Several years ago I was a panelist at a National Summit on Race and Racism in Chicago. There were about 250 people—mostly African Americans—present. Many were Chicago residents. I began my presentation by asking, "Does anyone here know about the 'Brown Condor'"? One hand was raised. I learned later that the person who raised his hand was a local Bronzeville (the historic South Side Black community) historian. He was the only one who indicated that he knew of the Ace World War II pilot, Colonel John C. Robinson, the "African American aviator and activist who was hailed as the 'Brown Condor' for his service in the Imperial Ethiopian Air Force against Fascist Italy" (Brownlee, 2012, p. 316). (For an image of Colonel John C. Robinson, see www.tadias.com/12/07/2012/understanding-mississippis-brown-condor.)

In New York City in May 1936, a rally of more than 5,000 people celebrated Colonel Robinson's return to the United States from Ethiopia. The next day in Chicago,

> Robinson, in an open limousine, led a procession of 500 cars from the airport to the South Side . . . A *Chicago Defender* reporter wrote without exaggeration how "Chicago [had] welcomed home its hero of the Ethiopian war Sunday afternoon when more than twenty thousand men, women, and children joined in a rip-roaring reception for Colonel John C. Robinson, the 'Brown Condor' of Emperor Haile Selassie's Royal air force" . . . and literally covered himself in glory, trying to preserve the independence of the last African empire.
>
> *(Tucker, 2012, n.p.)*

Today, however, his legacy is not taught and young people are not likely to identify with Africa's plight the way his generation did (Magubane, 1987). It also is worth noting that the Italian air force that Colonel Robinson fought to resist Italian colonization during the war had come to Chicago earlier in 1933. Italo Balbo, minister of fascist Italy's vaunted air force, "led a squad of 24 silver seaplanes on a transatlantic voyage, landing on Lake Michigan during the Chicago World's Fair of 1933, known as the Century of Progress" (Ackman & Schwarz, 2008, n.p.). A crowd of 1 million cheering Chicagoans welcomed the Italian pilots.

Vignette #2

In 1979 when my son was 6 years old and in the first grade, the Black school board in our district made Malcolm X's birthday a holiday. My son came home from school and reported that his teacher had told his class how much she disagreed with the district policy of making Malcolm X's birthday a holiday "because he had been sent to prison." I asked my son what he thought about what his teacher had said to the class. He said, "I think we should celebrate Malcolm X's birthday for a whole month because when he went to prison, he improved himself." Fascinated that a first-grader had such revolutionary thoughts, I asked him where he got that idea. He told me, "Baba Vulindlela taught us that in after-school." He was referring to the African-centered homeschool program my children attended after their day in public school. Vulindlela I. Wobogo (2011), an instructor/lecturer and Black Studies scholar at San Francisco State University and the City College of San Francisco, and his wife, Nozipo, provided children and families in East Palo Alto, California, where we lived, with an African-centered education in their homeschool/after-school program in the 1970s. The lesson Baba Wobogo taught the children about Malcolm X is a very good example of African epistemology and wisdom that a reparatory justice curriculum approach can provide. This example also suggests that families and communities will need to be organized to provide supplemental learning experiences beyond what is available in public schools settings.

Vignette #3

Recently, a member of my research group shared what her 8-year-old daughter said after learning what the Confederate flags flying outside of Atlanta represent. My colleague said she had explained to her daughter, "This flag stands for people who wanted to keep slavery." This child of two well-educated African American parents replied, "I wouldn't have minded being a slave. They had clothes, a place to live, and food to eat." This child's response is the same kind of justification for slavery that White student teachers in my classes proffered in the 1980s. Now, decades later, if only one individual among a gathering of politically conscious and engaged African American activists in a major Black metropolis like Chicago indicated knowing about the contributions to African liberation someone like Colonel John Robinson achieved in the last century, just 80 years ago, how can we expect young people in this generation to be capable of acting on behalf of African people's interests today? What legacy of heritage knowledge are we passing on to the children—not just about what was done to us but also about African people's agency and our humanity? Or shall our children remain defenseless against ubiquitous national narratives of forgotten, distorted, and erased history in American schools? What does "a reparatory justice curriculum for human freedom" look like? What must "rewriting the story of our dispossession and the debt owed" entail?

Part 2: Rewriting the Story of Our Dispossession

A reparatory justice curriculum requires accurate scholarship informed by African epistemology and wisdom to undo the mystifying, well-worn, ideological narratives of our dispossession that are justified by our so-called inferiority. This chapter demonstrates the importance of engaging both academic and community scholars to recover missing narratives of African people's agency and humanity affirmed by our own voices. Following are five premises of such a reparatory justice curriculum approach:

1. *Our story does not begin with enslavement but with humanity's origins in Africa* and thousands of years of our existence before either Arabs or Europeans enslaved people of African ancestry (King & Goodwin, 2006).
2. *The narrative that "Africans selling Africans" made European slaving possible is incomplete and therefore distorts history in several ways.* There is ample scholarship available to support this premise. First, Molefi Asante poses several questions to refute the prevailing orthodoxy that African people were either equally or primarily responsible for the European slave trade. Asante asks the following:

   • "Who traveled to Africa in search of captives?" "Who created an entire industry of shipbuilding, insurance, outfitting of crews and ships, and banking based on the slave trade?"
   • "Who benefited enormously from the evil and vile project of human kidnapping?"
   • "What countries held the Asiento from the Catholic Church and the King of Spain for regions of Africa used exclusively for capturing Africans?" (Asante, 2010)

Asante further explains: "There is no denying that some African peoples did assist the Europeans." However, these instances of collaboration represent "aberrations over a 300-year history" that amount not to African Peoples' generalized support for the European slave trade but to their minor role "vis-à-vis white slave traders."

Second, Saidiya Hartman (2007), another professor of African Studies, emphasizes, "In order to betray your race, you first had to imagine yourself as one. The language of race developed in the modern period and in the context of the slave trade" (p. 6). Notwithstanding the cultural unity of Black Africa (Diop, 2000), which carries the collective worldview and cultural concepts present in African epistemology, the diverse nations and ethnic groups from whom captives were taken did not understand their identity in pan-ethnic terms—as one racial or African family. Neither did the British, French, Dutch, Portuguese, and so forth understand themselves in pan-ethnic, racial terms as White Europeans, though the concept and practice of white supremacy racism evolved in the context of European enslavement.

Third, African understandings and experiences of free and servile status differed markedly from these categories among Europeans (Konadu, 2015; Nti, 2010). Prior to the European incursion, servitude in Africa included prisoners of war and wrongdoers, which bore no resemblance to chattel slavery in the Americas, with its dehumanizing bondage in perpetuity (Davidson, 1961). Moreover, in *Songhoy-senni*, the language of the West Africa's last great classical civilization and empire, as well as in the Twi language of Ghana, there is no indigenous word for prisons.

There was no word for prisons because prisons did not exist prior to the European presence (DeWolf, 2009; Maïga, 2010). Rather, those people who had lost their freedom and the protection and status afforded by their lineage through warfare or as punishment for wrongdoing were consigned to domestic servitude. Conversely, freedom and elevation in social status could be gained through hard work, merit, and ingenuity that brought benefit to the head of the household, who valued and rewarded such achievements.

Fourth, as European nations advanced into Africa in the fifteenth century, their strategy of economic control and divide and conquer tactics involved ongoing provocation of internal conflicts, weapons trade, and purposeful devaluing of local currencies (Davidson, 1961). As European-instigated wars and demand for captives intensified, African societies were significantly altered. The resulting social upheaval and political breakdown over the course of several centuries made it possible for Europeans to institute an extensive system of race-based chattel slavery that had never existed in Africa. Nor has there ever existed a slave-based African economy. In this culturally distorted context—and as Asante (2010) explained earlier—a small number of Africans played minor roles in European-financed raiding, capturing, and trading of others, sometimes in self-defense. But as Hartman points out, "they did not sell their brothers and sisters into slavery. They sold strangers"—that is to say, lineage-less persons—"outside the web of kin and clan relationships, nonmembers of the polity, foreigners and barbarians at the outskirts of their country, and lawbreakers expelled from society" (p. 5).

Thus, the prevailing narrative of slavery in school textbooks and academic scholarship collapses these different cultural conceptions and practices by referring to them with the same term—"slavery" (King, 1991). King and Swartz (2016) discuss assumptions and implications of the grand narrative of slavery (pp. 69–72). Without access to local language meanings, indigenous historical accounts, and the range of practices from domestic servitude to chattel slavery to hereditary castes, this prevailing narrative erroneously suggests that slavery is inherently African and that both Africa and Euro-America are equally responsible for the holocaust experienced by the former that brought benefits and worldwide dominance to the latter (Stern, 2007).

3. *Rewriting the debt owed requires a method of knowledge construction using accurate scholarship that affirms our own voices as well as our family-community consciousness as sources of validation.* Affirming the power of African Peoples' epistemological standpoints and narratives—that is, our indigenous wisdom and theorizing—must be informed by the study of African languages, which is essential for the recovery of our group memory, our cultural truths, historical consciousness, and heritage knowledge (Kunnie, 2006).

4. *After European enslavement and importation of Africans directly from the continent were outlawed, chattel slavery devolved into the lucrative business of domestic slave trading.* This business depended upon slave breeding in the United States that was fueled by legalized rape, and it propelled the forced movement of millions of enslaved African American men, women, and children who were "sold south." Enslaved concubinage, which was integral to this business of breeding and trafficking enslaved African Americans, was "explained away by what has become known as the 'Jezebel libel'"—the purported "incorrigible licentiousness" of Black women, "always willing and irredeemably dishonored from birth" (Sublette & Sublette, 2015, p. 35). Both slave breeding and concubinage were forms of systematic sexual exploitation of Black women and girls (Berry, 2017; Clayton, 2007; Fields, 1985). This practice, which constituted state-sanctioned terror, was destructive of Black familial relations.

5. *The ongoing global dehumanization of people of African ancestry is also rooted in the legacies of four centuries of Arab enslavement before Europeans kidnapped and enslaved Africans for 300 years.* During both periods, African women and girls, who were targeted for rape and sexual slavery, continued to be viewed as hyper-sexualized objects. Likewise, blackness continued to be equated with slavery and inferiority. This disparagement is evident in the Arabic language as well as associations with all that is negative in English (e.g., "black and evil," "black sheep," "black-balled"). Ongoing domination and depredations on the African continent include the kidnapping, rape, and forced marriage of women and girls in conflict zones in the Democratic Republic of the Congo, Sudan, Mali and northern Nigeria. Some African people, including those who identify as Arab, are fighting proxy wars in these

areas. Ostensible "religious" fighting and terrorism have entailed destroying Africa's indigenous cultural heritage (e.g., the destruction of sacred sites and the burning of ancient manuscripts in Timbuktu) and paving the way for the new "scramble" for Africa's natural resources, such as oil, gold, uranium, and so forth, in these conflict regions (Guzman, 2014). The 13th Organization of Islamic Cooperation (OIC) has called for a conference on slavery reparations, colonialism, and restitution (Chickrie, 2016). Thus, from a Pan-African perspective, rewriting the debt owed means bringing both Arab and European nations into the discussion of reparations for past and ongoing damages.

Recovering Our Memory/Rewriting Knowledge for Historical Consciousness

According Edward Ball (2015), in an article in the *Smithsonian Magazine*, the domestic slave trade, which he refers to as "Slavery's Trail of Tears,"

> is the blanked-out saga, an un-remembered epic . . . the great missing migration—a thousand-mile-long river of people, all of them black, reaching from Virginia to Louisiana. During the 50 years before the Civil War, about a million enslaved people moved from the Upper South—Virginia, Maryland, Kentucky—to the Deep South—Louisiana, Mississippi, Alabama. They were made to go, deported, you could say, having been sold.
>
> *(p. 62)*

Ball continues:

> This forced resettlement was 20 times larger than Andrew Jackson's "Indian removal" campaigns of the 1830s, which gave rise to the original Trail of Tears as it drove tribes of Native Americans out of Georgia, Mississippi and Alabama. It was bigger than the immigration of Jews into the United States during the 19th century, when some 500,000 arrived from Russia and Eastern Europe. It was bigger than the wagon-train migration to the West, beloved of American lore. This movement lasted longer and grabbed up more people than any other migration in North America before 1900. The drama of a million individuals going so far from their homes changed the country. It gave the Deep South a character it retains to this day; and it changed the slaves themselves, traumatizing uncountable families. But until recently, the Slave Trail was buried in memory.
>
> *(pp. 62–63)*

On the other hand, the story of our collectivist agency and communal resistance to these depredations is the story of our humanity that must be also told.

Moreover, our resistance, which is often rooted in ancestral memory, continues. Ball's *Smithsonian* article features the cultural heritage research and preservation campaign of an intrepid community historian, Ser Seshs Ab Heter (Clifford M. Boxley), who is almost single-handedly fighting to recover the history and protect the evidence of what happened at the Forks of the Road in Natchez, Mississippi, the site of the second largest domestic slave market in the United States.

> My aim is to preserve every inch of dirt in this area," Boxley says. "I am fighting for our enslaved ancestors. And this site speaks to their denied humanity, and to their contributions, and to America's domestic slave traffickers. The public recognition for Forks of the Road is for the ancestors who cannot speak for themselves.
>
> *(Ball, 2015, p. 76)*

Part 3: The Debt Owed

The National African American Reparations Commission (NAARC), "an extension of a global network of people of African ancestry who are committed to global reparatory justice," has endorsed Congressman John Conyers's 1989 HR 40 Bill, which he has presented to the U.S. Congress each year. HR 40 calls for a federal commission:

> To address the fundamental injustice, cruelty, brutality, and inhumanity of slavery in the United States and the 13 American colonies between 1619 and 1865 and to establish a commission to study and consider a national apology and proposal/process of reparations for the institution of slavery, subsequent *de jure* and *de facto* racial and economic discrimination against African-Americans, and the impact of these forces on living African-Americans, to make recommendations to the Congress on appropriate remedies, and for other purposes. (See HR 40 Full Text of the revised bill Introduced at the 115th Congress, Jan 3 2017—"What's New with HR 40?"https://ibw21.org/reparations/hr-40-primer/#whats-new-with-hr40)

The National African American Reparations Commission (NAARC) has affirmed "the foundational role and relevance of HR-40" and has supported this call for a commission to study and consider reparation proposals/a process for African Americans as a result of

(1) the institution of slavery, including both Trans-Atlantic and the "domestic trade" which existed from 1565 in colonial Florida and from 1619 through 1865 within the colonies that became the United States, and which included the Federal and State governments which constitutionally and statutorily supported the institution of slavery;

(2) the *de jure* and *de facto* discrimination against freed slaves and their descendants from the end of the Civil War to the present, including economic, political, educational, and social discrimination;

(3) the lingering negative effects of the institution of slavery and the discrimination on living African-Americans and on society in the United States;

(4) the manner in which textual and digital instructional resources and technologies are being used to deny the inhumanity of slavery and the crime against humanity of people of African descent in the United States;

(5) the role of Northern complicity in the Southern based institution of slavery;

(6) the direct benefits to societal institutions, public and private, including higher education, corporations, religious and associational;

(7) and thus, recommend appropriate ways to educate the American public of the Commission's findings;

(8) and thus, recommend appropriate remedies in consideration of the Commission's findings (HR 40 Full Text / Sec 2(b). Purpose. https://ibw21.org/reparations/hr-40-primer/#whats-new-with-hr40)

There have been various African American movements calling for reparations as far back as Paul Cuffe's 1780 demand for reparations and repatriation, Belinda's 1782 petition (Winbush, 2009), Callie House's remarkable 1899 mobilization, and The National Ex-Slave Mutual Relief, Bounty and Pension Association, the first mass movement for reparations (Berry, 2005), as well as an ongoing record of activism, engaged scholarship, lawsuits, legislation (Wittmann, 2013) and more recently, calls for a reparations Superfund "to address the dire circumstances" (Franklin, 2012, p. 371) faced by African American youth (America, 1995, 1999; Brophy, 2008; Coates, 2014; Henry, 2007; Winbush, 2009; Worrill & Winbush, 2015).

Calling for a Reparatory Justice Curriculum

In calling for a reparatory justice curriculum, this chapter builds upon and extends historian Vincent P. Franklin's (2012) appeal for the establishment of a reparations Superfund that would include providing educational alternatives. In addition, this reparatory justice curriculum approach takes inspiration from but also goes beyond the "African Knowledge Program" proposed in the CARICOM (Caribbean Community) 10-Point Plan:

> **African Knowledge Program**: The forced separation of Africans from their homeland has resulted in cultural and social alienation from identity and existential belonging. Denied the right in law to life, and divorced by space from the source of historic self, Africans have craved the right to return and knowledge of the route to roots.
>
> A program of action is required to build "bridges of belonging." Such projects as school exchanges and culture tours, community artistic and

> performance programs, entrepreneurial and religious engagements, as well as political interaction, are required in order to neutralize the void created by slave voyages . . . Such actions will serve to build knowledge networks that are necessary for community rehabilitation.
>
> *(http://ibw21.org/commentary/caricom-reparations-ten-point-plan)*

The argument here is that a reparatory justice curriculum for "community rehabilitation" to heal our "cultural and social alienation from identity and existential belonging," as the 10-Point CARICOM reparations agenda proposes, must undo the denial of our human right to identify with and to know ourselves and to act in the world as people of African ancestry (King, 2015). Lacking such an epistemological grounding in Pan-African perspectives on knowledge of our sociohistorical existence obstructs our capacity to care about and to act in the interests of our global African community in particular and for the benefit of humanity in general.

The absence of Pan-African perspectives on knowledge in education at all levels permits others to act out the dehumanized conceptions of us that slavery engendered, thus justifying our treatment as less than human—at times with our own participation. This legacy continues in our daily experiences of dehumanization and dispossession as documented in the evidence of arbitrary detentions and police killings and torture, as well as the criminalization and brutalization of our children—both boys and girls, even as young as 5 years old, in schools and in our communities.

For example, the Chicago police have brutalized children, as documented in a September 2014 grassroots research report young activists presented to the UN Committee Against Torture, titled "We Charge Genocide" (Lazare, 2017; MXGM, 2012).

It is important to recognize that "building bridges of belonging" to our African heritage and identity to reclaim our humanity is a condition not only of *our* repair but also for human freedom. Carter G. Woodson described this as a problem of miseducation; he stated there would never be any lynching in the street if it did not first take place in the classroom (Woodson, 1933). What researchers now describe in psychological terms as (unconscious) "implicit bias" can be understood as what I have described as dysconscious racism, a habit of mind that is a consequence of miseducation, which a reparatory justice curriculum would address.

Dysconscious Racism

In an article that I published in 1991, I introduced the concept of dysconscious racism into the academic literature on race and education to explain how student teachers in my courses identified poverty and other forms of black-white inequality as a legacy of slavery. That is, poverty and racial inequality in their minds—as well as discrimination—are the consequence of something that Black people lack as a result of slavery (King, 1991). The article, based on a study of student teachers' understanding of racial inequality, explained that dysconsciousness is a cognitively limited form of thinking, a habit of mind that accepts existing inequality as a result of the benefits White people have as given. In other words, their thinking is not "implicitly" biased but is a result of their miseducation. Dysconscious racism denotes the tacit acceptance of dominant white norms and privilege. It also is not the *absence* of consciousness (i.e., unconsciousness) but an *impaired* consciousness or distorted way of thinking about race and inequity as compared to critical consciousness, for example. Uncritical ways of thinking (or not thinking) about racial inequity accept certain culturally sanctioned assumptions, myths, and beliefs that justify the social and economic advantages White people have as a result of subordinating diverse others. What we teach, learn, and do not teach about slavery is fundamental (King, 1992). Thus, miseducation is a significant source of our "cultural and social alienation from identity and existential belonging"—that is to say, our dispossession and dehumanization that are inscribed in school textbooks, pedagogy, and the academic disciplines, as well as multimedia instructional resources, as the examples that follow will illustrate.

(Mis)Representing Slavery in a Global Online Game and Other Teaching Materials

Teaching about slavery remains a particularly vexing problem—in the United States and on a global level (Gonçalves e Silva, 2005; Seck, 2005). In the 1990s when I served on the Curriculum Development and Supplemental Materials Commission for the State of California, I was particularly distressed by ideological representations of the beginnings of the European slave trade in school textbooks, which presented slavery as essentially the fault of African people themselves (King, 1992). African kings, who were depicted as greedy for European goods, such as leather boots, were shown as eager to sell their "own people" into slavery. One textbook asked students to role-play a scenario as villagers decided whether to sell people in their village to the Portuguese ("who are arriving tomorrow").

Missing from this narrative is a culturally informed, historically accurate explication of this complex history. For example, missing from the focus in textbooks are any references to the resistance to slavery by African leaders like Songhoy emperor Sonni Ali Ber (who was head of the imperial Songhoy state between 1464 and 1492) or Queen Njinga Mbande of Ndongo (queen between 1624 and 1663), whose nations were caught up in but who also fought Arab, Tuareg, and Portuguese enslavers, respectively (Konadu, 2015; Maïga, 2010; Schwarz-Bart, 2001).

During the 1991 California textbook adoption process, I challenged these (mis)representations of slavery's beginnings as "half-truths" following historian

Basil Davidson's suggestion that slavery in Africa should be compared with slavery, serfdom, and vassalship in Europe—not represented as a social practice endemic to African people. I concluded,

> As a systematic and deliberate process of forced cultural amnesia, the slave trade and the Middle Passage are apt metaphors for the travesty of alienating texts that suppress the cultural knowledge students need . . . If the loss of [African people's] cultural memory aided the process of chattel slavery, textbooks aid contemporary processes of mental enslavement by making the "anarchy and terror" slavery engendered seem to be a natural state of existence for African people.
>
> *(King, 1992, p. 332)*

Since publishing this article in 1992, I have determined that "heritage knowledge" is a more appropriate term than "cultural knowledge" to describe what students need to know about their own cultural background and history (King, 2006, p. 345). Cultural knowledge refers to what teachers need to know about their students. It is utterly lamentable that currently available teaching materials remain emblematic of the ideological justifications for African enslavement. Consider a "serious" interactive learning game designed to teach about slavery produced by Dutch game designers, a high school textbook being used in Texas, and a children's book—each indicates that teaching and learning about slavery remain dangerously distorted.

The slavery game aimed at elementary and middle school students—and available online via the Internet—is called "Playing History 2—Slave Trade" (http://store.steampowered.com/app/386870/Playing_History_2__Slave_Trade). This game was released in Europe in 2013. Twitter users in the United States leveled accusations of racism against the game and the outcry was soon international. The designers issued a perfunctory "apology" and deleted the portion of the game that required children playing this game to "stack as many slaves in the bottom of a ship" as possible.

Other remaining aspects of this "Slave Trade" game that are equally problematic include the role of a young African who is the helper for the Europeans when they return to Africa "to buy more slaves." According to a 2015 *LA Times* article critical of the game, here is an example of the instructions this game provides the players:

> Yes—you [the player], a black slave, pilot the slave ship. Twice. To "win" this section, you are literally tasked with being a good slave driver. As time expires, your boat runs out of rations. So you need to steer the boat, avoid wind blasts that blow you off course, and collect items that replenish your food gauge . . . If you try to go back to Africa, you fail. If you don't sail

your boat fast enough, you fail . . . "Winning" here means getting all of the slaves (including yourself) to America.

(Thomas, 2015)

Additionally, the visual imagery in this game is equally egregious: The African characters look especially grotesque as compared to the way Europeans are depicted. In response to the controversy, the game website now includes this disclaimer:

> Update: The game and trailer has [*sic*] been updated. Slave Tetris has been removed as it was perceived to be extremely insensitive by some people. This overshadowed the educational goal of the game. Apologies to people who was [*sic*] offended by us using game mechanics to underline the point of how inhumane slavery was. The goal was to enlighten and educate people—not to get sidetracked discussing a small 15 secs part of the game.
>
> *(http://store.steampowered.com/app/386870/Playing_History_2__Slave_Trade)*

So much for an apology that isn't one!

A second controversial example is the international protest that occurred about how slavery is presented in a Texas high school textbook. It is worth mentioning that Texas state standards diminish slavery's role in the Civil War, and the Ku Klux Klan and Jim Crow segregation are not mentioned (Collins, 2012; Klein, 2014). The following passage erupted in a social media uproar when a Black student sent a text message containing a photo of this textbook content to his mother: "The Atlantic Slave Trade between the 1500s and the 1800s brought millions of workers from Africa to the southern United States to work on agricultural plantations" (Finley, 2015).

Fortunately, this young man had enough critical understanding of our history to recognize the distortion in referring to enslaved Africans as "workers" who were "brought" to the plantations in the South. His mother, who is also a teacher, posted a video critique of the text on social media. Her posting went viral and the ensuing wave of reactions reached the publisher, McGraw-Hill, at company headquarters in London. The CEO apologized and promised to change the online version of the textbook immediately; he also stated that changes would be made in the next print run. But who knows when that will be? Many complained that this response is inadequate.

A third example also generated immediate and widespread social media protest, including several online petitions. *A Birthday Cake for George Washington*, the title of a Scholastic Publications children's book released in January 2016, celebrated President George Washington's birthday with a colorful story about the cake his "happy" slave Hercules, his cook, was baking for him (Ganeshram, 2016).

After vigorously defending this book by highlighting the "multicultural" credentials (identities) of the author and the illustrator and their own responses to the avalanche of critiques, "amid an outcry over its visual depiction of the former president's slaves as happy, smiling workers," the publisher announced the distribution of the book would be halted (Stack, 2016).

In a statement reversing its previous position, the publisher acknowledged that the book sanitized the evils of slavery, despite its good intentions:

> "[W]e believe that, without more historical background on the evils of slavery than this book for younger children can provide, the book may give a false impression of the reality of the lives of slaves and therefore should be withdrawn."
>
> *(Wang, 2016, n.p.)*

An online Change.org petition, which requested that Amazon and Barnes and Nobles not sell the book, stated,

> The book, *A Birthday Cake for George Washington*, is a vile exemplification of the distortion of history. Slavery should not and cannot be portrayed as anything other than what it was—the abuse of people of color for centuries in order to build the America we know. America was built on the backs of slaves on the land of Native Americans.
>
> *(www.change.org/p/amazon-com-remove-a-birthday-cake-for-george-washington-from-amazon-com)*

The question that needs to be asked as part of a reparatory justice curriculum approach, with attention to rigorous culturally informed research and praxis, is the following (Swanson, 2009).

What exactly should be the content and pedagogy for teaching, not only about "the evils of slavery" but also about the reality of the lives of African people as human beings with agency before, during, and after enslavement, and with particular attention to younger children and the education of teachers (King, 2011; King, Goss, et al., 2014; Michelle 2012)?

This African-centered knowledge perspective would include a focus on resistance, as well as African agency in education, cultural expression, and community building, and forms of group self-determination and spiritual resilience (Behrendt et al., 2001). The following *Criterion Standard for Teaching and Learning About People of African Ancestry* (1 of 19), which my colleague Dr. Susan Goodwin and I developed, is indicative:

> Europeans and their descendants in the Americas targeted, enslaved and dehumanized African peoples in order to exploit and profit from African technical knowledge, skills, expertise, and cultural assets. People of African

descent not only survived enslavement but *lived* life in the midst of it, creating and inventing new cultural forms, variations and representations of Black life (#13).

(King & Goodwin, 2006, p. 4)

Meanwhile, for a fourth example, Black students are being directed to participate in humiliating "slavery reenactments" and classroom games in which they are "slaves being caught" or sent back to the plantation after trying to escape or pretending to be on the auction block. Outraged Black parents and students as young as third grade have complained bitterly about such demeaning instructional activities that assault children's dignity in dehumanizing history lessons, as well as math word problems focused on slavery:

"Each tree has 56 oranges. If eight slaves pick them equally, how much would each slave pick?"

"If Frederick got two beatings per day, how many beatings did he get in 1 week?"

(Evans, 2011)

It is worth noting that these teaching incidents are occurring throughout the country, not just in the South (DeLatorre, 2013; Hibbard, 2012; Mazza, 2017; see also, King, 2011, pp. 348–349).

Conclusion

The vignettes presented at the beginning of this chapter as well as the examples of controversial educational materials/resources and pedagogy just discussed, which are continuing to miseducate students (and their teachers) about slavery—controversies that have reached a global audience—underscore the need to prepare not only educators but also our students and parents to remain vigilant and armed with accurate scholarship informed by African epistemology and African historical consciousness (Mburu, 2012; Thornhill, 2016). We need a modern-day WPA-type (Works Project Administration) program to develop and implement a reparatory justice curriculum—for schools, families, and communities. Supported by a proposed reparations Superfund (Franklin, 2012), this is a call for sound curriculum and pedagogical alternatives to educate young people wherever they are, in public schools, private schools, homeschool and church settings, using African epistemology and the wisdom embodied in our African heritage (Mazama & Musumunu, 2015). Such a curriculum approach can and should support youth in inquiry activities working with both academic scholars and community educators like Ser Boxley with the aim of engaging young people in the recovery and production of liberating heritage knowledge (King, 2006; King & Swartz, 2016).

A reparatory justice curriculum approach is needed to train young people to capture and document critical sites of memory about our heritage in our neighborhoods, especially the stories of our elders, in order to produce engaging, culturally informed multimedia learning tools that counter dysconsciousness and the cultural amnesia that are systematically transmitted in distorted curricula as well as the corporate-controlled mass media (King, Swartz et al., 2014). Reparations movements must include attention to preparing our communities, our accomplices (Gutiérrez, 2017), and our allies, including young people, for the broadest active engagement in the global battle for knowledge not only to repair ourselves psychically and emotionally but also to heal the ongoing global wounds the legacies of slavery made in the world we have inherited (Baptist, 2014; Beckles, 2013; Sublette, 2009). Moreover, there is an underdeveloped role and opportunity for Black studies departments in this call for a reparatory justice curriculum. As Randall Robinson (2013) reminds us, "We have to know the world and we have to feel that we can change it."

References

Ackman, S., & Schwarz, C. (2008). "Dubious Legacy," Chicago Blog. Retrieved January 17, 2017 from www.chicagomag.com/Chicago-Magazine/August-2008/Dubious-Legacy/

America, R. F. (1995). Racial inequality, economic dysfunction, and reparations. *Challenge*, 40–45.

America, R. F. (1999). Reparations and public policy. *The Review of Black Political Economy* 26(3), 77–83.

Asante, M. K. (2010). *Henry Louis Gates is wrong about African involvement in the slave trade.* Retrieved from www.asante.net/articles/44/afrocentricity/

Asante, M. K. (2015). *African pyramids of knowledge: Kemet, Afrocentricity and Africology.* Brooklyn, NY: Universal Write.

Ball, E. (2015). Retracing slavery's trail of tears: America's forgotten migration: The journeys of a million African-Americans from the tobacco south to the cotton south. *Smithsonian Magazine, 46*(7), 58–82.

Baptist, E. P. (2014). *The half has not been told: Slavery and the making of American capitalism.* New York, NY: Basic Books.

Beckles, H. M. (2013). *Britain's Black debt: Reparations for Caribbean slavery and native genocide.* Kingston, JA: University of the West Indies Press.

Behrendt, S., Eltis, D., & Richardson, D. (2001). The costs of coercion: African agency in the pre-modern Atlantic World. *The Economic History Review, 54*(3), 454–476.

Berry, D. R. (2017). *The price for their pound of flesh: The value of the enslaved, from womb to grave, in the building of a nation.* Boston, MD: Beacon Press.

Berry, M. F. (2005). *My face is Black is true: Callie house and the struggle for ex-slave reparations.* New York, NY: Alfred A. Knopf.

Brophy, A. L. (2008). *Reparations: Pro and con.* New York, NY: Oxford University Press.

Brownlee, R. A. (2012). John C. Robinson: Father of the Tuskegee Airmen and the Tuskegee Airmen: An illustrated history: 1939–1949 (review). *Alabama Review, 65,* 316–319. Retrieved November 3, 2017, from https://muse.jhu.edu/login?auth=0type=summaryurl=/journals/alabama_review/v065/65.4.brownlee.html

Chickrie, R. (2016, April 18). Islamic bloc calls for international conference on slavery reparations. *Caribbean News Now.* Retrieved from http://caribbeannewsnow.com/headline-Islamic-bloc-calls-for-international-conference-on-slavery-reparations-30054.html

Clarke, J. H. (1994). *Christopher Columbus and the Afrikan holocaust: Slavery and the rise of European capitalism.* Brooklyn, NY: A & B.

Clayton, R. (2007). *Cash for blood: The Baltimore—New Orleans domestic slave trade.* Westminster, MD: Heritage Books.

Coates, T.- N. (2014). The case for reparations. *The Atlantic, 313*(5), 54–71.

Collins, G. (2012, June 12). How Texas inflicts bad textbooks on us. *The New York Review of Books.* Retrieved from www.nybooks.com/articles/archives/2012/jun/21/how-texas-inflicts-bad-textbooks-on-us/

Davidson, B. (1961). *Black mother.* Boston, MA: Little, Brown.

DeLatorre, V. (2013, September 19). Parent files complaint against Hartford schools over slavery re-enactment on field trip. *Hartford Courant.* Retrieved from http://articles.courant.com/2013-09-19/community/hc-hartford-parent-complaint-0920-20130919_1_parent-files-complaint-hartford-schools-classroom

DeWolf, T. N. (2009). *Inheriting the trade: A northern family confronts its legacy as the largest slave-trading dynasty in US history.* Boston: Beacon Press.

Diop, C. A. (2000). *The cultural unity of Black Africa: The domains of matriarchy and of patriarchy in classical antiquity.* London: Karnak House.

Evans, E. E. (2011, March 5). Mock slave auction: Ohio student humiliated in class. *The Root.* Retrieved from www.theroot.com/mock-slave-auction-ohio-student-humiliated-in-class-1790863010

Fields, B. J. (1985). *Slavery and freedom on the middle ground: Maryland during the nineteenth century.* New Haven, CT: Yale University Press.

Finley, T. (2015, October 8). McGraw-Hill Education CEO says it has done enough to fix its description of slaves as "workers." *Huffington Post.* Retrieved from www.huffingtonpost.com/entry/mcgraw-hill-ceo-says-it-has-done-enough-to-fix-its-description-of-slaves-as-workers_5616ad0ce4b0e66ad4c6df26

Franklin, V. P. (2012). Commentary: Reparations superfund: Needed now more than ever. *The Journal of African American History, 97*(4), 371–375.

Ganeshram, R. (2016). *A birthday cake for George Washington.* New York: Scholastic Press.

Gonçalves e Silva, P. B. (2005). A new millennium research agenda in Black education: Some points to be considered for discussion and decisions. In J. E. King (Ed.), *Black education: A transformative research and action agenda in the new millennium* (pp. 301–308). Mahwah, NJ: Erlbaum.

Gutiérrez, R. (2017). Commentary. Why mathematics (education) was late to the backlash party: The need for a revolution. *Journal of Urban Mathematics Education, 10*(2), 8–24.

Guzman, T. A. (2014). As war lingers in Mali, Western powers target its natural resources. *Global Reach.* Retrieved from www.globalresearch.ca/as-war-lingers-in-mali-western-powers-target-its-natural-resources/5364079

Hartman, S. (2007). *Lose your mother: A journey along the Atlantic slave route.* New York: Farrar, Straus & Giroux.

Henry, C. (2007). *Long overdue: The politics of racial reparations: From 40 acres to atonement and beyond.* New York, NY: New York University Press.

Hibbard, L. (2012, March 27). "Slave game" reported at Georgia's Camp Creek Elementary School outrages parents. *Huffington Post.* Retrieved from www.huffingtonpost.com/2012/01/26/alleged-slave-game-at-camp-creek-elementary-school-outrages-parents_n_1234096.html

King, J. E. (1991). Dysconscious racism: Ideology, identity and the miseducation of teachers. *Journal of Negro Education, 60*(2), 133–146.

King, J. E. (1992). Diaspora literacy and consciousness in the struggle against miseducation in the Black community. *Journal of Negro Education, 61*(3), 317–340.

King, J. E. (2006). "If justice is our objective": Diaspora literacy, heritage knowledge and the praxis of critical studyin' for human freedom. In A. Ball (Ed.), *With more deliberate speed: Achieving equity and excellence in education: Realizing the full potential of Brown v. Board of Education: National Society for the Study of Education, 105th Yearbook, Part 2* (pp. 337–360). New York, NY: Ballenger.

King, J. E. (2011). "Who dat say (we) too depraved to be saved?" Re-membering Katrina/Haiti (and beyond): Critical studyin' for human freedom. *Harvard Educational Review, 81*(2), 343–370.

King, J. E. (2015). Transformative curriculum praxis for the public good. In J. E. King (Ed.), *Dysconscious racism, Afrocentric praxis, and education for human freedom: Through the years I keep on toiling: The selected works of Joyce E. King* (pp. 235–247). New York: Routledge.

King, J. E., & Goodwin, S. (2006). *Criterion standards for teaching and learning about people of African ancestry*. Rochester, NY: Rochester Teacher Center.

King, J. E., McArthur, S. A., & Goss, A. (2014). Recovering history and the "parent piece" for cultural well-being and belonging. In J. King, E. Swartz et al., *Re-membering history in student and teacher and learning: An Afrocentric culturally-informed praxis* (pp. 155–188). New York, NY: Routledge.

King, J. E., & Swartz, E. E. (2016). *The Afrocentric praxis of teaching for freedom: Connecting culture to learning*. New York, NY: Routledge.

King, J. E., Swartz, E. E. et al. (2014). *"Re-membering" history in student and teacher learning: An Afrocentric culturally informed praxis*. New York, NY: Routledge.

Klein, R. (2014, October 22). These biased ideas are presented as fact in Texas curriculum standards. *Huffington Post*. Retrieved from www.huffingtonpost.com/2014/10/22/texas-social-studies-standards_n_6029224.html

Konadu, K. (2015). *Transatlantic Africa, 1440–1888*. New York, NY: Oxford University Press.

Kunnie, J. E. (2006). Indigenous African knowledge: Human rights and globalization. In J. E. Kunnie & N. I. Goduka (Eds.), *Indigenous people's wisdom and power: Affirming our knowledge through narratives* (pp. 246–270). Burlington, VT: Ashgate.

Lazare, S. (2017, January 15). Chicago police assaulted children, got away with murders: DOJ report echoes what residents have long known. *Alternet*. Retrieved from www.alternet.org/activism/chicago-police-assaulted-children-murdered-doj-report-echoes-resident-complaints

Magubane, B. M. (1987). *The ties that bind: African American consciousness of Africa*. Trenton, NJ: Africa World Press.

Maïga, H. O. (2010). *Balancing written history with oral tradition: The legacy of the Songhoy people*. New York, NY: Routledge.

Mazama, A., & Musumunu, G. (2015). *African Americans and homeschooling: Motivations, opportunities and challenges*. New York, NY: Routledge.

Mazza, E. (2017, January 25). Mom: Teacher made Black kids act as slaves for history lesson. *Huffington Post*. Retrieved from www.huffingtonpost.com/entry/school-kids-slaves-history-lesson_us_58898804e4b0737fd5cb90e2?

Mburu, W. (2012). Indigenous conceptions of civic education: Reinventing the past. In
A. Asabere-Ameyaw, G. J. Sefa Dei, & K. Raheem (Eds.), *Contemporary issues in African
sciences and science education* (pp. 175–193). Rotterdam, the Netherlands: Sense.

McLaurin, M. A. (1991). *Celia, a slave.* Athens: The University Press of Georgia.

Michelle (2012, January 29). "Catch a Slave" game played by teacher with students in
Georgia. *Motley News.* Retrieved from https://motleynews.net/2012/01/29/
catch-a-slave-game-played-by-teacher-with-students-in-georgia

MXGM (2012). Every 28 hours: Operation Ghetto Storm: 2012 Annual Report on the
Extrajudicial Killing of 313 Black People. *Malcolm X Grassroots Movement.* Retrieved
from https://mxgm.org/operation-ghetto-storm-2012-annual-report-on-the-extrajudicial-
killing-of-313-black-people/

Nti, K. (2010, May 5). The role of Africans in the slave trade. *Ghana Web.* Retrieved
from www.ghanaweb.com/GhanaHomePage/NewsArchive/The-Role-Of-Africans-
In-The-Slave-Trade-181302

Robinson, R. (2000). *The debt: What America owes to Blacks.* New York, NY: Plume.

Robinson, R. (2013). *The debt: What America owes to Blacks, an unbroken agony, quitting
America.* Retrieved from www.youtube.com/watch?v=r0pixo4bKYg

Schwarz-Bart, S. (2001). Ana de Souza Nzinga: The queen who resisted the Portuguese
conquest. In S. Schwarz-Bart (Ed.), *In praise of Black women, Volume 1: Ancient African
queens* (pp. 174–187). Madison: University of Wisconsin Press.

Seck, I. (2005). Worldwide conspiracy against Black culture and education. In J. E. King
(Ed.), *Black education: A transformative research and action agenda in the new millennium*
(pp. 285–290). Mahwah, NJ: Erlbaum.

Stack, L. (2016, January 16). Scholastic halts distribution of *A Birthday Cake for George
Washington. New York Times.* Retrieved from www.nytimes.com/2016/01/18/business/
media/scholastic-halts-distribution-of-a-birthday-cake-for-george-washington.
html?_r=0

Stern, S. M. (2007). It's time to face the whole truth about the Atlantic slave trade. *History News Network.* Retrieved from http://historynewsnetwork.org/article/41431

Sublette, N. (2009). *The world that made New Orleans: From Spanish silver to Congo Square.*
Chicago, IL: Chicago Review Press.

Sublette, N., & Sublette, C. (2015). *The American slave coast: A history of the slave-breeding
industry.* New York, NY: Lawrence Hill.

Swanson, D. M. (2009). Where have all the fish gone? Living Ubuntu as an ethics of
research and pedagogical engagement. In D. Caracciolo & A. M. Mungai (Eds.), *In
the spirit of Ubuntu: Stories of teaching and research* (pp. 3–21). Rotterdam, the Netherlands:
Sense.

Thomas, D. (2015, September 7). I played "Slave Tetris" so your kids don't have to. *LA
Times.* Retrieved from www.latimes.com/entertainment/herocomplex/la-et-hc-played-
slave-tetris-kids-20150904-htmlstory.html

Thornhill, T. E. (2016). Resistance and assent: How racial socialization shapes Black
students' experience learning African American history in school. *Urban Education,
51*(9), 1126–1151.

Tucker, P. T. (2012). *John C. Robinson: Father of the Tuskegee Airmen.* Washington, DC:
Potomac Books.

Wang, Y. (2016, January 19). Scholastic pulls children's book starring George Washington's
"happy" slaves. *The Washington Post.* Retrieved from www.washingtonpost.com/news/

morning-mix/wp/2016/01/19/scholastic-pulls-childrens-book-starring-george-washingtons-happy-slaves/

Winbush, R. A. (Ed.). (2003). *Should America pay? Slavery and the raging debate on reparations*. New York, NY: HarperCollins.

Winbush, R. A. (2009). *Belinda's petition: A concise history of reparations for the transatlantic slave trade*. Bloomington, IN: Xlibris.

Wittmann, N. (2013). *Slavery reparations time is now: Exposing lies, claiming justice for global survival—an international legal assessment*. Vienna, Austria: Power of the Trinity.

Wobogo, V. I. (2011). *Cold wind from the north: The prehistoric European origin of racism explained by Diop's two cradle theory*. Charleston, SC: Books on Demand.

Woodson, C. G. (1933). *The mis-education of the Negro*. Washington, DC: Associated.

Worrill, C. W., & Winbush, R. A. (2015). *Chronology of the reparations movement of Africans in America, Monograph*. Retrieved from www.drconradworrill.com/Chrono.ofRMofAA.pdf

7

RETURNING WHAT WE LEARN TO THE PEOPLE

Theory and Practice

Joyce E. King

> The only question that concerns us here is whether these educated persons are actually equipped to face the ordeal before them or unconsciously contribute to their own undoing by perpetuating the regime of the oppressor.
>
> (Carter G. Woodson, *Mis-Education of the Negro*, 1933)

> African resurgence will never take place until Africans champion a renaissance grounded in a new paradigm of dramatic narratives of victory.
>
> (Molefi K. Asante, 2015)

Introduction

This chapter invokes the transformative power and possibilities of education research in the Black intellectual (liberation) tradition of study and delineates the African philosophical and epistemological roots of this tradition in the works of historical Black educators and theoreticians as well as scholar activists whose inquiries also challenge the myth of "objectivity" in social science research. This eurocratic paradigm, which admonishes us to be "objective," often creates role conflict and alienates us from our people (King, 2005a). Instead, the Black intellectual (liberation) tradition in education research and practice favors partisan scientific inquiry and praxis in the interest of equity, racial justice, and human freedom. It is in this way that we are able to return to the people what we have learned from their everyday and ongoing practices in a form that is useful and uplifting to us all.

In *The Art of Clear Thinking* Rudolph Flesch (1951, p. 1), who also wrote *Why Johnny Can't Read*, quotes the British novelist E. M. Forster: "Unless we remember, we cannot understand." I would say, unless we "re-member" (King, Swartz et al., 2014) or reconnect the fragments and distorted information we have been "given" in schools and society in general—unless we recover what Cheikh Anta Diop (1991) described as our "historical conscience" or "cultural identity," we can neither understand or think for ourselves (p. 212). Carter G. Woodson, who is remembered as "the Father of Black History," understood this necessity as our responsibility to "think Black" (Hine, 1986, p. 409). In this final chapter we draw upon diverse examples of what heritage knowledge teaches us so that we can "re-member" and return that knowledge to others. This communal ethos of reciprocity is a fundamental tenet of Afrocentric praxis, Black Studies theorizing, and African philosophy. This chapter is organized into seven sections: (1) Liberating Theory, Method, and Pedagogy, (2) The UN International Decade of People of African Descent, (3) "I Know I Been Changed," (4) Study, Struggle, and Learning/s From Experience, (5) The Black Intellectual (Liberation) Tradition, (6) Seeking the Source of Returning What We Learn, (7) Toward Historical/ Cultural Consciousness in Afrocentric and Black Studies Education Research.

Liberating Theory, Method, and Pedagogy

Afrocentricity and Black Studies recognize that eurocratic social science theory and methods are neither universal nor neutral. Rather, theory and method can help or hinder intellectual independence and obscure the moral demands on education research/ers to resist, critique, and contribute to the struggle to overcome domination (King, 2016, 2017). As Jacob Carruthers (1999) noted in his book *Intellectual Warfare*,

> [T]he "science of oppression" . . . works for the master and . . . produces a master's mentality . . . We have to understand where it came from, what it does and has done to us, and what it does to humanity in general . . . We must replace it with a methodology and metaphysics that restores the world and gives light to everybody.
>
> *(p. 294)*

Regarding the possibility of resisting this "master's mentality," George Lipsitz (2016) aptly observed, "It's hard because we've been made into the kinds of people who fit into this society and we [academics] have a lot to unlearn" (p. 28). This experience is common among scholars of African ancestry, as suggested by the similar conclusion Guyanese historian Walter Rodney (1990) reached when he reflected upon his student experience: "It was necessary to come to grips with the way in which one's being, and the presentation of one's being, was so hopelessly distorted in the sources to which one went for scholarship" (p. 13). My search for liberating theory and method involved developing education research-as-pedagogy inquiries that benefit the Black community. I sought ways to overcome miseducation and the myth of objectivity in social science research since I began grappling with these concerns as an undergraduate in the Sociology Department at Stanford University (King, 1992, 1999).

This was a time when Black students were relatively new arrivals on predominately white colleges and universities and we were assaulted with ideologies of Black people's cultural deprivation and genetic deficiency masquerading as objective scientific theory. At all-Black Ravenswood High School in the Black community of East Palo Alto, California, where I was teaching a human relations class in 1968, students were alienated from their education as well. They were constantly cutting class and hanging out across the street and the local hamburger joint, and I discovered some of these students in my class could not read. For my senior honors thesis I designed a study to investigate the way these young people understood their reality. With the assistance of a school guidance counselor, I constructed a set of fictional but authentic-looking academic profiles that resembled the students I was teaching and I interviewed them about these fictional students. When I asked one student in my study to explain why she thought a kid with failing grades was missing so many classes and getting into so much trouble at school, what she said became a touchstone for my scholarship and activism. She said, "Maybe if somebody had told him what happened to his mother and father and why his parents are the way they are, he could do better."

Nothing in my Stanford courses had prepared me respond to her observation, not until Black students demanded the establishment of Black Studies programs on our campuses (Rogers, 2009). The Black Student Union strike nearby at San Francisco State College "marked the first serious effort by a group of black students to remold an American college" (Karagueuzian, 1971, p. 1). At Stanford Black students sought to integrate real community problems in our studies and this included a role for research in meeting community needs. Partnering with community elders and activists, we established the Community Development Workshop as part of the "Afro-Am" program.

St. Clair Drake came to Stanford as the founding director of the African and African American studies program (not a department). Sylvia Wynter succeeded Drake and, by the time I completed my doctorate, I had worked closely with both of them over the years. I had a long running "conversation" with "Drake," as we fondly called him, about partisanship versus objectivity in research. While he agreed with the necessity to resist oppression, he was unequivocal: "You do your activism after 5 pm." However, the intellectual warfare that I experienced in my studies was unrelenting. For instance, my comprehensive examination in the graduate school of education at Stanford required me to write a response to Arthur Jensen's (1969) publication proclaiming the scientific basis of Black people's supposed genetic inferiority (e.g., the "heritability of I.Q.") in the *Harvard Educational Review*. Such ideologically inflected knowledge production necessitated scholarly refutation, not abdication. It is worth noting that Jensen continued to pursue this line of investigation (Rushton & Jensen, 2005).

Initially, I found support for intellectual activism in the scholarly activism of Grace Lee Boggs (1974) and Jimmie Boggs (1968) and in the theories, methods, and pedagogy of Paulo Freire (1978), who acknowledged that education is not neutral, and Orlando Fals Borda's (1980) critique of the self-deceptive "wig of neutrality" and "mask of objectivity" in research. Although I succeeded in articulating a culturally affirming Black education analysis in my dissertation (Reeves/King, 1974), I had not yet fully grasped the significance for theory, method, and pedagogy of the Black intellectual (liberation) tradition of marrying intellectual activism to the everyday experiences of the people whose interests our education ought to serve (King, 2005b; Wynter, 1992, 2006, 2012). Several examples follow to illustrate this tradition in the contributions of W.E.B. Du Bois, Carter G. Woodson, Septima Clark, and Ella Baker.

W.E.B. Du Bois

According to Reiland Rabaka, in addition to his prodigious body of *"solution providing"* scholarship, W.E.B. Du Bois also emphasized that "the methods which we [Diaspora Africans] have evolved for opposing slavery and fighting prejudice are not to be forgotten, but learned for our own and others' instruction" (Du Bois, 1973, p. 144). Thus, Du Bois broadened the social theory of his era to include African people's unique contributions to "civilization and humanity" and theories of social transformation (Rabaka, 2008, pp. 18–19). His educational philosophy not only emphasized a critical study of history, cultural inquiry, and "understanding of present and future vital needs" (p. 44–45) but also sought ways to bring that knowledge to the masses. For example, in 1911 Du Bois created a theatrical pageant, "Star of Ethiopia," to educate the masses about African Diasporan history (Du Bois, 1985). From 1920–1921 he used his *Brownies' Books*, a magazine written by Black writers for Black children, to disseminate research on the Black experience that could prepare Black children for present realities and future possibilities (Brownies' Books, n.d.; Lewis, 2000; "Star of Ethiopia," n.d.). As discussed in Chapter 4, Du Bois's communal, reciprocal, and justice-oriented worldview was an epistemic expression of African worldview and cultural concepts, such as *sharing responsibility for communal well-being and belonging* and *pursuing freedom and justice as communal responsibilities*.

Carter G. Woodson

After Woodson founded Negro History Week in 1926, he disseminated his research in a collection of books that he arranged for Lorenzo Johnston Greene (1996) to sell door-to-door in towns and cities across the United States. Pero D. Dagbovie (2007) details the major roles Black women also played in "popularizing" Woodson's studies of Black history. Black clubwomen, teachers, librarians, and grassroots social activists helped to raise funds for Woodson's programs and they "set up activities in schools, such as book displays and pageants" (p. 94). Dagbovie notes that Black women

> worked to advertise Negro History Week celebrations and they established branches, clubs, and study groups throughout the country . . . Black women at the grassroots level were key organizers and participants in the Association for the Study of Negro Life and History's annual meetings throughout the country.
>
> *(p. 94)*

Nannie Helen Burroughs, an avid Woodson supporter, was active in his organization—the Association for the Study of Negro Life and History (King Papers, 1961). As an educator, social activist, and businesswoman of African ancestry, Burroughs understood the significance of having knowledge of history. She required her students at the National Training School for Women and Girls, which she founded in Washington, DC, "not only to study black history using Woodson's texts but also to pass a written and oral black history examination in order to graduate" (Dagbovie, 2007, p. 95).

Septima Clark

Thirty years later in 1956 when activist-educator Septima Clark was fired from her teaching job in Charleston, South Carolina, because of her membership in the NAACP, she went to work with Myles Horton at Highlander Folk School in Tennessee. Highlander began as a center for worker education, where Horton and his colleagues defied segregation laws by bringing Black and White people together in workshops using a liberation pedagogy that engaged people who came to Highlander—people like Rosa Parks—in analyzing their reality in order to engage in social change. Septima Clark and Myles Horton accepted an invitation to help set up an adult literacy program to enable the disenfranchised people of John's Island off the coast of South Carolina to register to vote. Drawing on her earlier experiences teaching adults on the island to read and, after systematic investigation, analysis, and reflection, Septima Clark and her team established a citizenship education program (Wigginton, 1992). Her work is a clear example of the Black intellectual (liberation) tradition of marrying intellectual activism to the everyday experiences of the people whom our education ought to serve.

Working with a local leader, Esau Jenkins, and Septima Clark's cousin, beauty shop owner Bernice Robinson, who taught the adult literacy classes, they developed a liberation pedagogy that respected and valorized community knowledge. This pedagogy includes Bernice Robinson's mutually respectful interactions with the adult learners in this community and the way the curriculum used the people's life experiences and everyday needs. In fact, she was selected to teach the literacy classes because she was not a professional educator whose training might have distanced her from the people. Rather, the citizenship school curriculum and pedagogy demonstrated liberatory possibilities in the way teaching and learning built upon what the people knew and multiple ways of knowing. The curriculum used hands-on, familiar materials, such as checks, postal money orders, catalogue order forms, driver's license exams, and voter registration information to teach literacy as well as political skills (Olsen, 2001, p. 214). This program became the foundational model for literacy instruction and political education across the South during the civil rights movement. By the time she retired in 1970 after the Southern Christian Leadership Conference (SCLC) had adopted the citizenship schools education program, Septima Clark and her staff (including Dorothy Cotton, Bernice Robinson, and Andrew Young) had trained 10,000 citizenship school teachers and taught "more than one hundred thousand black people to read and write and to demand their citizenship" (Olsen, 2001, p. 224).

Ella J. Baker

Septima Clark and Ella J. Baker were friends and colleagues who shared the same community-minded philosophy and emancipatory praxis as activist-community-educators. Ella Baker was a formidable (usually behind-the-scenes) organizer who had worked alongside major figures, like Du Bois, A. Phillip Randolph, and others in worker education and human rights/civil rights movements. As the highest-ranking woman in the NAACP, she risked her life traveling alone throughout the South in the 1940s, recruiting members, raising funds, and organizing chapters, including youth chapters. The relationships that she formed and her reputation were crucial later on in successful collective grassroots mobilizations and campaigns that she organized. In an effort to build on the successful Montgomery Bus Boycott, for example, Ella Baker was instrumental in launching the SCLC, the organization that Dr. Martin Luther King Jr. led. She mentored and facilitated the coordination of the activist leadership that emerged in the Student Nonviolent Coordinating Committee, with young people like Stokely Carmichael, Bob Moses, Julian Bond, and Diane Nash, for whom she was a trusted and revered adult advisor. "Miss Baker" was actively involved in and favored direct action, like the freedom rides and the Mississippi Freedom Democratic Party. Critical of racism, sexism, and elitism in the movement and emphasizing mass grassroots collective leadership versus the prevailing hierarchical, charismatic, domineering male leadership style, Ella Baker said, "Strong people don't need strong leaders." Describing her as a "radical humanist" and a "Freirian teacher and practitioner of a "radical democratic pedagogy" (though her work precedes Freire), biographer Barbara Ransby notes,

> In Baker's view, people had many of the answers within themselves; teachers and leaders simply had to facilitate the process of tapping and framing that knowledge, of drawing it out . . . her view of *teaching for liberation*

was based on the need to empower ordinary people to dig within themselves and their collective experiences for answers to social and political questions.

(Ransby, 2003, pp. 358–359, emphasis added)

Ransby also discusses similarities between Baker's and Paulo Freire's pedagogical style, as well as the thought and practice of Italian Marxist theorist Antonio Gramsci, who also regarded every teacher as a student and every student as a teacher. Ella Baker's courage was legendary and her method of participatory grassroots leadership for democratic social change profoundly valued the knowledge, experience, and wisdom of the people with whom she worked. She is an excellent example of an educator-activist who valued and learned from the heritage knowledge extant in communities and returned what she learned to strengthen their liberation-seeking practices. This knowledge is excluded from the standard school curriculum—as we have shown throughout this text. As discussed ahead, such knowledge is identified in the United Nations 2014 establishment of the International Decade of People of African Descent, which places the education and human rights of African people on an international stage.

The UN International Decade of People of African Descent

The main objective of the UN International Decade is the protection, promotion, and fulfillment of "all human rights and fundamental freedoms" for people of African descent recognized by the Universal Declaration of Human Rights. The theme of the International Decade is "Recognition, Justice and Development," which emphasizes education, including curriculum, textbooks, and teaching for racial-social justice. "Recognition" means that member states are expected to raise awareness "by supporting research and educational initiatives" ensuring that

> textbooks and other educational materials reflect historical facts accurately as they relate to past tragedies, atrocities, in particular slavery, the slave trade, the transatlantic slave trade and colonialism, so as to avoid stereotypes and the distortion or falsification of these historic facts which may lead to racism, racial discrimination, xenophobia and related intolerance.
>
> *(2015–2024 International Decade of*
> *People of African Descent-Recognition, n.d.)*

"Development" emphasizes the right to education. Thus, UN member states should

> ensure that public and private education systems do not discriminate against or exclude children of African descent, and that they are protected from direct or indirect discrimination, negative stereotyping, stigmatization and

violence from peers or teachers; to this end, training and sensitization should be provided to teachers and measures should be taken to increase the number of teachers of African descent working in educational institutions.

(2015–2024 U.N. International Decade of People of African Descent-Development, n.d.)

In January 2016 "at the invitation of the government of the United States" the UN's Working Group of Experts on People of African Descent, then chaired by Frantz Fanon's daughter, Mireille Fanon Mendès-France, conducted a fact-finding mission in five U.S. cities: Washington, DC, Baltimore, Maryland, Jackson, Mississippi, Chicago, Illinois, and New York (Oakford, 2016; United Nations, Office of the High Commissioner of Human Rights, 2017). The news media reported their findings under banner headlines, such as "U.N. Experts Seem Horrified by How American Schools Treat Black Children" and "UN Committee Urges U.S. Government to Pay Reparations for Slavery" (Klein, 2016).

The Final Report of the Working Group of Experts submitted to the Thirty-Third Session of the Human Rights Council of the UN General Assembly focuses on structural barriers in the areas of criminal justice, police brutality, housing discrimination, food insecurity, school closings, and disparities in access to health and employment, as well as reparations for slavery. For example, "to assist the United States in its efforts to combat all forms of racism, racial discrimination, Afrophobia, xenophobia and related intolerance," the report's recommendations pertain to various life and death matters, such as mass incarceration, police killings of unarmed African Americans with apparent state impunity, and racial discrimination in the justice system. Item Number 118 refers to ensuring that curricula "appropriately reflect the history of the transatlantic slave trade in Africans, enslavement and segregation" (Report of the Working Group of Experts, 2016, Number 118). While appropriately reflect[ing] the history of enslavement is important, education in the Black intellectual (liberation) tradition is about the restoration of African people's historical and cultural consciousness. And as Asa Hilliard so often advised, we do not start our story with slavery (Hilliard, 1997; King, 1992, 2011). See Chapter 4 for further development of this admonition.

The Working Group of Experts report calls upon the U.S. government to take concerted action to end racial oppression. However, in addition to a top-down approach, holding the government accountable for meaningful change also requires informed bottom-up participation in the struggle by those who are most aggrieved by the issues the report delineates. This is exactly what Septima Clark realized was necessary in order to transform nonreading Black adults into registered voters ready to reclaim their civil and human rights (Olsen, 2001, p. 220). The next section illustrates examples of knowledge and consciousness "born of struggle" in the 1950s and 1960s (Harris, 1983) that enabled everyday Black people to lay their lives on the line to transform this society. Of particular relevance for education research in the Black intellectual (liberation) tradition are the practices that can be seen in sites of study and struggle that facilitated such learning/s and changed consciousness.

"I Know I Been Changed"

Voter registration campaigns in the mid- to later twentieth century involved mass popular education that included literacy instruction and political organizing (Morris, 1984). Despite racial terror and deadly violence, local leaders emerged conscious of the life-transforming experiences, personal strength, and communal spiritual reserves that enabled them collectively to resist, reclaim their humanity, and transcend the enforced lack of knowledge that defined the "systematic racial terrorism" of the Jim Crow regime (Payne, 1995, p. 7). That regime's hegemony was relentless but never complete—from the *Maafa* to the present day—given the presence of African heritage knowledge or cultural memory that has been a wellspring of resistance to oppression. Efforts to transform unjust systems over centuries can be situated in heritage knowledge that *freedom is an inherent right [state of being]* and that *love, dignity, and decency are shared by all*—two of the African cultural concepts delineated throughout this text.

In twentieth-century civil rights history, consider what brought Mrs. Fannie Lou Hamer into the Black freedom struggle. Mrs. Hamer recounted what happened during a mass meeting in a Mississippi church, where "a gospel that embraced the longings and desires of a disenfranchised people" was preached and practiced: "We hadn't heard anything about registering to vote . . . but when they asked for those to raise their hands who'd go down to the courthouse the next day, I raised mine . . . as high as I could get it" (Marsh, 1997, p. 12). White theologian Charles Marsh explains that Mrs. Hamer had known all along that something was wrong with the harsh life her family and community had been forced to endure, and in the passage ahead he offers his interpretation that the "faith of the black church had prepared her for this moment" (p. 13). "[James] Bevel's sermon followed by SNCC member James Forman's talk on the constitutional right to vote spoke deeply to Mrs. Hamer's longing for justice. Her imagination was charged by new moral and spiritual energies" (p. 12).

An African-centered interpretation suggests, however, that rather than the awakening of "*new* moral and spiritual energies," the "longing for justice" inherent within Mrs. Hamer's imagination can be understood as an expression of the continuity of African consciousness in Black life and culture that has never been obliterated (King & Swartz, 2016). This inherent longing resisted the nihilation (e.g., total abjection) of her humanity (King, 2017; Nobles, 2015; Rucker, 2006); and African Diasporan scholarship avers that although the Black church has served as a site of struggle for justice in Black communities, Black Christianity was Africanized before it was absorbed within the Black community (Semmes, 1995, p. 8). While we know that European religion has been a powerful force for African people's cultural negation, Michael Gomez (1998) and Sterling Stuckey (1987) demonstrate that European religion did not erase Black people's African spirituality, which "persisted behind the oppressive veneer of European sacred, mythological, and supremacist symbol systems" (Semmes, 1995, p. 8).

The modern civil rights movement provided culturally affirming and sustaining contexts for "critical studyin'" (King, 2006) in which the leadership capacity of "local people" like Mrs. Hamer was forged (Dittmer, 1995) as they analyzed their reality with others and learned with and from each other about their common experiences with systems of oppression. These sites of "study and struggle" (Kelley, 2016) afforded learning/s from experience that facilitated Black people's historical and cultural consciousness and bolstered their courage and their collective pride in their identity and humanity as a people. I imagine they sang old soul-stirring songs, like "I know I've been changed, the angels in Heaven done signed my name," with reenergized enthusiasm.

Study, Struggle, and Learning/s From Experience

Educators have little or no opportunities to study or theorize civil rights movement teachings and organizing and certainly not regarding how Black educational thought contributed to theorizing, research methods, and pedagogy in the Black intellectual (liberation) tradition. While the students I teach are usually familiar with Freire's *Pedagogy of the Oppressed* as a founding critical pedagogy text (first published in Brazil in Portuguese in 1968 and translated into English in 1970), they are uninformed about the liberation pedagogy and research foundation upon which Black citizenship schools were established in the United States before Freire was known here. My students are also unaware of the systematic research that Freire undertook in Brazil in order to develop his method of adult literacy instruction ("in 30 hours"), nor do they know anything about Freire's literacy work with and his respect for the thought, research, and pedagogical praxes of revolutionary African leaders (Brown, 1970; Freire, 1970; Rabaka, 2008).

Freedom Schools

Other significant sites for study and struggle, critical pedagogy, morally engaged research, and community organizing are the 41 Mississippi Summer Project Freedom Schools taught by SNCC field secretaries and other volunteers during "Freedom Summer" in 1964 (Carmichael, 1974). Freedom schools were organized in Alabama as well (House, 2012). Accounts of the development and implementation of the curriculum and question-driven pedagogy in the freedom schools show that lessons learned at Highlander and the citizenship education schools on John's Island were incorporated into the curriculum and education-activists like Septima Clark, Myles Horton, and Ella Baker were directly involved (Emory et al., 2004). Of particular importance is that both African and local history were essential elements in the collectively constructed curriculum and pedagogy that were designed to raise the consciousness, political awareness, and civic engagement of Black youth.

Saul Alinsky's Organizing Tradition

There are notable parallels among the inquiry methods and political skill-building activities implemented at Highlander Folk School, the citizenship schools, the freedom schools, Freire's pedagogy of the oppressed, and Saul Alinsky's community organizing (Bell et al., 1990). (I participated in a national workshop led by Saul Alinsky before I learned about Freire.) Alinsky mobilized impoverished people beginning in the 1930s, and by the 1950s was organizing oppressed Black communities in Chicago and other cities (Alinsky, 1971). College students began using Alinsky's methods in campus struggles in the 1960s. It is worth noting that the first item on a list of Alinsky's training/teaching activities is "research—both on proposed solutions to problems and on power structures" (Schutz & Miller, 2015, p. 35).

Organizing in Communities

A comprehensive analysis of pedagogy and research and the nature of learning/s across social contexts of organizing and struggle is needed. Although such an analysis is beyond the scope of this chapter, a comparative inquiry would examine learning/s in contexts, such as: Black radical labor mobilizing among auto workers in Detroit, including the League of Revolutionary Black Workers (Ahmad, 2007; Boggs, 1968) and the more recent movement to "re-spirit" Detroit, "Detroit Summer," organized by Grace and Jimmy Boggs; the anti-apartheid campaigns led by Leo Robinson (2008), the ILWU longshoremen (stevedores) in the ports of San Francisco and Oakland who refused to unload cargo ships from South Africa during the apartheid regime (Marable & Rickford, 2011), and the Revolutionary Black Workers at Polaroid in Massachusetts ("Polaroid and Apartheid," 2013); and the collective leadership and civil rights organizing tradition "in the spirit of Ella" (Moses et al., 1989; Moye, 2013; Payne, 1995), as well as union-building activities among coal miners in impoverished Appalachian mountain communities that inspired Myles Horton (and his collaborators) to establish Highlander, which began with labor education workshops (Horton, 1997; Wigginton, 1992)—to cite a few examples.

The Black Intellectual (Liberation) Tradition

How and what have people learned in such sites of study and struggle? Is there a demonstrated role for research in the process of learning to act as agents of our own liberation (King, 2005a)? Educators-organizers in the examples cited earlier engaged in systematic prior study and empirical investigation, sometimes including (participant) observation and analysis, in order to construct pedagogical possibilities that democratize learning from experience. However, it is worth remembering what the late Black Marxist scholar Cedric Robinson said to Robin D. G. Kelley: "Experience is important, but consciousness is what matters most" (Kelley, 2017).

Preston Wilcox, an educator/organizer/leader in the movement for community control of schools in New York, emphasizes consciousness in his description of how Black Studies developed as an educational paradigm for "Black humanism." Wilcox (1978) explains:

> The thrust for Black Studies programs developed not on white college campuses but at Selma, at Birmingham, at the March on Washington. It was on the civil rights battlefield that Blacks learned that an appeal to white conscience had to be replaced by an appeal to Black consciousness.

Wilcox notes this Black Studies educational paradigm was intended

> to provide the framework on which new and substantive bodies of knowledge about the Black condition were to be linked. It would require that such issues as self-concept, reparations, collective and cooperative economic enterprises, psychological and political liberation, and a reordering of values be systematically addressed and understood.
>
> *(p. 92)*

Of course, it must also be clearly understood that Black studies and Afrocentric praxis offer vital knowledge we all need as a consequence of what Elizabeth Spelman (2007) describes as the socially generated epistemology of ignorance in our society. Our response to this epistemological ignorance is to exemplify how content and pedagogy can "re-member" or reconnect Africa and the Diaspora— an epistemic connection that we have shown to exist in scholarship and the practices it builds upon. The next section recounts my search for a source of this directive: "Return what you learn to the people," meaning that scholars in the Black intellectual (liberation) tradition have learned from people's/communities' practices and return that knowledge in order to enhance those people and communities.

Seeking the Source of Returning What We Learn

I queried several colleagues to locate a specific source of "Return what you learn to the people," since it so clearly expresses the importance of how education researchers can use African concepts to achieve an emancipatory stance in our work. I called upon Professors Kofi Lomotey (Western Carolina University) and Mwalimu Shujaa (Southern University), both leading intellectual-activists who have expertise in African Diasporan education in the United States and Africa (Milner & Lomotey, 2014; Shujaa & Shujaa, 2015). Professor Lomotey referred me to Tanzanian president Mwalimu Julius K. Nyerere's philosophy of education for self-reliance in the parable ahead. This educational philosophy made a deep impression on Black students in the 1960s:

> Those who receive this privilege (of education) therefore have a duty to repay the sacrifice, which others have made. They are like the man who has been given all the food available in a starving village in order that he might have strength to bring supplies back from a distant place. If he takes this food and does not bring help to his brothers, he is a traitor. Similarly, if any of the young men and women who are given an education by the people of this republic adopt attitudes of superiority, or fail to use their knowledge to help the development of this country, then they are betraying our union.
>
> *(Nyerere, 2007)*

Professor Shujaa suggested the relevance of the following passage in Ghanaian novelist Ayi Kwei Armah's (1979) *The Healers*:

> Healing is . . . the work of inspiration, not manipulation. If we the healers are to do the work of helping to bring our people together again, we need to know such work is the work of a community . . . It should not depend on any single person, however heroic he may be. And it can't depend on people who don't understand the healing vocation—no matter how good such people may be as individuals . . . The work of healers is work for inspirers working long and steadily, in a group . . . able to bring us together again.
>
> *(p. 308)*

Professor Shujaa also suggested that I look at Jacob Carruthers's discussion of Cheikh Anta Diop's "massive project to restore African culture to us," and "cure the amnesia of African peoples" (Carruthers, 1999, p. 221). Carruthers states that for Diop, "such a project must be the work of a group of leaders and intellectuals who commit themselves to the vocation of the restoration of African historical and cultural consciousness" (Carruthers, 1999, pp. 221–222). Diop called upon African intellectuals to use rigorous scientific methods in this project of African rehabilitation—to correct the false doctrine of white superiority. As Carruthers explains, "Diop's devotion to science was not for the sake of science" but for the benefit of African people: "Much more important is the practice of taking the scientifically supported arguments into the arenas of politics, education, and scholarly debate in defense of our people and for the advancement of our people" (p. 227). According to Carruthers, the real intellectual battle is the war between the champions of African-centered thought and the defenders of Western civilization. Carruthers and other Nile Valley scholars, including Asa G. Hilliard, embraced and used Diop's Afrocentric argument to assert the African identity of ancient Egyptians and the cultural and linguistic unity of African people. For many years Hilliard presented a slide show that depicted stunning images of the visual evidence of Diop's argument, titled "Free Your Mind: Return to the Source," our African heritage in ancient Egypt (Kemet). In all of these examples, African Diasporan scholars teach and remind us of our heritage knowledge—of our *shared responsibility for communal well-being and belonging*, of *pursuing knowledge [through science and other epistemologies] as inseparable from pursuing wisdom*, and *knowing as a communal experience in which everyone has something to contribute*. These African cultural concepts are able to more fully restore our cultural memory, and they teach us that we are responsible to enhance our communities with the knowledge we have learned.

I also discussed my search with Dr. Sylvia Hill (2008), who teaches at the University of the District of Columbia and who was an activist in the Pan-African Congress and anti-apartheid movements. We agreed that I should look for the source of "return what you learn to the people" in the civil rights movement/freedom schools pedagogy (Clark, 1964; Cobb, 2011) and the works of Paulo Freire or Amilcar Cabral, leader of the Guinea-Bissau-Cape Verde Islands national liberation movement for independence from Portuguese colonialism. I located a reference for this dictum in the letters Paulo Freire exchanged with Amilcar Cabral.

The *Routledge Dictionary of Twentieth-Century Political Thinkers* includes this description of Cabral:

> In the early 1960s Amilcar Cabral emerged from the national liberation struggle of Guinea-Bissau and Cape Verde as one of the foremost Third World revolutionary theorists and activists of the century. His work on revolutionary organization and ideology, on imperialist exploitation and on African peasantry and national liberation placed him at the forefront of black intellectuals like Frantz Fanon, Julius Nyerere, Kwame Nkrumah and Patrice Lumumba.
>
> *(Benewick & Green, 1992, p. 46)*

Indeed, Cabral remains a revered political figure in the pantheon of African/Black leaders and the PAIGC motto, "A luta continua" ("The struggle continues" in Portuguese), and his speeches ("Tell no lies . . . claim no easy victories") were watchwords among Black activists (Minter et al., 2008). Black Americans followed the struggles and thinking of African revolutionary leaders—many who were assassinated—including Patrice Lumumba, Eduardo Mondlane, and Josina Machel, a courageous FRELIMO leader in Mozambique who also gave her life to free her people.

Freire visited Guinea-Bissau and worked with Amilcar Cabral to develop an adult literacy program in the liberated zones in the countryside. The World Council of Churches (WCC) sponsored this collaboration during Freire's exile from Brazil when it was being ruled by a military dictatorship. Freire documented his correspondence with Cabral and other leaders of the *Partido africano de independência da Guiné e Cabo Verde* (African Party for the Independence of Guinea and Cape Verde—PAIGC) in *Pedagogy in Process: The Letters to Guinea-Bissau* (Freire, 1978). In the book's introduction Freire explains his literacy approach for the benefit of the reader:

> The act of learning to read and write . . . is a creative act that involves a critical comprehension of reality . . . What is implied is not the transmission to the people of a knowledge previously elaborated, a process that ignores what they already know, but the act of returning to them, in an organized form, what they have themselves offered in a disorganized form.
>
> *(pp. 24–25)*

In a footnote citing the statement "We must teach the masses with precision what we receive from them with confusion," Freire identifies its source as Mao Tse Dung in an interview with André Malraus (*Antimémoires* [Paris 1967], p. 531). When I retrieved my copy of *Selected Readings From the Works of Mao Tsetung*, I found that Mao's idea of revolutionary leadership during the Chinese Revolution in 1943 was to put together the ideas of the masses, study them, and return them to the people so they could "translate them into action, and test the correctness of these ideas in such action" (Tsetung, 1971, p. 290). While Mao applied Marxist-Leninist theory to the conditions of the Chinese masses, revolutionary African leaders like Cabral and Nyerere were skeptical of the idea that European historical development (and theory of revolution) should be mistaken as universal—that is to say, that Europe's Marxist theory of class warfare could serve as the guide for African liberation. Accordingly, for Mwalimu (President) Nyerere in Tanzania, "African socialism or *Ujamaa* (familyhood/brotherhood) is rooted . . . within African pre-colonial practices . . . [Nyerere's] prescription . . . is that Africans must look to their own past and accept the inspiration found there" (Benewick & Green, 1992, p. 241). Cabral's thought was grounded in Marxism but he felt free to develop his own analysis of revolution in his society (Chabal, 1983, p. 186). Rather than privilege economic determinism, Cabral's "return to the source" meant returning to indigenous culture, to "the 'memory' of historical development," which contains "the seeds of opposition" (Cabral, 1973, p. 186). Thus, Cabral understood the culture of the masses as a sociological reality to be studied and analyzed (not romanticized) as the source of the ideology of the liberation struggle, which the colonizers necessarily sought to usurp and suppress (Benewick & Green, 1992, p. 48). He knew that colonial domination required suppressing the people's cultural identity and cultivating in its place alienated, de-Africanized, (mis)educated, assimilated "petty bourgeoisie" (middle-class) individuals in the colonizers' image. "Returning to the source(s)" meant joining with the masses in the national liberation struggle (Cabral, 1973). To do so, however, these "educated" individuals would have to achieve a "nationalist consciousness" and identify with and respect the local culture, not the colonizers' foreign culture, which was represented as "superior in every respect" (Chabal, 1983, p. 184).

Ramon Grosfoguel (2013) poses a challenging set of questions for those educated in the intellectual tradition of Western universities that merit consideration here:

> How is it possible that the canon of thought in all the disciplines of the Social Sciences and Humanities in the *Westernized* University . . . is based on the knowledge produced by a few men from five countries . . . Italy, France, England, Germany and the USA? How is it possible that men from these five countries achieved such an epistemic privilege to the point that their knowledge today is considered superior over the knowledge of the rest of the world? . . . Why is it that what we know today as social, historical, philosophical, or Critical Theory is based on the socio-historical experience and world views of men from these five countries?
>
> *(p. 74, emphasis in the original)*

Likewise Black Studies scholar Clovis E. Semmes asked, "Where is the social philosophy, the social, political and economic [or educational] theory that could change the condition of African Americans?" (Semmes, 1992, p. 72). This chapter concludes in the next section with seven examples of education research that illustrate the social uses of research needed to restore the historical and cultural consciousness of people of African ancestry.

Toward Historical/Cultural Consciousness in Afrocentric and Black Studies Education Research

There is striking congruence in the way that community activists, emancipatory educators, and revolutionary political leaders valued the knowledge, cultural heritage, and wisdom of ordinary people. The Black intellectual (liberation) tradition they represent recognizes and defends the unique contribution that people of African origin have to make to civilization and humanity. Education research in this tradition is both "answerable" to our community and based in evidence (Asante, 2015; Patel, 2014). This stance toward knowledge production for historical and cultural consciousness centered in the lived experience of people of African ancestry is the antidote to what I have described as epistemological nihilation—"the imposition of an ideological conception of blackness . . . which involves the inherent denial or total abjection of one's identity and beingness and falsely elevates whiteness" (King, 2017, p. 212). It is a stance that accords with W.E.B. Du Bois's commitment to social advocacy through activist scholarship and his rejection of the eurocratic paradigm's racialized use of the false standard of objectivity (Byrd, 2016; Marable & Rickford, 2011; Morris, 2015). According to Manning Marable (2000), the Black intellectual (liberation) tradition has always been *prescriptive*, and while the study of history has been central, as Du Bois also recognized, history has often been nothing more than an "ideological ruse" (Rabaka, 2008, p. 44). This applies to research across the disciplines (Semmes, 1981). Seven examples of contemporary education research and intellectual activism ahead illustrate the problem-solving possibilities for research in this Black intellectual (liberation) tradition:

1. *Morally engaged, culturally informed research.* Vernon Polite's (2000) study of predominately Black Catholic schools with a tradition of student success identified four categories of "effective curriculum" for African American students. Some schools taught "basic knowledge of African American history and culture" (Category 1), others made an effort to center instruction around African American culture (Category 2), and still fewer schools offered a curriculum centering instruction for all students' cognitive and affective development in African American history and culture (Category 3). Polite found no evidence of curriculum for teaching Black cultural values that would prepare students to be agents of social change (Category 4), the Afrocentric curriculum approach that he deemed is most needed for African American students' development. He nevertheless included this missing Category 4 in the study's published findings to point prescriptively toward an educational ideal based on Black cultural values: the type of education needed to prepare Black students, particularly Black Catholics in the United States, as "agents of social change for the betterment of the African American people" (p. 149).

2. *Public scholarship for advocacy.* Publishing commentaries in *Education Week*, the *Boston Globe*, and the *Washington Post*, for instance, Leslie T. Fenwick (2006, 2013) has waged a vigorous public scholarship campaign on behalf of Black educators and saving public schools to serve Black children. Demonstrating the uses of empirical research in advocacy, Fenwick's forthcoming book, titled *Jim Crow's Pink Slip: Public Policy and the Near Decimation of Black Educational Leadership After Brown* (cited in McIntyre, 2016), investigates the dearth of Black teachers and principals in the wake of the 1954 Brown decision (Chimurenga, 2016; Garcia, 2016).

3. *The education cartel exposed.* Walter C. Farrell's policy analysis of the "education cartel," published in the online magazine *BlackCommentator.com*, is a hard-hitting empirical, political, and partisan exposé. This investigative research series documents and disseminates evidence of organized attacks to dismantle and privatize public education by "conservative corporate, intellectual and political reformers" (Farrell, 2015).

4. *The People's Report.* "Street ethnographer" and Black studies professor Yasser Payne (2013) has trained 15 formerly incarcerated people to research their experiences with violence, unemployment, racialized educational disparities using sites of resilience theory (Payne, 2011). This participatory action research (PAR) project is an ethnographic community needs assessment of two inner-city neighborhoods in Wilmington, Delaware (Nardone, 2013). A documentary film, *The People's Report,* makes the findings of this assessment broadly accessible in addition to Payne's scholarly publications and more than 100 presentations the research team has made (Hitchens & Payne, 2017; Payne & Brown, 2016).

5. *The Youth Bucket Brigade.* A nonprofit grassroots group originally formed in Gainesville, Georgia, by Black women in 1956 to provide funeral wreaths, the Newtown Florist Club was established under the leadership of "Mrs. Ruby Wilkins by club members who felt a civic responsibility to their community . . . to fill a void of activism" (Newtown Florist Club Facebook page). After discovering an alarming pattern—that their neighbors were succumbing to illnesses apparently related to toxic contamination—they asked state environmental agencies to investigate industrial pollution from several nearby plants (Christ, 2010). However, the community's needs were not addressed, as the club's Facebook page recounts: "As acts occurred related to racist violence, police brutality, insensitive and intolerant public officials, voting rights, and environmental racism, and deplorable living conditions, the group was led to shift its focus" (Newtown Florist Club Facebook page).

   In keeping with their focus on youth leadership training, in 2005 the club sent their "Youth Bucket Brigade," children aged 8–18, to investigate the candy manufactured in Mexico contaminated with lead being sold in Hispanic groceries in Gainesville, Georgia. Unable to prevent its sale, the African American children in the Youth Bucket Brigade, who also consumed this candy, emphasized using their findings to educate their peers (Gilbert, 2005).

6. *Songhoy (African) language for cultural recovery.* We acknowledge that what we as educators know comes from the lived realities of people, and that our responsibility is to return what we have learned to the people. As described in Chapter 3, one way to "re-member" heritage knowledge or recover cultural memory is through access to curriculum in multiple languages that can fill the gaps in our knowledge that exist because we have been effectively kept away from the languages of our ancestors. In Mali, West Africa, Hassimi Maïga's (2010, 2015) intellectual activism serves an African community that is in danger of losing its connections with its history and heritage. Recently he led a team that has translated the *Holy Qur'an* into the Songhoy language, which can correct distortions in the religious instruction people in this community are receiving, especially regarding the treatment of women and girls.

7. *Archaeological research in Kemet.* Funded by the ASA Restoration Project, Anthony T. Browder (2011) is the only African American leading an archaeological excavation in Kemet (Egypt). He explains that Twenty-Fifth Dynasty rulers were instrumental in engaging in "retroactive remembrances" to rehabilitate Kemet and were responsible for introducing the first "renaissance" (or "repetition of births"—*Wehem mesut* in the ancient Kemetic language) in recorded history. Browder and his team recently discovered Sankofa symbols painted on the ceilings of two Twenty-Fifth Dynasty tombs near the temple of Hatshepsut "during a conference that was organized to commemorate the opening of the restored 2nd pillared hall in the tomb of Karakhamun" (personal communication, October 2016).

The foregoing seven examples demonstrate researchers who are returning what they learn to the people in various ways—from policy analysis and cultural restoration to youth action research. As Beverly Gordon (1990) suggested, education [research] can assist people of color (and their teachers) in challenging the societal structures that maintain and reproduce inequality. Noting that its broad-based epistemology is one of its strengths, Gordon stressed that African American scholarship takes the actual experience of the African American community as its starting point.

Conclusion

In this chapter I (Joyce King) have attempted to demonstrate the transformative power and possibilities of education research in the Black intellectual (liberation) tradition that obligates us to return what we learn to the people to restore our collective historical and cultural amnesia (King, 2017). The education and advocacy efforts described in this final chapter were generated within an African episteme—that is, within African ways of knowing based on an African worldview and the cultural concepts that express that worldview. When there is access to knowledge about the collective African family—passed on from Africa to the Diaspora and from one generation to the next—this episteme is visible in the heritage knowledge (a group's cultural memory) and practices of a people. Our task as emancipatory African Diasporan scholars, PK-12 teachers, administrators, and community educators and activists is to learn from this knowledge and these practices in order to transform eurocratic and distorted representations of the past and in turn the present. We can return what we have learned by breaking through the entrenched hegemonic curriculum that continues to systematically miseducate our children by distorting knowledge in every discipline (King, 1995).

W.E.B. Du Bois's and Carter G. Woodson's monumental efforts, the civil rights and African liberation movements, and over a century of African Diasporan scholarship have prepared the ground for transforming education, yet the vast majority of educators fail to grasp the real nature of oppression and education's role in maintaining it (King, 2000). We need to deepen our knowledge of African Peoples' traditional practices *that foster communal well-being, belonging, and the sharing of love, dignity, and decency by all*—the same practices that have supported ongoing efforts to overcome injustice and inequality in Africa and the Diaspora. This requires that we use the authority of our African cultural heritage to examine how theory and research, including the eurocratic myth of objectivity, have been used to obfuscate our moral reasoning and to legitimize oppression as inevitable (King, 1996; Mazama, 2001). A precept of African epistemology is that the African person "thinks not only with the head but also with the heart" (Nkulu-N'Sengha, 2005, p. 42). And as African people, we bring this essentially spiritual rationality to the intellectual battle and to our struggle for an education that is liberating. By retrieving an African episteme, we can produce emancipatory curricula, pedagogies, and research to return what we have learned for the benefit of our people and humanity.

References

2015–2024 International Decade of People of African Descent, Recognition. (n.d.). Retrieved from www.un.org/en/events/africandescentdecade/development.shtml

Ahmad, M. (Max Stafford, Jr.). (2007). *We will return in the whirlwind: Black radical organizations 1960–1975*. Chicago, IL: Charles H. Kerr.

Alinsky, S. (1971). *Rules for radicals: A pragmatic primer for realistic radicals*. New York, NY: Random House.

Armah, A. K. (1979). *The healers*. London: Heinemann.

Asante, M. K. (2015). *African pyramids of knowledge: Kemet, Afrocentricity and Africology*. Brooklyn, NY: Universal Write.

Bell, B., Gaventa, J., & Peters, J. (Eds.). (1990). *Myles Horton and Paulo Freire: We make the road by walking: Conversations on education and social change*. Philadelphia: Temple University Press.

Benewick, R., & Green, P. (1992). *The Routledge dictionary of twentieth-century political thinkers*. London: Routledge.

Boggs, G. (1974). Education the great obsession. In Institute of the Black World (Ed.), *Education and Black struggle: Notes from the colonized world* (pp. 61–81). Harvard Educational Review Monograph, No. 2.

Boggs, J. (1968). *The American revolution: Pages from a Negro worker's notebook*. New York, NY: Monthly Review Press. Retrieved from www.historyisaweapon.com/defcon1/amreboggs.html

Browder, A. T. (2011). *Finding Karakhamun: The collaborative rediscovery of a lost tomb*. Washington, DC: IKG.

Brown, C. (1970). *Literacy in 30 hours: Paulo Freire's literacy process in North East Brazil*. London: Writers and Readers.

Brownies' Books. (n.d.). *DuBoisopedia*. Retrieved from http://scua.library.umass.edu/duboisopedia/doku.php?id=about:brownies_book

Byrd, B. (2016, August 13). The Black intellectual tradition and the myth of objectivity. *Black Perspectives, AAIHS*. Retrieved from www.aaihs.or/author/bbyrd/

Cabral, A. (1973). *Return to the source: Selected speeches of Amilcar Cabral.* New York, NY: Monthly Review Press.

Carmichael, S. (1974). Stokely's speech class. In M. Wasserman (Ed.), *Demystifying school* (pp. 327–330). New York, NY: Praeger.

Carruthers, J. (1999). *Intellectual warfare.* Chicago, IL: Third World Press.

Chabal, P. (1983). *Amilcar Cabral: Revolutionary leadership and people's war.* New York, NY: Cambridge University Press.

Chimurenga, T. (2016, September 5). Of course Black educators matter: But do we know why? *Daily Kos.* Retrieved from www.dailykos.com/story/2016/9/6/1566580/-Of-course-Black-educators-matter-but-do-we-know-why

Christ, C. (2010, October 10). "Carry the struggle": Newtown Florist Club at 60. *Gainesville Times Viewpoint.* Retrieved from www.gainesvilletimes.com/archives/39227/

Clark, S. P. (1964). *Literacy for liberation.* Freedomways, 1st Quarter. New York: Freedomways Associates.

Cobb, C. (2011, July–August). Freedom's struggle and Freedom schools. *Monthly Review, 63*(3). Retrieved from https://monthlyreview.org/2011/07/01/freedoms-struggle-and-freedom-schools/

Dagbovie, P. (2007). *The early Black history movement: Carter G. Woodson and Lorenzo Johnston Greene.* Chicago, IL: University of Illinois Press.

Diop, C. (1991). *Civilization or barbarism: An authentic anthropology.* Brooklyn, NY: Lawrence Hill Books.

Dittmer, J. (1995). *Local people: The struggle for civil rights in Mississippi.* Champaign, IL: University of Illinois Press.

Du Bois, W.E.B. (1985). "The star of Ethiopia: A pageant" 1915. In H. Aptheker (Ed.), *Pamphlets and leaflets (W.E.B. DuBois works)* (pp. 161–165, 206–309). White Plains, NY: Kraus-Thomason.

Du Bois, W.E.B. (1973). *The education of Black people: Ten critiques, 1906–1960.* (Herbert Aptheker, Ed.). New York, NY: Monthly Review Press.

Emory, K., Braselmann, S., & Gold, L. R. (2004). *Mississippi Freedom School Curriculum.* Retrieved from www.educationanddemocracy.org/FSCfiles/A_02_Introduction.htm

Fals Borda, O. (1980). Science and the common people. In F. Dubell et al. (Eds.), *Research for the people: Research by the people* (pp. 13–40). Linkoping, Sweden: Linkoping University.

Farrell, W. C. (2015). Dismantling public education from Reagan to Obama: Public School privatization, Race to the Top (RTTT) and Common Core. BlackCommenator.com, September, Issue #621. Retrieved from http://blackcommentator.com/621/621_cover_dismantling_public_education_from_reagan_to_obama_farrell_guest.html

Fenwick, L. T. (2006). *Putting school and community on the map: Linking school reform, neighborhood revitalization, and community building.* Columbia, MD: Enterprise Atlanta Community Partners. Retrieved from http://community-wealth.org/sites/clone.community-wealth.org/files/downloads/report-fenwick.pdf

Fenwick, L. T. (2013, May 28). Urban school reform is really about land development (not kids). *The Washington Post.* Retrieved from www.washingtonpost.com/news/answer-sheet/wp/2013/05/28/ed-school-dean-urban-school-reform-is-really-about-land-development-not-kids/?utm_term=.682a0f21fefd

Flesch, R. (1951). *The art of clear thinking.* New York, NY: Collier Books.

Freire, P. (1970). *Pedagogy of the oppressed.* New York, NY: Continuum.

Freire, P. (1978). *Pedagogy in process: The letters to Guinea-Bissau.* New York, NY: Continuum.

Garcia, L. E. (2016, September 9). Black teachers matter. *Lily's Blackboard/Blog.* Retrieved October 3, 2016, from http://lilysblackboard.org/2016/09/black-teachers-matter/

Gilbert, D. (2005, October 7). Hall stores found with toxic treats: 2004 study revealed many types of imported candy contain lead. *The Gainesville Times.* Retrieved from http://gainesvillelegals.com/news/stories/20051007/localnews/24146.shtml

Gomez, M. (1998). *Exchanging our country marks: The transformation of African identities in the colonial and antebellum south.* Chapel Hill, NC: University of North Carolina Press.

Gordon, B. (1990). The necessity of African-American epistemology for educational theory and practice. *The Journal of Education, 172*(3), 88–106.

Greene, L. J. (1996). *Selling Black history for Carter G. Woodson: A diary, 1930–1933.* Columbia: University of Missouri Press.

Grosfoguel, R. (2013). The structure of knowledge in westernized universities: Epistemic racism/sexism and the four genocides/epistemicides of the long 16th century. *Human Architecture: Journal of the Sociology of Self-Knowledge, 11*(1), 73–90. Retrieved from http://scholarworks.umb.edu/humanarchitecture/vol11/iss1/8

Harris, L. (Ed.). (1983). *Philosophy born of struggle: An anthology of African-American philosophy from 1917.* Dubuque, IA: Kendal/Hunt.

Hill, S. (2008). Sylvia Hill: From the Sixth Pan-African Congress to the Free South Africa Movement. In W. Minter, G. Hovey, & C. Cobb (Eds.), *No easy victories: African liberation and American activists over a half century, 1950–2000* (pp. 167–169). Trenton, NJ: African World Press.

Hilliard, A. G. III (1997). *SBA: The reawakening of the African mind.* Gainesville, FL: Makare.

Hine, D. C. (1986, May). Carter G. Woodson, White philanthropy and Negro historiography. *The History Teacher, 19*(3), 405–425.

Hitchens, B. K., & Payne, Y. A. (2017). "Brenda's got a baby": Black single motherhood and street life as a site of resilience in Wilmington, Delaware. *Journal of Black Psychology, 43*(1), 50–76.

Horton, M. (1997). *The long haul: An autobiography.* New York: Teachers College Press.

House, G. (2012). We'll never turn back. In F. S. Holsaert, M. Prescod Norman Noonan, J. Richardson, et al. (Eds.), *Hands on the freedom plow: Personal accounts by women in SNCC* (pp. 503–514). Urbana: University of Illinois Press.

Jensen, A. (1969). How much can we boost I.Q. and scholastic achievement? *Harvard Educational Review, 39*, 1–123.

Karagueuzian, D. (1971). *Blow it up! The Black student revolt at San Francisco State and the emergence of Dr. Haykawa.* Boston: Gambit.

Kelley, R.D.G. (2016, March 7). Black study, Black struggle. *Boston Review.* Retrieved from http://bostonreview.net/forum/robin-d-g-kelley-black-study-black-struggle

Kelley, R.D.G. (2017, February 17). Robin D. G. Kelley Interview UWI TV. Cave Hill Campus, University of West Indies. Retrieved from www.uwitv.org/prog/pelican-pride-robin-d-g-kelley-interview-feb-17-2017

King, J. E. (1992). Diaspora literacy and consciousness in the struggle against miseducation in the Black community. *Journal of Negro Education, 61*(3), 317–340.

King, J. E. (1995). Culture-centered knowledge: Black studies, curriculum transformation and social action. In J. Banks & C. A. Banks (Eds.), *Handbook of research on multicultural education* (1st Rev. ed., pp. 265–290). San Francisco, CA: Jossey-Bass.

King, J. E. (1996). Bad luck, bad blood, bad faith: Ideological hegemony and the oppressive language of hoodoo social science. In J. Kinchloe, S. Steinberg, & A. Gresson (Eds.), *Measured lies: The Bell Curve re-examined* (pp. 177–192). New York, NY: St. Martin's Press.

King, J. E. (1999). In search of a method for liberating education and research: The half (that) has not been told. In C. A. Grant (Ed.), *Multicultural research: A reflective engagement with race, class, gender and sexual orientation* (pp. 101–119). Philadelphia, PA: Falmer Press.

King, J. E. (2000, Fall). White teachers at the crossroads: A moral choice for White teachers. *Teaching Tolerance Magazine, 18,* 14–15.

King, J. E. (2005a). A transformative vision of Black education for human freedom. In J. E. King (Ed.), *Black education: A transformative research & action agenda for the new century* (pp. 3–17). Washington, DC: AERA/Mahwah, NJ: Lawrence Erlbaum.

King, J. E. (2005b). Rethinking the Black/White duality of our times. In A. Bogues (Ed.), *Caribbean reasonings: After man, toward the human: Critical essays on Sylvia Wynter* (pp. 25–56). Kingston, Jamaica: Ian Randle.

King, J. E. (2006). "If justice is our objective": Diaspora literacy, heritage knowledge and the praxis of critical studyin' for human freedom. In A. Ball (Ed.), *With more deliberate speed: Achieving equity and excellence in education: Realizing the full potential of Brown v. Board of Education* (pp. 337–360). NSSE 105th Yearbook, Part II. New York: Ballinger.

King, J. E. (2011, Summer). "Who dat say (we) too depraved to be saved?" Re-membering Katrina/Haiti (and beyond): Critical studyin' for human freedom. *Harvard Educational Review, 81*(2), 343–370.

King, J. E. (2016). "We may well become accomplices": To rear a generation of spectators is not to educate at all. *Educational Researcher, 45*(2), 159–172.

King, J. E. (2017). 2015 AERA Presidential Address. Morally engaged research/ers dismantling epistemological nihilation in the age of impunity. *Educational Researcher, 46*(5), 211–222.

King, J. E., & Swartz, E. E. (2016). *The Afrocentric praxis of teaching for freedom: Connecting culture to learning.* New York, NY: Routledge.

King, J. E., Swartz, E. E., et al. (2014). *Re-membering history in student and teacher learning: An Afrocentric culturally informed praxis.* New York, NY: Routledge.

King Papers. (1961). *Burroughs, Nannie Helen, biography.* Retrieved from https://kinginstitute.stanford.edu/encyclopedia/burroughs-nannie-helen

Klein, R. (2016, February 2). U.N. experts seem horrified by how American schools treat Black children. *The Huffington Post.* Retrieved from www.huffingtonpost.com/entry/school-discrimination-united-nations_us_56b141e1e4b01d80b24474d3; www.rt.com/usa/330934-un-recommends-usa-reparations-slavery/

Lewis, D. L. (2000). *W.E.B. Du Bois: The fight for equality and the American century, 1919–1963.* New York: Henry Holt.

Lipsitz, G., Green, P., Kelley, R. D. G., Poe, T., & Rogers, J. (2016). Generations of struggle: Panel discussion on protest before, during and after the Ferguson rebellion. *Kalfou, 3*(1), 7–35.

Maïga, H. O. (2010). *Balancing written history with oral tradition: The legacy of the Songhoy people.* New York: Taylor & Francis.

Maïga, H. O. (2015). Africana sociocultural heritage. In M. J. Shujaa & K. J. Shujaa (Eds.), *The SAGE encyclopedia of African cultural heritage in North America* (pp. 158–166). Thousand Oaks, CA: SAGE.

Marable, M. (Ed.). (2000). *Dispatches from the Ebony tower: Intellectuals confront the African American experience* (pp. 1–2). New York: Columbia University Press.

Marable, M., & Rickford, R. (2011). *Beyond boundaries: The Manning Marable reader*. New York: Paradigm.

Marsh, C. (1997). *God's long summer: Stories of faith and civil rights*. Princeton, NJ: Princeton University Press.

Mazama, A. (2001). The Afrocentric paradigm: Contours and definitions. *Journal of Black Studies, 31*(4), 387–405.

McIntyre, E. (2016). Fewer Black male teachers leading K12 classrooms. *Education Dive*. Retrieved from www.educationdive.com/news/fewer-black-male-teachers-leading-k-12-classrooms/414256/

Milner, H. R., & Lomotey, K. (2014). *Handbook of urban education*. New York: Routledge.

Minter, W., Hovey, G., & Cobb, C. (Eds.). (2008). *No easy victories: African liberation and American activists over a half century, 1950–2000*. Trenton, NJ: African World Press.

Morris, A. D. (1984). *The origins of the civil rights movement: Black communities organizing for change*. New York: The Free Press.

Morris, A. D. (2015). *The scholar denied: The scholar denied*. Oakland: University of California Press.

Moses, R. P., Kamii, M., McAllister, S., & Howard, J. (1989). The Algebra Project: Organizing in the spirit of Ella. *Harvard Educational Review, 59*(4), 423–443.

Moye, J. T. (2013). *Ella Baker: Community organizer of the civil rights movement*. Lanham, MD: Rowman & Littlefield.

Nardone, M. (2013). Can Payne end violence? *Delaware Today*. Retrieved from www.delawaretoday.com/Delaware-Today/September-2013/University-of-Delaware-Professor-Yasser-Paynes-Efforts-to-Decrease-Wilmingtons-Crime-Rate/index.php?cpa rticle=6&siarticle=5#artanc

Nkulu-N'Sengha, M. (2005). African epistemology. In M. K. Asante & M. A. Mazama (Eds.), *Encyclopedia of Black Studies* (pp. 39–44). Thousand Oaks, CA: SAGE.

Nobles, W. W. (2015). African cultural consciousness as cultural continuity. In M. J. Shujaa & K. J. Shujaa (Eds.). *The SAGE encyclopedia of African cultural heritage in North America* (Vol. 1, pp. 44–48). Los Angeles: SAGE.

Nyerere, J. (2007, November). On higher education, 1960s. *UDSM Alumni Newsletter*, 2. Retrieved from https://en.wikiquote.org/wiki/Julius_Nyerere

Oakford, S. (2016). In US visit, UN experts insist that Washington needs to consider reparations for slavery. *Muhammad Speaks, 20*(19), 5, 7.

Olsen, L. (2001). *Freedom's daughters: The unsung heroines of the civil rights movement from 1830 to 1970*. New York, NY: Simon & Schuster.

Patel, L. (2014). Countering coloniality in educational research: From ownership to answerability. *Educational Studies, 40*(4), 357–377.

Payne, C. (1995). *I've got the light of freedom: The organizing tradition and Mississippi freedom struggle*. Berkeley, CA: University of California Press.

Payne, Y. A. (2011). A reconceptualization of resiliency and resilience in street life-oriented Black men. *Journal of Black Psychology, 37*(4), 426–451.

Payne, Y. A. (2013). *The people's report: The link between structural violence and crime in Wilmington, Delaware*. http://www.thepeoplesreport.com/images/pdf/Executive_Summary_final_draft_9_2013.pdf

Payne, Y. A., & Brown, T. M. (2016). "I'm still waiting on that Golden ticket": Attitudes toward and experiences with opportunity in the streets of Black America. *Journal of Social Issues, 72*(4), 789–811.

Polaroid & Apartheid: Inside the beginnings of the boycott, divestment movement against South Africa (2013, December 13). *Democracy Now*. Retrieved from www.democracynow. org/2013/12/13/polaroid_apartheid_inside_the_beginnings_of

Polite, V. C. (2000). Cornerstones: Catholic high schools that serve predominately African American student populations. In J. Youniss & J. J. Convey (Eds.), *Catholic schools at the crossroads: Survival and transformation* (pp. 137–156). New York, NY: Teachers College Press.

Rabaka, R. (2008). *Du Bois's dialectics: Black radical politics and the reconstruction of critical social theory*. Lanham, MD: Lexington Books.

Ransby, B. (2003). *Ella Baker and the Black freedom movement: A radical democratic vision*. Chapel Hill, NC: University of North Carolina Press.

Reeves/King, J. E. (1974). *An experimental evaluation of a behavior change curriculum for Black high school students*. (Ph.D. dissertation). Stanford University, Stanford, CA.

Report of the Working Group of Experts on People of African Descent on Its Mission to the United States of America. (2016, August 18). *Human Rights Council thirty-third session of the UN General Assembly, agenda item 9*. Retrieved from www.ushrnetwork. org/sites/ushrnetwork.org/files/unwgepad_us_visit_final_report_9_15_16.pdf

Robinson, L. (2008). From local to national—Bay Area connections. In W. Minter, G. Hovey, & C. Cobb, Jr. (Eds.), *No easy victories: African liberation and American activists over a half century, 1950–2000* (pp. 182–183). Trenton, NJ: Africa World Press.

Rodney, W. (1990). *Walter Rodney speaks: The making of an African intellectual*. Trenton, NJ: Africa World Press.

Rogers, I. (2009). Remember the Black campus movement: An oral history interview with James P. Garrett. *The Journal of Pan-African Studies, 2*(10). Retrieved from www. jpanafrican.com/docs/vol2no10/2.10_Remembering_the_Black_Campus_Movement. pdf

Rucker, W. C. (2006). *The river flows on: Black resistance, Black culture and identity formation in early America*. Baton Rouge, LA: Louisiana State University.

Rushton, J. P., & Jensen, A. R. (2005). Thirty years of research on race differences in cognitive ability. *Psychology, Public Policy, and Law, 11*(2), 235–294.

Schutz, A., & Miller, M. (Eds.). (2015). *People power: The community organizing tradition of Saul Alinsky*. Nashville, TN: Vanderbilt University Press.

Semmes, C. E. (1981). Foundations of Afrocentric social science. *Journal of Black Studies, 12*(1), 3–17.

Semmes, C. E. (1992). *Cultural hegemony and African American development*. Westport, CT: Praeger.

Spelman, E. V. (2007). Managing ignorance. In S. Sullivan & N. Tuana (Eds.), *Race and epistemologies of ignorance* (pp. 119–131). Albany: State University of New York Press.

Star of Ethiopia. (n.d.). *DuBoisopedia*. Retrieved from http://scua.library.umass.edu/ duboisopedia/doku.php?id=about:star_of_ethiopia

Stuckey, S. (1987). *Slave culture: Nationalist theory and the foundation of Black America*. New York: Oxford University Press.

Tsetung, M. (1971). Some questions concerning methods of leadership. In *Selected readings from the works of Mao Tsetung* (pp. 287–294). Peking: Foreign Language Press.

United Nations, Office of the High Commissioner of Human Rights. (2017, February). Retrieved from www.ohchr.org/EN/NewsEvents/Pages/DisplayNews.aspx?NewsID= 21239&LangID=E#sthash.ObT5Dyqu.dpuf

Wigginton, E. (Ed.). (1992). *Refuse to stand silently by: An oral history of grassroots social activism in America, 1921–1964*. New York: Anchor Books.

Wilcox, P. (1978). The thrust for Black Studies. In M. Wolf-Wasserman & L. Hutchinson (Eds.), *Teaching human dignity: Social change lessons for every teacher* (p. 92). Minneapolis, MN: Education Exploration Center.

Woodson, C. G. (1933). *The miseducation of the Negro.* Washington, DC: Associated.

Wynter, S. (1992). "No Humans Involved": An open letter to my colleagues. *Voices of the African Diaspora, 8*(2), 13–16.

Wynter, S. (2006). On how we mistook the map for the territory, and re-imprisoned ourselves in our unbearable wrongness of being, of désêtre: Black studies toward the human project. In L. R. Gordon & J. A. Gordon (Eds.), *Not only the master's tools: African American studies in theory and practice* (pp. 107–169). Boulder, CO: Paradigm.

Wynter, S. (2012). *We must learn to sit together and talk about a little culture: Decolonizing essays, 1967–1984.* Leeds, UK: Peepal Tree Press.

AFTERWORD

Vera L. Nobles, PhD, and Wade W. Nobles, PhD

In our opinion, there is no afterword to the reading of *Heritage Knowledge in the Curriculum: Retrieving an African Episteme*. It is more appropriate to comment on it as a profound and bold continuation of Black intellectual dialogue that is currently being framed or defined as African-centered discourse. Drs. King and Swartz have continued to pry open the historical treasure chest of the intellectual heritage of African people. They place attention on diasporic retentions and residuals relative to the unaddressed African episteme and grand narrative. The connection between continental and diasporic knowing revealed in this text is a critical key in shattering the ideology of whiteness and its false claim of universality.

While extremely important, the major gift of this text, in our opinion, is its irrefutable establishment of a Pan-African system of knowing and knowledge production. In so doing, this text helps to mend the shattered consciousness and fractured identity and imposed rupture between Continental and Diasporan Peoples. It fortifies the recognition that African people worldwide, regardless of oppression and domination, have always maintained systems of knowing that represent our own subjective possibilities and potential and by so doing supported the reproduction and refinement of the best of ourselves. *Heritage Knowledge in the Curriculum: Retrieving an African Episteme* inspires the reader, especially teachers, to recognize the relationship between memory and imagination as the twin pillars of every community's quest for authenticity.

While the entire text serves as a flashlight in the dark tunnel of Western (White) hegemonic ignorance, we believe its real value is that through an African lens it shines a brilliant light on the hidden Black emancipatory narrative and provides an accurate (culturally congruent) reading and understanding of African scholarship, worldview, and agency. In this regard, Chapter 3 is a special lighthouse. In our own work (Nobles, V. L., 2015; Nobles W. W., et al., 2016) we have stressed the importance of African language and logic, and their retentions, in revealing knowing and the overall meaning of being and human functioning of African Peoples. The Afro-Trinidadian historian, journalist, and socialist C.L.R. James is quoted in Gutman (1976) as saying that the enslaved Africans brought into slavery the content of his mind, his memory, and the language and logic of his people and by so doing brought the selfhood of being African. While mostly not recognized or honored, African people (both Continental and those of the Diaspora) have always possessed a full language and systems of beliefs (logic).

Language is, though often overlooked, the arbiter of intelligence, the production of knowledge, and the sharing of knowing. It is no less than a critical definer of what it means to be human. Most languages spoken in Africa belong to one of three large language families—that is, Afro-Asiatic, Nilo-Saharan, and Niger-Kongo. Parenthetically, the so-called Niger-Kongo or more correctly BaNtu-Kongo represents about three-fourths of sub-Saharan Africa. The millennia-long series of migrations of speakers of the original proto- BaNtu language group include the Benue-Kongo branch that is found throughout West, Central, Southern, and Eastern Africa. We believe that the great empires of Mali, Songhoy, and Ghana should be reexamined as all having pre-Islamic roots as BaNtu. With regards to language families, what should be obvious but seemingly less appreciated is that people create language to communicate about what is most important to them—that is, environment, experience, belief, thought, and so on. The BaNtu-Kongo language family represents the need of the BaNtu people to communicate their thoughts, beliefs, and experiences. Hence, if there is a common language family, then there must be common experiences, environment, beliefs, and thoughts that bind that language family. What is clear is that the BaNtu people with their culture, language, family, spiritual beliefs, and philosophical ideas are the very people stolen and captured in the transatlantic slave trade. In effect, BaNtu beliefs and ideas were embedded in the various peoples who were stolen and kidnapped. All human communities, especially African prior to invasion and colonization, used their own intrinsic essence (spiritness), epistemic reflections, cultural appreciations, and apperceptions about reality to inform their knowing framework and intellectual mind-set (ergo, episteme), from which, in turn, they recognized and recorded their story (narrative) as well as "made sense" of the world.

Chapter 3 is most informative. Hassimi's story in this chapter powerfully demonstrates the logic found in the language of African tongues. It is no small revelation that the word for slave in *Songhoy-senni* language (Baanya) means "does not even have a mother." The logic embedded speaks to relationship and to be a slave is to have the most crippling and unhealthy relationship imaginable, to not even have a mother. It is clear, as Joyce and Hassimi point out, that when our ancestors engaged in epistemic reflections about their new world condition, the *Songhoy-senni* word would be expressed as Black sounds in our mouths. We sang the sorrow song, "*Sometimes I feel like a motherless child, far, far from home.*" The discussion in Chapter 3 inspires us to note that, through Ebonics, the African American use of language, particularly names and naming, is more than simple transliterations. The linguistic rule structure of the BaNtu-Kongo helps us to understand African American names and naming. In deciphering contemporary African American names, for instance, the similarity to the BaNtu-Kongo is intriguing. Note, for instance, the most common patterns of syllables for BaNtu-Kongo names are generally CVCV or CVC. Hence, we can find CVCV or CVC in BaNtu-Kongo names, such as Lesiba, and CVCV or CVC in African American names, such as Lakeesha. African American naming is not randomly searching for similar African sounds or made-up names in the service of uniqueness. The new creation and adoption of names in the African American community are rule-governed Ebonics expressions. African American names and naming should be thought of as both cultural retentions and epistemic reflections.

Expressed as Ebonics, the speech from our mouths, though vilified and stigmatized, is an expression of our resistance to linguistic hegemony and the retention of our epistemic resistance. The use of language (i.e., Ebonics) for African American people was (is) an expression of the power to think, communicate, care, cure, and know. It was and is this memory and imagination as filtered through the retention of African language and the imagination of being free and African that was the source of the liberatory instinct of our ancestors. As reinforced and documented in Chapter 3, our ancestors came with a language and a system of beliefs (logic) about what it meant to be human and to whom they belonged and why they existed.

In sharing their classroom encounter, Joyce and Hassimi have demonstrated that they are *Shushukulu Nkindis*. In BaNtu-Kongo language a *shushukulu nkindi* is not only one qualified to deal with physical issues but also one capable of communicating and addressing issues of the spirit. They have "eyes" in both worlds. They are not only wise men and women but also therapists and teachers. They are healers and epistemologists.

In "returning what we learn to the people," Dr. King has gifted us with a treatise, technique, and critical epistemic lens for knowing and understanding African heritage, knowledge, and historical consciousness, which have shaped and are shaping our intellectual tradition, cultural struggle, and vision of human freedom. The flashlight on the text, *Heritage Knowledge in the Curriculum: Retrieving an African Episteme*, is showing us, especially teachers, that it is through a penetrating epistemic reinterpretation of the "language and logic" of our African ancestry that both Continental and Diasporan Africans can rescue and remember their humanity, wholeness, wellness, and knowing.

There is no afterthought or afterword for *Heritage Knowledge in the Curriculum: Retrieving an African Episteme*. This important work is a guiding light for all oppressed peoples, especially African American people, to know and express their authentic selves.

References

Gutman, H. (1976). *The Black family in slavery and freedom, 1750–1925*. New York, NY: Vintage Press.

Nobles, V. L. (2015). Ebonics: The retention of African tongues. In M. J. Shujaa & K. J. Shujaa (Eds.), *The SAGE encyclopedia of African cultural heritage in North America* (pp. 388–391). Thousand Oaks, CA: SAGE.

Nobles, W. W., Baloyi, L., & Sodi, T. (2016). Pan African humanness and Sakhu Djaer as praxis for indigenous knowledge systems. *Alternation Special Edition, 18*, 36–59.

ABOUT THE AUTHORS

Joyce E. King, PhD, holds the Benjamin E. Mays Endowed Chair for Urban Teaching, Learning and Leadership at Georgia State University, where she is Professor of Educational Policy Studies and affiliated faculty in the Department of African American Studies and the Institute for Women's, Sexuality and Gender Studies. Her research and publications address a transformative role for culture in teaching and teacher preparation, Black studies curriculum theorizing, community-mediated research, and dysconscious racism, the term she coined. King has international experience teaching, lecturing, and providing professional development in Brazil, Canada, China, England, Jamaica, Japan, Kenya, Mali, New Zealand, and Senegal. She served as the 2014–2015 president of AERA and she is a member of the National African American Reparations Commission.

Ellen E. Swartz, PhD, is an education consultant in curriculum development and the construction of culturally informed instructional materials for K-12 teachers and students. As the former Frontier Chair in Urban Education at Nazareth College, Dr. Swartz conducted research on the knowledge base of preservice teachers in urban education as part of identifying how teacher educators can more effectively prepare teachers for urban schools. She has also published in the areas of education history, emancipatory pedagogy, and the concept of "re-membering" as an approach to achieving more comprehensive accounts of the past.

Dr. Hassimi O. Maïga is a Distinguished Researcher, appointed by Presidential Decree (2001), and *Amiiru*, Paramount Chief of Songhoy. He holds a PhD from the University of Caen, France (with honors), in Letters and Human Sciences, and a master's degree in International Development Education and Evaluative Research from Stanford University. For his BA degree he studied Philosophy and Psycho-Pedagogy at the Ecole Normale Supérieur, and he holds a Diploma in Teacher Education (English-as-a-Second Language) from the Ecole Normale Sécondaire, also in Bamako, Mali. Dr. Maïga was Regional Director of Education (Deputy Minister) and Inspector of Psycho-pedagogy in Gao, Mali, and he is Professor of Education Emeritus, having supervised doctoral and master's students at ISFRA, the higher education institute at the University of Bamako. He taught French and Songhoy language at Southern University in New Orleans, and he taught the history of education, urban education, and multicultural education at Medgar Evers College (CUNY). His book *Balancing Written History With Oral Tradition: The Legacy of the Songhoy People* and other publications address African history and culture. In 2016 as Editor, he spearheaded the team that translated the *Holy Qur'an* into the Songhoy language. Currently, he serves as Vice President and Director of Research for the Academy for Diaspora Literacy, Inc. (Atlanta and New York).

INDEX

Note: Page locators in bold indicate tables, italic indicate figures.

impaired 165 (*see also dysconsciousness*);
  victorious 65
continuity: between Africa and the Diaspora
  3, 85, 88; African Diasporan 12, 74;
  cultural 3–4, 8–10, 17, 57, 74, 88, 130–134
Cooper, A. J. 19, 61, 80
Counts, G. 19
cultural: amnesia 57, 166, 170, 193; assets
  9, 19–20, 168; concepts 94–96, *101*;
  knowledge 2–3, 9, 166; legacy 8, 98,
  108; memory 1–2, 5, 79, 106, 183,
  192–193; recovery 57, 192
cultural continuity 3–4, 8–10, 57, 88, 130,
  132–134, 44; between Africa and the
  Diaspora 17, 74, 85; between Europe
  and the Americas 11
culturally: authentic assessment 9, 104;
  informed principles 10, 26, 41, 126
culturally informed principles and
  emancipatory pedagogies 32–37
curriculum violence, nihilating erasure of
  epistemic 57

Dagbovie, P. 178–179
Davidson, B. 167
Dei, G. 68–69
democracy 13–15, 27–32, 82–85, 88,
  103–105, 108, 122–123; African
  Democracy: Continental and *Diasporan*
  82–85; retention of 79
democratized account: "remembered" 10
developing character 98–99
Dewey, G. 61
Dewey, John 19, 80, 122–123, 125–126,
  128, 131
Diaspora: Africans 178; can rescue and
  remember their heritage 203; collective
  African family 193; continuity between
  Africa and the Diaspora 85; heritage
  knowledge 74
Diop, C. A. 176, 187–188
dominant Euro-American cultural
  concepts 104–134; *see also* eurocratic
"double-consciousness" 90–92; African
  epistemic reading of 94; African side of
  93; as epistemological location 92–93; as
  strategic asset 93
double consciousness revisited 91–95
Douglas, F. 10
Du Bois, W.E.B. 16, 79, 88–90; Du Boisian
  themes 79; W.E.B. Du Bois: Recognition
  and Silence 88; Making African Epistemic
  Continuity Visible 90; Rewriting W.E.B.
  Du Bois: Du Boisian themes 95–96

dysconsciousness 165; *see also* double
  consciousness revisited

education: for life and community uplift
  (Du Bois) 100; a means to develop
  character 99; research-as-pedagogy 176
eldership 2, 60, 101, 107, 142–143
emancipatory: African epistemic
  foundation of 101; pedagogies 32, 48,
  101–102, 108, 137; pedagogy 33, *33*,
  34, 58, 66–67, 74, 143, 205; *see also*
  culturally informed principles and
  emancipatory pedagogies
environmental: activists 4; pollution 4;
  racism 5, 7, 192
epistemic foundation of afrocentric
  theoretical concepts 28–32, *31*
epistemological: ignorance 186;
  nihilation 190
eurocratic: biography of Benjamin
  Banneker 37; constraints on knowledge
  13; content 32, 38; cultural concepts
  136–137; curriculum content 49, 108;
  episteme 49; master scripts 26; paradigm
  175, 191; rather than "Eurocentric" 13;
  school knowledge 79; scripts 14; social
  science theory 176; system of education
  143; textbook account 38; view of Black
  scholarship 14; *see also* Black scholarship
European: civilizations 17; cosmology 131;
  enslavement 40, 60, 159–160; Europeans
  disconnected from their heritage of
  enslavement 13; heritage knowledge 86;
  slave trade 158–159, 165; supremacist
  ideology 94; system of chattel slavery 95,
  98–99; worldview 19–20, 28, 35, 90–91,
  94, 131, 134; worldview elements 20, 39,
  86, 133; *see also* worldview

family 40; and elders 107; and
  emancipatory pedagogy 33–34;
  families 8, 45, 48, 108, 142–143, 157;
  families' heritage knowledge 38;
  family knowledge 9; and knowledge
  of community standards 102; and
  reparations 22
Farrell, W. C. 191
Fenwick, L. T. 191
folktale: African 70; African American
  folk narrative *73*; *Black Folktales* (Lester)
  70; Songhoy 68; folkstories 70; *see also*
  Songhoy, folktale
Franklin, V. P. 163
Freire, P. 181, 184–185, 188–189

Made in the USA
Middletown, DE
15 January 2022

58744220R00129